外贸单证实务

主　编　周锰珍
副主编　陈　倩　廖万红　石薇尔

北京理工大学出版社
BEIJING INSTITUTE OF TECHNOLOGY PRESS

内 容 简 介

《外贸单证实务》以外贸单证员工作过程为逻辑主线，介绍了国际贸易单证的基础知识，设计审核和修改信用证，制作商业发票、海运提单、保险单、检验检疫单证以及报关单等国际贸易业务中所涉及的各类主要单证。

本教材撰写体例新颖独特，结构条理清晰，语言表达流畅。教材结构采用概念学习+样单结构拆解+案例实训的模式，学生在学习概念、掌握单证结构的同时，进行模拟实操训练，更好地掌握外贸单证的概念、制单方法，提高缮制单证的有效性和准确性，培养学生的理解和实践操作能力。

本教材注重理论联系实际，坚守为党育人、为国育才的初心使命，紧扣立德树人根本任务，体现"课程思政"理念。一是体现思想性：在教学设计上，融入"零差错""高效率""求极致"的工匠精神、精益求精和诚实守信的单证观；二是体现前沿性：教材内容涉及中国-东盟自贸区、RCEP 原产地证书等新内容；三是体现时代性：教案顺应贸易强国建设要求，融入敢于担当的使命意识和责任意识，让学生在潜移默化中感受贸易强国的崛起，增强民族自信心和崇高爱国主义精神。

教材具有突出的实用性和时效性特点：一是双语教材，既可以适用于双语教学，也适合学生专业课程和专业英语学习使用，具有一定的实用性；二是时效性，教材收集最新的外贸原产地证书材料，符合中国-东盟自贸区 3.0 版以及 RCEP 成员国之间国际贸易高质量发展的需要。

本教材内容理论知识丰富，实训操作性强，配有习题作业和操作训练，适合国际贸易新变化和职业新需求，可作为大学院校学生、外贸业务员、外贸单证员学习和应用外贸单证知识的工具书，还可作为国际商务单证员考试、培训的参考书。

图书在版编目（CIP）数据

外贸单证实务：英汉对照 / 周锰珍主编. --北京：
北京理工大学出版社，2023.7
　　ISBN 978-7-5763-2628-4

　　Ⅰ.①外… Ⅱ.①周… Ⅲ.①进出口贸易-原始凭证
-教材-英、汉 Ⅳ.①F740.44

中国国家版本馆 CIP 数据核字（2023）第 134881 号

出版发行 / 北京理工大学出版社有限责任公司
社　　址 / 北京市海淀区中关村南大街 5 号
邮　　编 / 100081
电　　话 / （010）68914775（总编室）
　　　　　（010）82562903（教材售后服务热线）
　　　　　（010）68944723（其他图书服务热线）
网　　址 / http：//www.bitpress.com.cn
经　　销 / 全国各地新华书店
印　　刷 / 北京广达印刷有限公司
开　　本 / 787 毫米×1092 毫米　1/16
印　　张 / 13.75　　　　　　　　　　　　　　　　责任编辑 / 武丽娟
字　　数 / 322 千字　　　　　　　　　　　　　　　文案编辑 / 武丽娟
版　　次 / 2023 年 7 月第 1 版　2023 年 7 月第 1 次印刷　　责任校对 / 刘亚男
定　　价 / 79.00 元　　　　　　　　　　　　　　　责任印制 / 李志强

图书出现印装质量问题，请拨打售后服务热线，本社负责调换

前　言

随着"一带一路"倡议的提出以及 RCEP 的生效实施，我国对外贸易得到进一步高质量发展，越来越多的企业走向国际市场，国际贸易的日益发展对从业人员提出了更高的要求，不仅要掌握国际贸易的理论与实务、法律与法规，而且还需要具有较强的实际操作能力。在对外贸易业务中，进出口外贸单证是个重要业务内容，它覆盖了国际贸易的整个流程，单证是国际贸易的基础，也是确保准确、及时、顺利的国际贸易结算的前提条件。

本教材共分为 10 章，详细介绍了进出口业务中单证的基础知识、信用证的审核与修改、商业发票、运输单、保险单、原产地证书、检验证书以及报关单等外贸单证的内容及缮制方法。教材的结构为概念学习+样单结构拆解+案例实训，通过这些环节的学习和模拟实操训练，帮助使用者在较短的时间内掌握外贸单证的概念、制单方法，确保单证的有效性和缮制单证的准确性，强化他们对于外贸单证概念、格式和内容的理解及实践动手能力。

教材体现了"思政+专业"的理念，在教学设计上不但让学生们切实掌握相关专业知识，而且更传授"祖国利益高于一切"的社会责任感、民族自信心和崇高爱国主义精神，使用者可以在教学实践中以"润物无声"的方式将正确的价值观、民族责任感、遵守国际贸易法律法规和家国情怀等思想在专业课学习中有效地体会。

教材具有突出的实用性和时效性特点：一是双语教材，既适用于双语教学，也可用于学生专业课程和专业英语学习，具有一定的实用性；二是融入最新的外贸原产地证书材料，收集了中国−东盟自由贸易区原产地证书、RCEP 原产地证书，符合中国−东盟自贸区 3.0 版以及 RCEP 成员国之间贸易高质量发展的需要。本教材可作为大学院校学生、外贸业务员、外贸单证员学习和应用外贸单证知识的工具书，还可作为国际商务单证员考试、培训的参考书。

由于编者学识水平和能力有限，加之外贸政策的不断变化，书中难免存在不妥与疏漏，敬请读者批评指正。

编　者
2023 年 4 月

目录

Chapter 1 Basic Knowledge of International Trade Documents 单证的基础知识

Key Points and Difficulties

- To Understand the Definition of International Trade Documents
- To Know the Classifications of International Trade Documents
- To Understand the Function of International Trade Document
- To Understand the Requirement of Making up International Trade Document

Learning Objectives

- The Definition of International Trade Documents
- The Functions of International Trade Documents
- Some Rules of Making out International Trade Documents

Section One   The Definition of International Trade Documents 外贸单证的含义

Documents refer to a set of certificates or papers used in merchandise transaction. In international trade settlement or payment, documents play an important role in safe exchange between goods and proceeds. It is important to note that the technical name for letters of credit is documentary credits and, along with documentary collections, that documents are at the heart of all forms of international trade payment.

单证是指在商品交易中所用到的一套证书或者文件。在国际贸易结算或支付中，单证在货物的安全交易中发挥着非常重要的作用。值得注意的是，信用证的专业术语为跟单信用证和单据托收。单证是所有国际贸易支付方式的核心。

With all matters involving money and payments, the form and content of these documents are of great importance to all parties to the transaction. Subtle differences between forms and subtle changes in wording can mean the difference between a successful and an unsuccessful transaction. Before specifying the required documents, the buyer should ensure that the seller is willing and able to provide the documents called for and that they can be provided in the form and with the details stipulated.

在涉及金钱和支付的所有问题中，这些单证的内容和格式对于交易各方都是很重要的。在格式上细微的差别和构词上细微的变化都决定着此交易成功与否。在具体说明所要求的单证之前，买方应该确保卖方愿意并且能够提供符合所规定的格式和内容的单证。

Importance of various documents in international trade payment is different.

Some are indispensable in all transactions, namely, key documents, such as commercial invoices, transport documents and insurance documents; some are called complementary documents, which are occasionally called for according to the nature of goods and the trade regulations of nations.

各种单证在国际贸易支付中的重要性是不同的。有些是所有交易中不可或缺的，即关键文件，如商业发票、运输单证和保险单证；有些文件被称为补充文件，指根据货物的性质和各国的贸易规则，需要补充的文件。

Section Two   The Classifications of International Trade Documents
外贸单证的分类

Normally, documents can be classified into 4 groups according to different issuers：通常，根据发证人的不同，单证分为四种：

- Business documents issued by business people；由商务人士开立的商业单据
- Transport documents issued by carriers；由运输方开立的运输单据
- Insurance documents issued by the insurers；由保险方开立的保险单据
- Official documents issued by state authorities. 由官方发布的官方文件

1. Commercial Documents 商业单据

（1）Commercial Invoice 商业发票

（2）Packing Documents 包装单据

- Packing List 装箱单
- Weight List 重量单

（3）Manufacturer's Invoice 厂商发票

2. Transport Documents 运输单据

- Ocean bill of Lading 海运提单
- Air Waybill 空运运单
- Rail Waybill 铁路运单
- Combined Transport Documents 多式联运单据
- CMR Consignment Notes 公路运单
- Post Receipt 特快专递和邮政收据

3. Insurance Policy 保险单据

- 保险单 Insurance Policy
- 保险凭证 Insurance Certificate
- 联合凭证 Combined Certificate
- 预约保单 Open Policy

4. Official Documents 官方单据(政府机构、社会团队签发的各种证件)

(1)Certificate of Origin 产地证明书

(2)Inspection Certificate 商品检验证明

- Inspection Certificate of Quality 品质检验证书
- Inspection Certificate of Weight or Quantity 重量或数量检验证书
- Inspection Certificate of Packing 包装检验证书
- Sanitary/Healthy Inspection Certificate 卫生或健康检验证书
- Veterinary Inspection Certificate 兽医检验证书
- Disinfection Inspection Certificate 消毒检验证书
- Inspection Certificate of Temperature 温度检验证书
- Inspection Certificate of Fumigation 熏蒸检验证书

(3)Pro-forma Invoice 形式发票

(4)Consular Invoice 领事发票

(5)Customs Invoice 海关发票

5. Financial Documents 金融单据

- Bill of Exchange/Draft 汇票
- Cheque/Check 支票
- Promissory Note 本票

6. Other Certificates 其他单据

- Beneficiary's Certificate 受益人证明
- Certificate of Itinerary 航程证明
- Certificate of Vessel's Age 船龄证明
- Certificate of Classification 船级证明
- Certificate of Conference Line Vessel 班轮工会船只证明

Section Three　The Function of International Trade Documents 外贸单证的作用

1. Documents are the Foundation of International Trade 单证是国际贸易的基础

There are four steps included in international trade: making a deal, stocking, exporting and receiving the payment. When making a deal, the seller and the buyer begin to fulfill the contract; at the same time, the cooperation among all the departments of both sides(such as import and export departments, financial departments, document departments and storage and transport departments etc.), the correspondence between the enterprises of both sides and other relative departments(such as shipping company, insurance company, commodity inspection organizations, customs, departments responsible for trade, etc.), the consignment of goods and the monetary settlement and payment are all carried out by making and circulating business documents. In fact, documents go through the whole process of trade. So the commercial documents are the foundation of international trade.

国际贸易包括四个步骤：交易、储存、出口和接收付款。在达成交易时，买卖双方开始履行合同；同时，双方各部门进行合作(如进出口部、财务部、单证部、储运部等)，双方企业与其他相关部门之间的通信(如船运公司、保险公司、商检机构、海关、贸易主管部门等)，货物的寄售和货币结算与支付都是通过制作和流通商业单据来进行的。事实上，单证贯穿整个贸易过程。因此，商业单证是国际贸易的基础。

2. Documents are the Basic Tool of International Settlement 单证是国际贸易结算的基本工具

In international trade, the object is goods. But the settlement is, in fact, the dealing of documents. As a basic tool of settlement, the commercial documents are indispensable for dealing goods; and it is also the basis of payment for the buyer. If the trade is based on the term of CIF, the seller delivers goods against documents and the buyer will pay against documents, that is, the "payment against document", which is a process of exchanging documents and payment.

The process of international trade relies on the documents so that selling and buying goods must be realized against documents. As the marine transportation develops rapidly, Marine Bill of Lading or Ocean Bill of Lading is not only shipping document but the certification of transferable title of goods. In the way of international settlement, documents are the foundation as well as the certification. So business documents are the basic tool of international settlement.

国际贸易中的实施对象是货物。但是，结算是货物的交易过程。作为结算最基本的工具，商业单证是货物交易中必不可少的凭证，也是买方付款的依据。如果交易以 CIF 术语为基础，卖方凭单证交货，买方凭单证付款，即"付款交单"，这是一个交换单证和付款的过程。

国际贸易的过程依赖于单证，因此买卖货物必须凭单证进行。随着海运业的迅速发展，海洋提单或海运提单不仅是海运单证，而且是货物所有权转移的证明。在国际结算方式中，单证是基础，也是证明。因此，商业单证是国际结算的基本工具。

3. Documents are the Benefits of Enterprises Lie in 单证是企业的利益所在

In dealing international goods, the business document is the basis of maintaining rights and duties between the buyer and the seller; moreover, it is which the benefits of import and export enterprise lie in. If any mistake occurs in the management of document, the goods can't be delivered in time, the client will lose the fund's interest because of the delayed payment. If any mistake occurs in the document itself, the client will refuse to pay for the goods, the issuing bank will refuse to pay for the L/C, and the enterprise will probably take the risk of not taking money back. Therefore, it is very important to ensure that the documents are precise and accurate so that any problems mentioned above would be avoided.

在国际货物交易中，商务单证是维护买卖双方权利和义务的基础；此外，这也是进出口企业的利益所在。如果单证管理出现错误，货物不能及时交付，客户将因延迟付款而失去资金的利益。如果单证本身出现任何错误，客户将拒绝支付货款，开证银行将拒绝支付信用证，企业很可能会承担不能收回款项的风险。因此，确保单证的精确性和准确性非常重要，从而避免上述任何问题。

4. Documents are Important Foreign-Related Legal Files 单证是重要的涉外法律文件

Documents go through the whole process of international trade. Their manifestations, circulation, exchange and utilization reflect not only the contract-fulfilling process but the rights and duties of relative parties in the delivery process, such as importer and exporter, consignor and carrier, insurer and insurant, bank and customer, customs officer and those who go in or out of customs. If there is any dispute, documents will be the certification of settling claims between the contract parties. Thus the commercial documents are important foreign-related legal files. They must comply with laws and regulations related with international trade, international transportation, international insurance, and international settlement, etc.

单证贯穿于整个国际贸易过程。单证的各种形式、流通、交易以及使用不仅反映履行合同的过程也反映货物交易过程中有关各方的责任和权利。如：进口方和出口方，发货人和承运人、保险人和被保险人、银行和客户、海关官员以及进出海关人员。如果在交易过程中有任何争议，单证将是合同双方解决索赔的凭证。因此，商业发票是最重要的涉外法律文件。单证必须遵守国际贸易、国际运输、国际保险、国际结算等方面的法律法规。

Section Four The Basic Requirements for Making out International Trade Documents 缮制单证的基本要求

Without documents, international trade can never be conducted. The information provided in the documents must be wholly accurate and appropriate to the particular purpose of each individual document. Inaccurate documentation will result in delays in processing, shipping and receipt of goods, which in turn may cause contract to be breached through delivery period. As a result, the exporter will lose money on the contract, and the importer will not be able to fulfill other orders according to imported components. Therefore, all parties involved in the transaction hope to ensure that the documentation should be correct, in time, complete, clear, and concise in order to make out documents without any discrepancies.

如果没有单证，国际贸易将无法实现。单证里的信息必须一致并且互相符合。不准确的单证会使交易延迟、收发货物延迟，最终导致违约。这些会使出口方遭受重大损失，进口方无法履行合同规定。因此，为了准确无误，交易各方应确保单证的缮制准确、及时、完整、清晰和简洁。

Accuracy: The detail in documents must be in strict conformity with those in the sales contract. No ambiguous words or expressions should be used. The documents are in conformity with the terms of the contract; The documents are in conformity with the provisions of the credit; The document is consistent with the contents of the document; The documents are consistent with the actual shipment; The documents are in conformity with relevant international practices and laws; The documents are consistent with the relevant laws and administrative regulations of the importing/exporting country.

准确性：单证内容必须完全符合销售合同。模糊性的词语或者表达方式不能使用。要做到单证与合同的规定相符，单证与信用证的规定相符，单证与单证的内容相符，单证与实际装运的货物相符，单证与有关国际惯例、法律的规定相符，单证与进口国/出口国有关法令、行政规章的规定相符。

Completeness：Every necessary detail should be included in each document. Ensure that the types of documents are complete, the contents of documents are complete and the number of copies of documents is complete.

完整性：每一条有必要的信息必须包含在单证内。确保单证的种类完整，单证的内容完整，单证的份数完整。

Promptness：Make sure the documents are ready when they are needed, so that unnecessary delay or confusion can be avoided. To ensure that the issuing date of various documents must be logical, the negotiation of presentation of documents shall not exceed the validity period of presentation stipulated in the letter of credit.

及时性：单证在双方需要时就应该准备好，应当避免任何不必要的延迟和混淆。要确保各种单证的出单日期必须符合逻辑，交单议付不得超过信用证规定的交单有效期。

Conciseness：Unnecessary words and expressions should not be used in the document, and there should be no trace of modification on the document. The contents of documents shall be concise and clear, and the layout of various contents shall be reasonable, clear hierarchy, prominent key projects, avoid complexity.

简洁性：单证中不应使用多余的词汇和表达，单证上不应出现修改痕迹。单证内容要力求简洁明了，各项内容布局合理，层次分明，重点项目突出，避免复杂烦琐。

The basic requirements for making out document are reflected in the course construction of "Foreign Trade Documents Practice", which adheres to the concept of integrating value into the practice of dual education and cultivating talent engineering for foreign trade. The basic principles of accuracy, complete, prompt, concise, and tidy is the basic requirements for making out International Trade Documents. It reflects the core educational elements of the course "Practice of Foreign Trade Documents", which are the craftsman spirit of "zero error", "high efficiency", and "seeking the ultimate", as well as the concept of excellence in documents. The "Foreign Trade Document Practice" takes the work process of foreign trade document clerks as the logic thread, and designs several work items such as verification and certificate change business operations, commercial invoice production and packing list operations, each work project incorporates a loving and dedicated work attitude, a spirit of continuous improvement as a craftsman, and an honest and trustworthy professional character, reflecting ideological values, And new technologies and standards such as customs inspection integration and INCOTERMS 2020 reflect cutting-edge characteristics. Comply with the requirements of building a strong trading country, integrate a sense of mission and responsibility that dare to take on responsibilities, reflect the times, and allow students to experience the rise of a trading country in a subtle way.

缮制单证的基本要求体现在《外贸单证实务》课程建设中，坚持价值融入、践行双元共育培养外贸工匠的育人工程的理念。"正确、完整、及时、简明、整洁"制单工作的基本原则，体现出《外贸单证实务》课程的核心育人元素是"零差错""高效率""求极致"的工匠精神和精益求精的单证观。《外贸单证实务》以外贸单证员工作过程为逻辑主线，设计审证与改证业务操作、制作商业发票和装箱单操作等多个工作项目，每个工作项目融入爱岗敬业的劳动态度、精益求精的工匠精神、诚实守信的职业品格，体现思想性；而海关检验一体化、INCOTERMS 2020 等新技术新规范，体现前沿性；顺应贸易强国建设要求，融入敢于担当的使命意识和责任意识，体现时代性，让学生在潜移默化中感受贸易强国的崛起。

Exercises 练习

一、判断题。(判断对与错，对的打"√"，错的打"×")

1. 外贸单证是合同履行的必要手段。　　　　　　　　　　　　　　　　　　　　（　　）

2. 外贸单证是在国际贸易中使用的各种单据、文件与证书的统称。　　　　　　　（　　）

3. 在国际贸易过程中，支票这种单证可以直接代表货币。　　　　　　　　　　　（　　）

4. 我国的进口报检需要到商品检验检疫局进行。　　　　　　　　　　　　　　　（　　）

5. 外贸单证中的各个条款必须订得严密体现的是单证的正确性的要求。　　　　　（　　）

6. 审单工作要求审核单证是否内容准确、格式完整、单证齐全、份数不缺、单证一致和单单相符，还要保证各种单证的签发日期无逻辑、惯例和条款规定上的矛盾。（　　）

7. 国际商务单证的制作原则是：准确、完整、及时、简洁，其中准确最为重要。
　　　　　　　　　　　　　　　　　　　　　　　　　　　　　　　　　　　（　　）

8. 在实务中，国际贸易的最终完成往往以单证交流的形式实现。　　　　　　　　（　　）

9. 信用证支付方式下，国际贸易单证工作除基本环节外还有审单、制单和交单环节。
　　　　　　　　　　　　　　　　　　　　　　　　　　　　　　　　　　　（　　）

10. 按照单证性质，外贸单证分为保险单证和包装单证。　　　　　　　　　　　（　　）

二、Translate the Following Information into Chinese. 将下列信息译为中文。

Bill of Lading is a contract between the owner of goods and the carrier(as with domestic shipments). There are two types: a straight bill of lading which is non-negotiable and a negotiable or shipper's order bill of lading. The latter can be bought, sold, or traded while the goods are in transit. The customer usually needs an original copy as a proof of ownership to take possession of goods.

Commercial Invoice is a bill recording a sale of goods by the seller to the buyer. These invoices are often used by governments to determine the true value of goods when assessing customs duties. Governments that use the commercial invoice to control imports will often specify its form, content，number of copies，language to be used，and others.

三、简答题

1. How much do you know about documentation that exporting requires?

2. Could you please list some commonly used international trade documents?

3. What is the function of foreign trade documents ?

4. What is the basic requirements for making out International Trade Documents?

Chapter 2 Examination and Amendment a Letter of Credit 信用证的审核和修改

Key Points and Difficulties

- To Underst and the Definition and Procedure of Letter of Credit
- To Understand the Functions of Letter of Credit
- To Know the Parties and the Types of Letter of Credit
- How to Review and Amend a Letter of Credit
- The Case Study of Amending a Letter of Credit

Learning Objectives

- The Main Contents and the Key Point of a Letter of Credit
- How to Examine and Amend a Letter of Credit
- Some Rules of Amending the Letter of Credit

Section One　Understanding Letter of Credit 认识信用证

一、Introduces the Concept and Procedure of L/C. 信用证的含义及业务流程

1. The Concept of Letter of Credit(L/C) 信用证的含义

The Concept of Letter of Credit(L/C)：Letter of Credit(L/C)is a written document. It is a written commitment made by the issuing bank to the beneficiary to pay a certain amount against the specified documents within a certain period of time according to the requirements and instructions of the applicant or due to its own needs.

信用证的概念：信用证是一种书面文件，是开证行根据申请人的要求和指示或因自身需要，在一定期限内凭指定的单证向受益人支付一定金额的书面承诺。

2. The Procedure of L/C. 信用证的业务流程(图2-1)

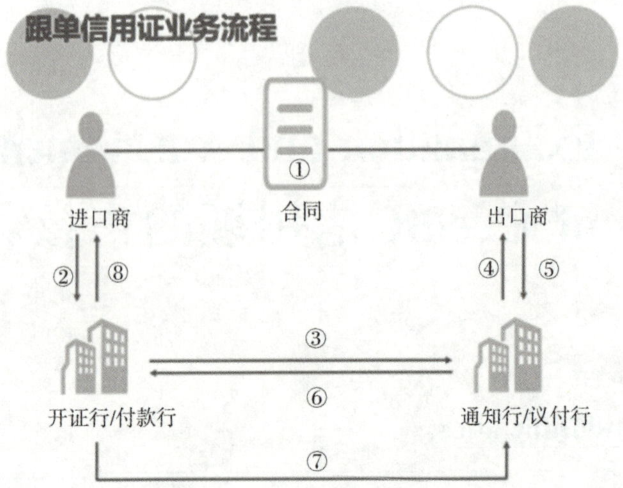

图2-1 信用证业务流程

① In trade contracts, It is stipulated that the payment shall be made by Letter of Credit for importers and exporters. 进出口商在贸易合同中，规定使用信用证方式支付货款。

② The importer shall apply to the local bank, fill in the L/C application form, fill in the regulations and requirements according to the contract, and pay the deposit or provide other guarantees. And ask the bank(issuing bank)to open the Letter of Credit. 进口商向当地银行提出申请，填写开证申请书，依照合同填写规定和要求，并交纳押金或提供其他保证，请银行（开证行）开证。

③ According to the content of the application, the issuing bank shall open a Letter of Credit to the exporter(beneficiary)and send it to the branch or agent bank where the exporter is located (collectively referred to as the advising bank). 开证行根据申请书内容，向出口商（受益人）开出信用证，寄交出口商所在地分行或代理行（统称通知行）。

④ After checking the seal, the advising bank shall submit the Letter of Credit to the exporter. 通知行核对印鉴无误后，将信用证交与出口商。

⑤ After checking that the L/C is in conformity with the contract, the exporter shall ship the goods according to the provisions of the L/C, prepare all shipping documents, draw a bill of exchange, and send it to the local bank(negotiating bank)for negotiation within the validity of the L/C. After reviewing the documents according to the terms of the Letter of Credit, the negotiating bank shall deduct the interest according to the amount of the bill and advance the payment to the exporter. 出口商审核信用证与合同相符后，按信用证规定装运货物，并备齐各项货运单据，开出汇票，在信用证有效期内，送请当地银行（议付行）议付。议付行按信用证条款审核单据无误后，按照汇票金额扣除利息，把货款垫付给出口商。

⑥ The negotiating bank will send the draft and shipping documents to the issuing bank(or its designated paying bank)for compensation. 议付行将汇票和货运单据寄开证行（或其指定的付款行）索偿。

⑦ The issuing bank(or its designated paying bank)shall make payment to the negotiating bank after checking the documents. 开证行(或其指定的付款行)核对单据无误后，付款给议付行。

⑧ The importer pays the redemption note. 进口商付款赎单。

二、The Functions of Letter of Credit 信用证的作用

(1)L/C payment plays the role of security guarantee and financing. 信用证支付起到安全保证作用和资金融通作用。

(2)For the seller：as long as the documents submitted comply with the provisions of the Letter of Credit, the payment can be obtained. 对于卖方：只要提交符合信用证规定的单据，就可以得到货款。

(3)For the buyer：as long as you apply for L/C issuance and pay a small deposit, the payment for goods can be paid after the arrival of documents to reduce the occupation of funds. 对于买方：只要申请开证，交少量押金，货款可在单据到达后支付，以减少资金占用。

(4)For banks：lend credit, master property documents, charge a certain handling fee and interest(negotiating bank), and use the deposit delivered by the applicant for capital turnover to drive other businesses. 对于银行：贷出信用，掌握物权单据，收取一定手续费和利息(议付行)，利用开证申请人交付的押金进行资金周转，带动其他业务。

三、The Parties of Letter of Credit 信用证的当事人

(1)Applicant/Operator：refers to the party issuing the Letter of Credit application. The applicant for issuing the Letter of Credit is the importer, which is also called the applicant or the applicant in the Letter of Credit. 开证申请人(APPLICANT/OPENER)：意指发出开立信用证申请的一方。开证申请人即进口方，在信用证中又称开证人或申请人。

(2)Issuing/Opening bank：refers to the bank that accepts the request of the applicant and agrees to issue the document. The issuing bank is generally the bank in the location of the importer. It undertakes the responsibility of ensuring payment according to the conditions stipulated in the Letter of Credit and becomes the first payer in the Letter of Credit instead of the applicant. 开证行(ISSUING /OPENING BANK)：意指接受开证申请人请求，同意开立信用证的银行。开证行一般为进口方所在地的银行，它承担按信用证规定条件保证付款的责任，代替开证申请人成为信用证中的第一付款人。

(3)Advising/Notifying bank：refers to the bank that notifies the Letter of Credit at the request of the issuing bank. The advising bank is generally the correspondent bank of the issuing bank or the designated bank of the exporter. It only proves the authenticity of the Letter of Credit and bears no other obligations. 通知行(ADVISING /NOTIFYING BANK)：意指应开证行的要求通知信用证的银行。通知行一般为开证行的往来行或出口方的指定银行，它只证明信用证的真实性，不承担其他义务。

(4)Beneficiary：refers to the party named in the Letter of Credit who has the right to use the Letter of Credit. The beneficiary is usually the exporter. 受益人(BENEFICIARY)意指信用证上指定的有权使用信用证的一方。受益人一般为出口商。

(5)Negotiating bank：also known as documentary bank, it is a bank that is willing to draw or submit bills of exchange or documents in accordance with the provisions of the Letter of Credit issued or submitted by the buyer or discount beneficiary under the authorization of the issuing bank. The negotiating bank is generally the exporters. 议付行(NEGOTIATING BANK):又称押汇银行,是根据开证行的授权愿意买入或贴现受益人开立或提交的符合信用证条款规定的汇票或单据的银行。议付行一般为出口方银行或开证行指定的银行。

(6)Paying bank:the bank designated by the issuing bank to pay under the Letter of Credit or act as the payer of the bill of exchange. The paying bank is generally the issuing bank or the bank designated by the issuing bank. No matter who the drawee of the bill is, the paying bank must fulfill the responsibility of payment to the exporter who has submitted the documents in accordance with the requirements of the Letter of Credit. 付款行(PAYING /DRAWEE BANK):开证行指定的对信用证项下付款或充当汇票付款人的银行。付款行一般为开证行,也可以是开证行所指定的银行。无论汇票的付款人是谁,付款行必须对提交了符合信用证要求的单证的出口商履行付款的责任。

(7)Confirming bank:refers to the bank that adds confirmation to the Letter of Credit at the authorization or request of the issuing bank. Both the confirming bank and the issuing bank bear the primary payment responsibility to the beneficiary. In actual business, the confirming bank is usually concurrently held by the advising bank. 保兑行(CONFIRMING BANK):指根据开证行的授权或要求在信用证上增加保兑的银行。保兑行和开证行均对受益人承担主要付款责任。在实际业务中,保兑行通常由通知行兼任。

(8)Reimbursing bank:also known as clearing bank, it refers to a third country bank entrusted by the issuing bank to repay the advance on its behalf in the Letter of Credit. The reimbursing bank is usually the deposit bank of the issuing bank or the branch or sub branch of the issuing bank. 偿付行(REIMBURSING BANK):又称清算银行(Clearing Bank),是指接受开证银行委托在信用证中代其偿还垫款的第三国银行。偿付行通常是开证行的存款银行或是开证行的分行、支行。

四、The Types of Letters of Credit 信用证的种类

Letter of Credit can be classified according to their nature, form, payment term and purpose. 信用证依其性质、形式、付款期限及用途的不同可进行不同的分类。

(1)Clean Letter of Credit and Documentary Letter of Credit. ①Clean Letter of Credit refers to a Letter of Credit payable by draft without documents. Such letters of credit are mainly used for trade ancillary expenses or non-trade settlement. ②Documentary credit means a Letter of Credit payable by documentary draft or documents only. A document representing the ownership of or delivery of goods.

跟单信用证和光票信用证(CLEAN CREDIT& DOCUMENT CREDIT)。①光票信用证指凭不附单证的汇票付款的信用证。此类信用证主要用于贸易从属费用或非贸易结算。②跟单信用证指凭跟单汇票或只凭单证付款的信用证。单证是指代表货物所有权或证明货物已经发运的单据。

(2)Sight Letter of Credit and Acceptance Letter of Credit. ①Sight Letter of Credit refers to the Letter of Credit that will be paid after the issuing bank or negotiating bank has passed the examination when the beneficiary presents the relevant documents. It can use sight draft or no draft. ②Usance letter of credit refers to a letter of credit in which the beneficiary can only issue usance bills, the issuing bank or negotiating bank accepts the bills after reviewing the documents and pays the payment on the due date of payment.

即期信用证和(SIGHT CREDIT& USANCE OR TIME CREDIT)。①即期信用证指受益人提示有关单据时，开证行或议付行审核合格后即付款的信用证，可使用即期汇票，也可不用汇票。②远期信用证指受益人仅可开立远期汇票，开证行或议付行审核单据合格后对该汇票予以承兑，在付款到期日支付货款的信用证。

(3) Payment credit & Acceptance credit. ①Payment credit refers to the letter of credit that stipulates that the issuing bank guarantees payment when the beneficiary submits documents in accordance with the provisions of the letter of credit to the issuing bank or its designated paying bank, or the letter of credit issued by the beneficiary and not allowed to be negotiated. ②Acceptance credit refers to the documentary letter of credit using usance bills. A letter of credit in which the issuing bank or the designated paying bank performs the acceptance formalities first when receiving the bills and documents in accordance with the provisions of the letter of credit, and then pays the bills when they are due.

付款信用证与承兑信用证(PAYMENT CREDIT & ACCEPTANCE CREDIT)。①付款信用证，是指信用证规定开证银行保证当受益人向开证银行或其指定的付款行提交符合信用证规定的单证时付款，或受益人开具而不准议付的信用证。②承兑信用证，是指使用远期汇票的跟单信用证。开证行或指定付款行在收到符合信用证规定的汇票和单据时，先履行承兑手续，待汇票到期再行付款的信用证。

(4) Confirmed and Unconfirmed letters of credit. ①Confirmed Letter of Credit refers to the Letter of Credit issued by the issuing bank and guaranteed to be honored by another bank. After the confirming bank confirms the Letter of Credit, its responsibility is equivalent to issuing the Letter of Credit itself. No matter what happens to the issuing bank, the confirming bank shall not unilaterally revoke its confirmation. ②An unconfirmed Letter of Credit refers to a Letter of Credit that is cashed without the guarantee of another bank.

保兑信用证和不保兑信用证(CONFIRMED CREDIT& UNCONFIRMED CREDIT)。①保兑信用证指开证行开出的信用证又经另一家银行保证兑付的信用证。保兑行对信用证进行保兑后，其承担的责任就相当于本身开证，不论开证行发生什么变化，保兑行都不得单方面撤销其保兑。②不保兑的信用证指未经另一银行加以保证兑付的信用证。

(5) Transferable Letter of Credit and Nontransferable Letter of Credit. ①Transferable Letter of Credit refers to a Letter of Credit in which the beneficiary can transfer part or all of the rights of the Letter of Credit to a third party. A transferable Letter of Credit must indicate "transferable" on the Letter of Credit. ②Nontransferable Letter of Credit refers to a Letter of Credit in which the beneficiary cannot transfer the right of the Letter of Credit to others. In international trade, the seller generally does not accept transferable Letter of Credit in order to ensure the safety of receiving payment for goods and do not know the credit of the third party.

可转让的信用证和不可转让的信用证(TRANSFERABLE CREDIT& NONTRANFERABLE CREDIT)。①可转让的信用证指受益人可将信用证的部分或全部权利转让给第三人的信用证。可转让的信用证必须在信用证上注明"可转让"（Transferable）的字样。②不可转让的信用证指受益人不能将信用证的权利转让给他人的信用证。在国际贸易中，卖方为了保障收取货款的安全，以及在对第三方的资信不了解的情况下，一般不接受可转让信用证。

（6）Revocable Letter of Credit and Irrevocable Letter of Credit. ①Revocable Letter of Credit refers to a Letter of Credit that can be modified or cancelled at any time without prior notice to the beneficiary. However, if the Letter of Credit has paid, accepted, negotiated or made a commitment of deferred payment in accordance with the terms of the Letter of Credit before receiving the cancellation notice from the issuing bank, the issuing bank shall reimburse the bank. ②Irrevocable Letter of Credit refers to a Letter of Credit that cannot be modified or cancelled without the consent of the issuing bank, confirming bank and beneficiary within the validity of the Letter of Credit. Irrevocable Letter of Credit is the most widely used Letter of Credit in international trade.

可撤销的信用证和不可撤销的信用证（REVOCABLE CREDIT & IRREVOCABLE CREDIT）。①可撤销的信用证指信用证在有效期内，开证行不必事先通知受益人，即可随时修改或取消的信用证。但如果在收到开证行撤销通知之前，该信用证已经按照信用证条款付款、承兑、议付或做出了延期付款的承诺，开证行应对该银行偿付。②不可撤销的信用证指在信用证有效期内，不经开证行、保兑行和受益人同意就不得修改或撤销的信用证。不可撤销的信用证对受益人收款比较有保障，是在国际贸易中使用最为广泛的一种信用证。

In addition, it also includes back-to-back Letter of Credit, counter Letter of Credit revolving Letter of Credit, standby Letter of Credit and other types of Letter of Credit. 此外，还包括背对背信用证、对开信用证、循环信用证、备用信用证等种类的信用证。

五、Sample and Content of a Letter of Credit 信用证的样本及内容

1. Specimen of a Letter of Credit 信用证样本（附中文说明）

Issue of a Documentary Credit——开证行

    BKCHCNBJA08E SESSION：000 ISN：000000

    BANK OF CHINA LIAONING NO. 5 ZHONGSHAN

    SQUARE ZHONGSHAN DISTRICT DALIAN CHINA

Destination Bank：——通知行

    KOEXKRSE ××× MESSAGE TYPE：700 KOREA EXCHANGE

    BANK SEOUL 178. 2 KA, ULCHI RO, CHUNG-KO

Type of Documentary Credit   **40A**IRREVOCABLE——信用证性质为不可撤销

Letter of Credit Number   **20**LC84E0081/99——信用证号码，一般做单时都要求标注此号

Date of Issue   **31G** 990916——开证日期

Date and Place of Expiry   **31D** 991015 KOREA——失效时间、地点

Applicant Bank   **51D** BANK OF CHINA LIAONING BRANCH——开证行

Applicant   **50D** DALIAN WEIDA TRADING CO., LTD. ——开证申请人

Beneficiary	**59** SANGYONG CORPORATION CPO BOX 110 SEOUL KOREA——受益人
Currency Code, Amount	**32B** USD 1,146,725.04——信用证总额
Available with … by …	**41D** ANY BANK BY NEGOTIATION——呈兑方式：任何银行议付，有的信用证为 ANY BANK BY PAYMENT，这两句有区别，第一个为银行付款后无追索权，第二个则有追索权，就是有权限要回已付给你的钱。
Drafts at	**42C** 45 DAYS AFTER SIGHT 见证 45 天内付款
Drawee	**42D** BANK OF CHINA LIAONING BRANCH　付款行
Partial Shipments	**43P** NOT ALLOWED——部分装船不允许
Transshipment	**43T** NOT ALLOWED——转船不允许
Shipping on Board/Dispatch/Packing in Charge at/ from	**44A** RUSSIAN SEA——起运港
Transportation to	**44B** DALIAN PORT, P. R. CHINA——目的港
Latest Date of Shipment	**44C** 990913——最迟装运期
Description of Goods or Services：	**45A** 货物描述 FROZEN YELLOW FIN SOLE WHOLE ROUND（WITH WHITE BELLY）USD770/MT CFR DALIAN QUANTITY：200MT ALASKA PLAICE（WITH YELLOW BELLY）USD600/MT CFR DALIAN QUANTITY：300MT
Documents Required：	**46A**——议付单据

1. SIGNED COMMERCIAL INVOICE IN 5 COPIES. ——签字的商业发票五份

2. FULL SET OF CLEAN ON BOARD OCEAN BILLS OF LADING MADE OUT TO ORDER AND BLANK ENDORSED, MARKED "FREIGHT PREPAID" NOTIFYING LIAONING OCEAN FISHING CO., LTD. TEL：411-3680288——

一整套清洁已装船提单，抬头为 TO ORDER 的空白背书，且注明运费已付，通知人为 **LIAONING OCEAN FISHING CO., LTD. TEL：411-3680288**

3. PACKING LIST/WEIGHT MEMO IN 4 COPIES INDICATING QUANTITY/GROSS AND NET WEIGHTS OF EACH PACKAGE AND PACKING CONDITIONS AS CALLED FOR BY THE L/C. ——装箱单/重量单四份，显示每个包装产品的数量/毛净重和信用证要求的包装情况。

4. CERTIFICATE OF QUALITY IN 3 COPIES ISSUED BY PUBLIC RECOGNIZED SURVEYOR. ——由 **PUBLIC RECOGNIZED SURVEYOR** 签发的质量证明三份。

5. BENEFICIARY'S CERTIFIED COPY OF FAX DISPATCHED TO THE ACCOUNTEE WITH 3 DAYS AFTER SHIPMENT ADVISING NAME OF VESSEL, DATE, QUANTITY, WEIGHT, VALUE OF SHIPMENT, L/C NUMBER AND CONTRACT NUMBER. ——受益人证明的传真件，在船开后三天内已将船名航次、日期、货物的数量、重量、价值、信用证号和合同号通知付款人。

6. CERTIFICATE OF ORIGIN IN 3 COPIES ISSUED BY AUTHORIZED INSTITUTION. ——当局签发的原产地证明三份。

7. CERTIFICATE OF HEALTH IN 3 COPIES ISSUED BY AUTHORIZED INSTITUTION. —— 当局签发的健康/检疫证明三份。

ADDITIONAL INSTRUCTIONS： **47A**——附加指示

1. CHARTER PARTY B/L AND THIRD PARTY DOCUMENTS ARE ACCEPTABLE. —— 租船提单和第三方单据可以接受。

2. SHIPMENT PRIOR TO L/C ISSUING DATE IS ACCEPTABLE. ——装船期早于信用证的签发日期是可以接受的。

3. BOTH QUANTITY AND AMOUNT 10 PERCENT MORE OR LESS ARE ALLOWED. ——允许数量和金额公差在10%左右。

Charges **71B** ALL BANKING CHARGES OUTSIDE THE OPENNING BANK ARE FOR BENEFICIARY'S ACCOUNT. ——费用说明

Period for Presentation **48** DOCUMENTS MUST BE PRESENTED WITHIN 15 DAYS AFTER THE DATE OF ISSUANCE OF THE TRANSPORT DOCUMENTS BUT WITHIN THE VALIDITY OF THE CREDIT. ——提示票据

Confirmation Instructions **49** WITHOUT——确认说明

Instructions to the Paying/Accepting/Negotiating Bank： **78**——付款/承兑/押汇银行指令

1. ALL DOCUMENTS TO BE FORWARDED IN ONE COVER, UNLESS OTHERWISE STATED ABOVE.

2. DISCREPANT DOCUMENT FEE OF USD 50.00 OR EQUAL CURRENCY WILL BE DEDUCTED FROM DRAWING IF DOCUMENTS WITH DISCREPANCIES ARE ACCEPTED.

"Advising Bank" **57A**——通知行

KOEXKRSE ××× MESSAGE TYPE：700

KOREA EXCHANGE BANK SEOUL 178.2 KA, ULCHI RO, CHUNG-KO——

2. SWIFT 信用证代码

SWIFT Society for Worldwide Interbank Financial Telecommunications is a private joint-stock company jointly owned by financial institutions. The SWIFT Code is usually used for international wire transfers or letter of credit telegrams. SWIFT can quickly process wire transfers between banks, similar to the bank's ID number. As long as you know the SWIFT code, you can accurately know the bank's information.

SWIFT 环球银行间金融通信协会(Society for Worldwide Interbank Financial Telecommunications)，是一个由金融机构共同拥有的私营股份公司。银行国际代码(SWIFT Code)通常情况下用于国际电汇或者信用证电报，SWIFT 可以快速地办理银行之间的电汇等业务，就像是银行的身份证件号码一样，只要知道了 SWIFT 代码就能准确地知道银行的信息(表 2-1)。

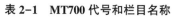

表 2-1　MT700 代号和栏目名称

Tag(代号)	Field Name(栏目名称)
20	documentary credit number(信用证号码)(MT 700)
20	documentary credit number(信用证号码)(MT 707)
21	receiver's reference(收报行编号)
23	issuing bank's reference(开证行号码)
26E	number of amendment(修改序号)
27	sequence(报文页数)
30	date of amendment(修改日期)
31C	date of issue(开证日期)
31D	date of expiry, place of expiry(到期日及到期地点)
31E	new date of expiry(新的到期日)
32B	currency code, amount(币别代号、金额)
33B	increase of documentary credit amount(信用证金额的增加)
34B	decrease of documentary credit amount(信用证金额的减少)
39A	percentage credit amount tolerance(信用证金额加减百分比)
39B	maximum credit amount(最高信用证金额)
39C	additional amounts covered(可附加金额)
40A	form of documentary credit(跟单信用证性质)
41A	available with … by …(信用证兑付方式)
42C	draft at …(汇票期限)
42A	drawee(汇票付款人)
42M	mixed payment details(混合付款指示)
42P	deferred payment details(延期付款指示)
43P	partial shipment(分批装运)
43T	transshipment(转运条款)
44A	loading on bard/dispatch/taking in charge at/from(装船发送/接管地点)
44B	for transportation to …(装运……至……)
44C	latest date of shipment(最后装船日)
44D	shipment period(装运期)
45A	description of goods and/or services(货物/劳务描述与价格条款)
45B	description goods and/or services(货物描述与交易条件)
46A	continued documents required(应具备单据)
47A	additional conditions(附加条件)

续表

Tag(代号)	Field Name(栏目名称)
48	period for presentation(提示期间)
49	confirmation instructions(保兑指示)
50	applicant(申请人)
51A	applicant bank(信用证开证行)
52A	issuing bank(开证行)
53A	reimbursement bank(偿付银行)
59	beneficiary(before this amendment)(修改以前的受益人)
71B	charges(费用条款)
72	sender to receiver information(银行间的备注)
78	instruction 给付款行、承兑行、议付行的指示
79	narrative(修改详述)

Section Two　Review and Amend the Letter of Credit
信用证的审核和修改

一、Review the Letter of Credit 信用证的审核

(一)Review the Letter of Credit 审核信用证

The examination of a letter of credit is an international trade in which the exporter reviews the shipping terms in the letter of credit. Key review points include: shipment date and port of shipment, destination port, transshipment and partial shipment, and foreign exchange settlement date. Reviewing and promptly modifying the letter of credit is crucial for exporters to ensure safe and timely collection of payment.

审核信用证是指在国际贸易中，出口商审核信用证中的装运条款。要重点审核：装运期和装运港、目的港、转船和分批装运、结汇日期。审核并及时修改信用证是出口商能否安全及时收回货款的关键。

(二)The Purpose of Reviewing a Letters of Credit 审核的目的

审核收到的信用证，有以下几点目的：

(1)The factors such as amount, description of goods, loading date and validity period of the letter of credit are consistent with the contract and the company's own production, including logistics arrangements.

金额、货物描述、信用证的装船期、效期等要素是否与合同以及企业自身的生产包括物流安排等相符。

(2)The credit standing of the issuing bank of the letter of credit, whether there is a paying bank, the duration of the letter of credit, and other factors that affect the payment effectiveness.

信用证的开证行的资信，是否有偿付行，信用证的期限等影响支付效力的因素。

（3）The key point is to review whether there are documents issued by the buyer or the buyer's agent in the requirements of the letter of credit documents. This clause is not acceptable.

重点是审核信用证单据要求中是否有由买方或买方的代理方出具的单据，这种条款是不能接受的。

（4）After receiving the letter of credit, after review, it is confirmed that it is consistent with one's own trading background, and at the same time, it is confirmed that one's export risk is controllable and will not be refused payment by the issuing bank, in order to ship and prepare documents in accordance with the requirements of the letter of credit and contract. Otherwise, if it is confirmed that there are terms that are not conducive to oneself, it is necessary to promptly contact the buyer to modify the letter of credit and inform them that if the letter of credit is not modified, they will refuse to fulfill the contract.

在收到信用证后，经过审核，与自己的交易背景等相符合，同时能确认自己出口的风险可控，不会被开证行拒付，才能按照信用证及合同要求发货并准备单据。否则的话，确认有不利于自身的条款，要及时联系买方修改信用证，并告知如果不修改就拒绝履行合同。

（三）The Key Points for Banks to Review a Letter of Credit 银行审核信用证的要点

（1）The issuing bank of the letter of credit better have good reputation.

信用证的开证行，最好是信誉比较好的银行。

（2）The advising bank of the letter of credit, the exporter generally chooses his own bank as the advising bank in order to facilitate business processing.

信用证的通知行，通常情况下出口方一般选择自己的银行为通知行，便于业务的处理。

（3）Is the letter of credit irrevocable?

信用证是不可撤销的吗？

（4）Does the letter of credit have restrictive validity or other reservation clauses?

信用证是否存在限制性生效或其他保留条款？

（5）Is the telegraphic letter of credit a simple telegraphic letter of credit?

电汇信用证是简单的电汇信用证吗？

（6）Does the letter of credit state the rules of international practice?

信用证是否规定了国际惯例？

（7）Is the letter of credit confirmed according to the contract requirements?

信用证是否按照合同要求加了保兑？

（8）The applicant and beneficiary of the L/C shall carefully check the names.

开证申请人和受益人应该仔细核对姓名。

（9）The payment term of the letter of credit, is it payment at sight or at usance?

信用证付款期限，是即期付款还是远期付款？

（10）The expiry date of the letter of credit shall comply with the provisions of the sales contract, generally 15 or 21 days after the shipment of the goods.

信用证的有效期应符合销售合同的规定，一般为货物装运后 15 或 21 天。

（11）The place where the L/C expires must be specified as the exporter's place, so that documents can be delivered in time; If it is overseas, then the documents should be presented in advance so as to have enough time to reach an effective bank.

信用证到期地点一定要规定为出口商的所在地，以便做到及时交单；如果是在海外，则应提前提交文件，以便有足够的时间到达有效的银行。

（12）Are the amount, currency and payment term of the letter of credit consistent with the contract?

信用证的金额、币种和付款期限，是否与合同一致？

（13）Is the name, specification, quantity, packaging and shipping mark of the goods in the letter of credit consistent with the contract?

信用证中的货物名称、规格、数量、包装、唛头等是否与合同一致？

（14）Are the provisions of the L/C on the port of shipment, port of discharge, time of shipment, partial shipment and transshipment consistent with the contract?

信用证中装运港口、卸货港口、装运时间、是否分批发货、转运的规定是否与合同一致？

（15）Beneficiary specified in letter of credit should submit the negotiation documents to the bank, including commercial invoice, bill of lading, insurance policy, packing list, certificate of origin, inspection certificate, etc. Pay attention to whether the documents can be issued, especially whether some documents have the provisions of the issuing unit and whether there are special document requirements.

信用证规定的受益人需要给银行提交的议付单据，包括商业发票、提单、保险单、装箱单、产地证、检测证书等。注意单据是否能够出具，尤其注意某些单据是否有出具单位规定，是否有特殊的单据要求条款。

（16）Note on the L/C, whether there is any supplement to the terms, so as not to cause losses.

信用证上的加注需要注意，是否有对条款的补充，以免做不到造成损失。

（17）The original letter of credit is the basis for foreign exchange settlement. Whether it is settlement by D/P or bill negotiation, the bank requires the original letter of credit, so it needs to be properly kept.

信用证的正本是办理结汇的依据，无论是交单结汇还是押汇，银行都要求提供信用证的正本，因此需要妥善保管。

（18）Whether the letter of credit number is clear; The date of issuance must be indicated on the letter of credit; If not, the date of power generation or the date of raising the head of the issuing bank shall be the date of issuance of the letter of credit; Who will bear the bank charges stipulated in the letter of credit; Whether the letter of credit is valid or conditional.

信用证号码是否清晰；信用证上必须注明签发日期；如果没有，发电日期或开证行行长的任命日期应为信用证的签发日期；信用证中规定的各项银行费用由谁来承担；信用证是否有效还是有条件的生效等。

（四）The Key points for Enterprise to Review a Letter of Credit 企业审核的要点

（1）The issuing bank of the letter of credit better have good reputation.

信用证的开证行最好是信誉良好的银行。

（2）The advising bank of the letter of credit, the exporter generally chooses his own bank as the advising bank in order to facilitate business processing.

信用证的通知行，通常情况下出口方一般选择自己的银行为通知行，便于业务的处理。

（3）Is the letter of credit irrevocable?

信用证是不可撤销的吗？

（4）Does the letter of credit have restrictive validity or other reservation clauses?

信用证是否存在限制性生效或其他保留条款？

（5）Is the telegraphic letter of credit a simple telegraphic letter of credit?

电汇信用证是简单的电汇信用证吗？

（6）Does the letter of credit state the rules of international practice?

信用证是否规定了国际惯例？

（7）Is the letter of credit confirmed according to the contract requirements?

信用证是否按照合同要求加了保兑？

（8）The applicant and beneficiary of the L/C shall carefully check the names.

开证申请人和受益人应该仔细核对姓名。

（9）The payment term of the letter of credit, is it payment at sight or at usance?

信用证付款期限，是即期付款还是远期付款？

（10）The expiry date of the letter of credit shall comply with the provisions of the sales contract, generally 15 or 21 days after the shipment of the goods.

信用证的有效期应符合销售合同的规定，一般为货物装运后的 15 或 21 天。

（11）The place where the L/C expires must be specified as the exporter's place, so that documents can be delivered in time; If it is overseas, then the documents should be presented in advance so as to have enough time to reach an effective bank.

信用证到期地必须指定为出口商所在地，以便及时交付单据；如果是在海外，则应提前提交文件，以便有足够的时间到达有效的银行。

（12）Are the amount, currency and payment term of the letter of credit consistent with the contract?

信用证的金额、币种和付款期限，是否与合同一致？

（13）Is the name, specification, quantity, packaging and shipping mark of the goods in the letter of credit consistent with the contract?

信用证中的货物名称、规格、数量、包装、唛头等是否与合同一致？

（14）Are the provisions of the L/C on the port of shipment, port of discharge, time of shipment, partial shipment and transshipment consistent with the contract?

信用证中的装运港口、卸货港口、装运时间、分批发货、转运的规定是否与合同一致？

（15）Beneficiary specified in letter of credit should submit the negotiation documents to the bank, including commercial invoice, bill of lading, insurance policy, packing list, certificate of origin, inspection certificate, etc. Pay attention to whether the documents can be issued, especially whether some documents have the provisions of the issuing unit and whether there are special document requirements.

信用证规定的受益人需要给银行提交的议付单据，包括商业发票、提单、保险单、装箱单、产地证、检测证书等，注意单据是否能够出具，尤其注意某些单据是否有出具单位规定，是否有特殊的单据要求条款。

(16) Note on the L/C, whether there is any supplement to the terms, so as not to cause losses.

注意信用证上是否有任何条款的补充，以免造成损失。

(17) The original letter of credit is the basis for foreign exchange settlement. Whether it is settlement by D/P or bill negotiation, the bank requires the original letter of credit, so it needs to be properly kept.

信用证的正本/原件是办理结汇的依据，无论是交单结汇还是押汇，银行都要求提供信用证的正本/原件，因此需要妥善保管。

(18) Requirements for documents: A letter of credit is a typical document transaction. If there are new special requirements for documents, it must be explicitly amended in the letter of credit. In addition, it also includes other agreed trading conditions.

单证要求：信用证是一种典型的单据交易。如果对单证有新的特殊要求，必须在信用证中明确修改。此外，它还包括其他商定的交易条件。

二、The Principles and Contents of Amending a Letter of Credit 修改信用证的原则和内容

(一) The Principle of Amending a Letter of Credit 修改信用证的原则

(1) Generally, it will not be changed if it is beneficial to us and does not affect the interests of the other party.

一般情况下，如果对我们有利且不影响对方利益，则不会更改。

(2) It is beneficial to us, but it will seriously affect the interests of the other party. Generally, it should be changed.

对我方有利，但会严重影响对方利益，一般要改。

(3) It's not good for us, but it can guarantee the safe collection of foreign exchange without increasing or basically increasing the cost, so it can be left unchanged.

对我方不利，但是在不增加或基本不增加成本的情况下可以保证安全收汇，可以不改。

(4) It's not good for us, and it can be completed at a higher cost. it will not be changed if the other party is willing to bear the cost, otherwise it will be modified.

对我方不利，又要在增加较大成本的情况下可以完成，若对方愿意承担成本，则不改，否则就要修改。

(5) We must change it if it's not good for us, and will seriously affect the safe collection of foreign exchange if we don't change it.

对我方不利，若不改会严重影响安全收汇，则坚决要改。

（二）The Contents of Amending a Letter of Credit 修改信用证的内容

（1）The shipment date of the Letter of Credit：If the shipment cannot be arranged according to the original provisions in the Letter of Credit, it needs to be amended.

信用证的装运期：如果不能按照信用证中原来的规定安排装运，就需要进行修改。

（2）The validity period and the place of expiry of the Letter of Credit：Generally, the validity period of the Letter of Credit should be revised along with the time of shipment. Most of the reasons are that the craftsman cannot deliver the documents within the validity period stipulated in the Letter of Credit. In addition, if the place of expiry is not in the beneficiary's place and it is not acceptable, it should be revised.

信用证的有效期与到期地：通常情况下，信用证的有效期应随装运时间而修改。大部分原因是持票人无法在信用证规定的有效期内交付文件。此外，如果到期地不在受益人所在地，并且不可接受，则应对其进行修订。

（3）Amount of L/C：It is usually caused by the change of transaction amount, for example, the change of unit price or quantity leads to the change of total amount.

信用证金额：通常是由于交易金额有变化所致，比如单价或者数量变化导致总金额变化。

（4）Conditions of shipment in the Letter of Credit：For example, when the conditions of the port of shipment, the port of destination, partial shipment and transshipment change, the relevant clauses in the Letter of Credit must be amended.

信用证内有关装运的条件：比如，装运港、目的港、分批装运、转运等条件发生变化时，必须对信用证内的相关条款进行修改。

（5）Modification of the conditions of goods：For example, if the quality, quantity and specifications of the traded goods need to be adjusted, the Letter of Credit must be modified, otherwise, the documents may be inconsistent and affect the collection of foreign exchange.

关于货物方面的条件的修改：比如，需要对交易货物的质量、数量、规格等方面进行调整时，必须修改信用证，否则就可能出现单证不符的情况，从而影响收汇。

（6）Usage of L/C：For example, the provisions on the transfer mode and revolving mode of L/C may be adjusted due to the actual needs of the transaction, so the relevant clauses must be amended.

信用证的使用方式：比如，对信用证的转让方式、循环方式等的规定，可能由于交易的实际需要而出现调整，于是就必须修改相关条款。

（7）Requirements for documents：A Letter of Credit is a typical document transaction. If there are new special requirements for documents, it must be explicitly amended in the Letter of Credit. In addition, it also includes other agreed trading conditions.

对于单证的要求：信用证是典型的单证交易，如果在单证方面出现了新的特殊要求，必须在信用证中明确修订，另外还包括其他约定的交易条件。

（三）The Requirements and Notes of Amending a Letter of Credit 修改信用证的要求和注意事项

Requirements（要求）：

Only the buyer（the applicant）has the right to decide whether or not to accept the amended Letter of Credit. The amendment of the Letter of Credit can only be proposed by the beneficiary to the applicant, and the applicant will notify the issuing bank after its consent.

只有买方（开证申请人）有权决定是否接受修改信用证。修改信用证只能由受益人向开证申请人提出，经开证申请人同意后再由其通知开证行。

Only the seller（beneficiary）has the right to decide whether to accept the amendment of the Letter of Credit. The amendment to the L/C is valid only after the beneficiary receives the amendment notice transmitted by the issuing bank through the advising bank. The application for amendment made directly by the beneficiary to the issuing bank is invalid.

只有卖方（受益人）有权决定是否接受信用证的修改。受益人只有在收到开证行通过通知行转递的修改通知后，对信用证的修改才有效。直接由受益人向开证行提出的改证申请是无效的。

Notes（注意事项）：

Anything that needs to be amended should be put forward to the other party at one time, so as to avoid amending the letter of credit many times.

凡是需要修改的内容应做到一次性向对方提出，避免多次修改信用证的情况。

Any amendment to an irrevocable Letter of Credit must be approved by the parties before it becomes effective.

对于不可撤销信用证中任何条款的修改，都必须取得当事人的同意后才能生效。

After receiving the amendment of the Letter of Credit, we should promptly check whether the amendment meets the requirements, and accept or propose a new amendment according to the situation. All the contents of the same amendment are either accepted or rejected, and partial acceptance of the amendment is invalid.

收到信用证修改后，应及时检查修改内容是否符合要求，并根据情况表示接受或提出重新修改；同一份修改书的内容，要么全部接受，要么全部拒绝，对修改书的部分接受是无效的。

The amendment of the relevant L/C must be notified by the original L/C to be true and effective. A copy of the modification application or modification letter sent directly by the buyer is not a valid modification.

相关信用证修改必须通过原信用证通知行才真实、有效；买方直接寄送的修改申请书或修改函的副本不是有效的修改。

It is clear who will bear the cost of modification, which is generally determined according to the attribution of responsibility.

明确修改费用由谁承担，一般按照责任归属来确定。

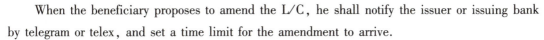
When the beneficiary proposes to amend the L/C, he shall notify the issuer or issuing bank by telegram or telex, and set a time limit for the amendment to arrive.

受益人提出修改信用证，应用电报或电传通知开证人或开证行，并规定修改到达的期限。

Section Three　Case Study 信用证的审核和修改的案例实训

【Case study】案例 1：Review and amend a Letter of Credit according to the following information 根据下面信息审核和修改信用证。

Issuing date：June 15, 2022

Expiry place and expiry date：Germany September 10, 2022

Issuing bank：China Construction Bank Xian Branch

Format of issuance：SWIFT

The L/C is negotiable with any bank in Germany.

The issuing bank can make payment against presentation of the documents specified below as well as a 30 days draft for full invoice amount issued by the beneficiary.

＊Documents required：

Commercial invoice in triplicate, indicating L/C number and contract number.

Packing list in triplicate, indicating the gross weight, net weight of each package and the packing conditions.

Certificate of Origin in duplicate issued by competent authority.

Full set of ocean Bill of Lading in triplicate made out to order with blank endorsement, marked "freight prepaid" and notify the applicant.

Certificate of quality in duplicate issued by the beneficiary.

Beneficiary's statement certifying that a copy of the full set of documents has been sent to the applicant.

A copy of shipping advice sent out within 24 hours after shipment, indicating shipment details.

＊Goods description：

NAME：1008-TL-02 H. S. 85423100. 00(52)

PRICE：USD 22. 00 PER PCS

QUANTITY：700 PCS

PACKING：PACKED IN 4 CARTONS ONLY

Period of presentation：15 days after issuance of transport documents

＊Remarks：

Applicant A/C No. （RMB）：06-039282536342058468

Contact person：LILY CHAO

Tel.：52365866

Sale Contract

CONTRACT						
Seller				Contract No.		PC141202510
KARSTADT WARENHAUS AG THEODOR-ALTHOFF-STRASSE 2 45133 ESSEN GERMANY				Date		JUN. 10,2022
				Signed At		XIAN
Buyer				L/C No.		
XIAN LIXING ELECTRONICS CO., LTD. NO. 29 HUOJU NORTH ROAD, XIAN HIGH TECHNOLOGY DEVE- LOPMENT ZONE, XIAN, SHAANXI, CHINA						

The undersigned Seller and Buyer have agreed to close the following transactions according to the terms and conditions stipulated below:

Shipping Marks	Item No.	Description	QTY	Unit	Unit Price	Amount
N/M		1008-TL-02 H. S. 85423100.00(52)	700	PCS	USD 22.00	USD 15,400.00
Total			700			USD 15,400.00

Price Terms:	CIP XIAN
Total Amount:	SAY U. S. DOLLARS FOURTEEN THOUSAND ONLY.
Percentage of allowance for amount and quantity:	% More or Less
Payment Terms:	IRREVOCABLE L/C AT 30 DAYS SIGHT
Time of Shipment:	NOT LATER THAN AUGUST 30 2019
Packing:	PACKED IN 4 CARTONS ONLY
Port of Loading:	HAMBURG
Port of Destination:	XIAN
Partial Shipment:	NOT ALLOWED
Transshipment:	NOT ALLOWED
Insurance:	TO BE EFFECTED BY THE BUYER
Special Clause:	
Remark:	

1. QUALITY/QUANTITY DISCREPANCY: In case of quality discrepancy, claim should be filed by the Buyer within 3 months after the arrival of the goods at port of destination, while of quantity discrepancy, claim should be filed by the Buyer within 15 days after the arrival of the goods at port of destination. It is understood that the Seller shall not be liable for any discrepancy of the goods shipped due to causes for which the Insurance Company, Shipping company, other transportation, organization/or Post Office are liable.

2. The Seller shall not be held liable for failure or delay in delivery of the entire lot or a portion of the goods under this Sales Contract on consequence of any Force Majeure incidents.

3. Arbitration: All disputes in connection with this Contract or the execution thereof shall be settled by negotiation between two parties. If no settlement can be reached, the case in dispute shall then be submitted for arbitration in the country of defendant in accordance with the arbitration regulations of the arbitration organization of the defendant country. The decision made by the arbitration organization shall be taken as final and binding upon both parties. The arbitration expenses shall be borne by the losing party unless otherwise awarded by the arbitration organization.

4. The Buyer are requested to sign and return one copy of this Sales Contract immediately after receipt of the same. Objection, if any, should be raised by the Buyer within five days after the receipt of this Sales Contract, in the absence of which it is understood that the Buyer has accepted the terms and conditions of the Sales Contract.

This Contract shall come into effect after signature by both parties. This Contract is made in two originals with same effects. Each party holds one.

THE SELLER:	THE BUYER:
KARSTADT WARENHAUS AG	XIAN LIXING ELECTRONICS CO., LTD.

Please amend the letter of credit below. 请修改下面的信用证。

不可撤销跟单信用证申请书	
APPLICATION FOR IRREVOCABLE DOCUMENTARY CREDIT	
To: CHINA CONSTRUCTION BANK XIAMEN Please establish by: SWIFT Date: 2022-8-15	
Applicant: XIAN LIXING ELECTRONICS CO., LTD. NO. 29 HUOJU NORTH ROAD, XIAN HIGH TECHNOLOGY DEVELOPMENT ZONE, XIAN SHAANXI, CHINA	IRREVOCABLE DOCUMENTARY CREDIT No.
	Valid IN GERMARNY until 10-SET-2022
	Advising Bank: (If cannot specify, left for bank to fill)
Beneficiary: KARSTADT WARENHAUS AG THEODOR-ALTHOFF-STRASSE 2 45133 ESSEN GERMANY	Amount(In figures and words) USD14,000.00
	SAY U. S. DOLLARS FOURTEEN THOUSAND ONLY
	Price term: CIP XIAMEN

Credit available with ANY BANK IN GERMARNY by NEGOTIATION
against the documents detailed herein and beneficiary's draft(s)for 100% of the invoice value
at 30 DAYS AFTER SIGHT drawn on ISSUING BANK
Documents required：（marked with√）
□√ Signed Commercial Invoice in 3 COPIES indicating L/C No. and Contract No. PC141202510
□√ Full set of clean on board Ocean Bill of Lading in 3/3 made out to ORDER marked FREIGHT PREPAID and endorsed   IN BLANK   showing freight amount notifying APPLICANT
□Air Waybills in _____ showing _____ indicating freight amount and consigned to _____
□Forwarding agent's Cargo Receipt consigned to _____
□Insurance Policy/Certificate in _____ for _____ of the invoice value showing claims payable at/in _____ in
currency of the draft endorsed _____ and covering _____
□√Packing List/Weight Memo in 3 COPIES indicating quantity/gross and net weight of each package and packing
conditions as called for by the L/C.
□√Certificate of Quantity/Weight in 3 COPIES issued by BENIFICIARY
□√Certificate of Quality in 1 COPIES issued by COMPETENT AUTHORITY
□√Beneficiary's certified copy of Fax/Telex advising applicant within 24 hours after shipment indicating SHIP-MENT DETAILS
_____
□√Certificate of Origin in 2 COPIES   issued by COMPETENT AUTHORITY
□Special Condition：
Evidencing Shipment of：
GOODS：1008-TL-02 H. S. 85423100. 00(52) PRICE：USD 20. 00 PER PCS QUANTITY：700 PCS PACKING：PACKED IN 4 CARTONS ONLY
Packing：PACKED IN 4 CARTONS ONLY
Manufacturer：

Shipping Mark：		
Documents must be presented within 15 days after date of issuance of the transport document（S）but within the validity of the credit.		
Shipment from GERMANY	Partial shipment	□Allowed □√Not allowed
to XIAN, CHINA latest on 30-AUG-2022	Transhipment	□Allowed □√Not allowed
□Documents issued earlier than L/C issuing date are not acceptable.		
□Third party as shipper is not acceptable. Short form/Blank back B/L is not acceptable.		
□All banking charges except issuing charge and acceptance commission if any are for account of beneficiary.		
For banks use only	我公司承担本申请书背面所列责任及承诺，并保证按照办理。 <div align="right">（申请人名称及印鉴章）</div>	
Seal and/or Signature　　　　checked by	RMB A/C No.	
L/C Margin　　%　　checked by	06-039282536342058468	
Credit Facility　　　　checked by	USD or（　　　　　）A/C No.	
Ent　　　　Ver　　　　App	联系人：LILY CHAO 电话：51365868	

案例答案：

不可撤销跟单信用证申请书	
APPLICATION FOR IRREVOCABLE DOCUMENTARY CREDIT	
To：CHINA CONSTRUCTION BANK XIAN　　Please establish by：SWIFT　　Date：2022-6-15	
Applicant： XIAN LIXING ELECTRONICS CO., LTD. NO. 29 HUOJU NORTH ROAD, XIAN HIGH TECH- NOLOGY DEVELOPMENT ZONE, XIAN SHAANXI, CHINA	IRREVOCABLE DOCUMENTARY CREDIT No.
	Valid　IN GERMANY　until 10-SEP-2022
	Advising Bank：（If cannot specify, left for bank to fill）
Beneficiary： KARSTADT WARENHAUS AG THEODOR-ALTHOFF-STRASSE 2 45133 ESSEN GERMANY	Amount（In figures and words）　USD15,400.00
	SAY U. S. DOLLARS FIFTEEN THOUSAND AND FOUR HUNDRED ONLY
	Price term：CIP XIAN
Credit available with ANY BANK IN GERMANY by NEGOTIATION	

against the documents detailed herein and beneficiary's draft(s) for 100% of the invoice value
at   30 DAYS AFTER SIGHT   drawn on ISSUING BANK
Documents required：（marked with√）
□√ Signed Commercial Invoice in 3 COPIES indicating L/C No. and Contract No. PC141202510
□ √Full set of clean on board Ocean Bill of Lading in 3/3 made out to ORDER marked FREIGHT PREPAID and endorsed   IN BLANK   showing freight amount notifying APPLICANT
□Air Waybills in _____ showing _____ indicating freight amount and consigned to _____
□Forwarding agent's Cargo Receipt consigned to _____
□Insurance Policy/Certificate in _____ for _____ of the invoice value showing claims payable at/in _____ in
currency of the draft endorsed _____ and covering _____
□√Packing List/Weight Memo in 3 COPIES indicating quantity/gross and net weight of each package and packing
conditions as called for by the L/C.
□Certificate of Quantity/Weight in _____ issued by _____.
□√Certificate of Quality in 2 COPIES issued by BENEFICIARY
□√Beneficiary's certified copy of Fax/Telex advising applicant within 24 hours after shipment indicating SHIPMENT DETAILS
_____
□√Certificate of Origin in 2 COPIES issued by COMPETENT AUTHORITY
□Special Condition：
Evidencing Shipment of：
GOODS：1008-TL-02 H. S. 85423100. 00(52)   PRICE：USD 22. 00 PER PCS   QUANTITY：700 PCS   PACKING：PACKED IN 4 CARTONS ONLY
Packing：PACKED IN 4 CARTONS ONLY
Manufacturer：
Shipping Mark：

Documents must be presented within 15 days after date of issuance of the transport document(S)but within the validity of the credit.		
Shipment from GERMANY	Partial shipment	□Allowed □√Not allowed
to XIAN, CHINA latest on 30-AUG-19	Transhipment	□Allowed □√Not allowed
□Documents issued earlier than L/C issuing date are not acceptable.		
□Third party as shipper is not acceptable. Short form/Blank back B/L is not acceptable.		
□All banking charges except issuing charge and acceptance commission if any are for account of beneficiary.		
For banks use only	我公司承担本申请书背面所列责任及承诺，并保证按照办理。 （申请人名称及印鉴章）	
Seal and/or Signature　　checked by	RMB A/C No.	
L/C Margin　%　checked by	06-039282536342058468	
Credit Facility　　checked by	USD or(　　　　)A/C No.	
Ent　　Ver　　App	联系人：LILY CHAO 电话：51365868	

　　案例 2：英国某公司来信用证的金额为："About USD4,200, less 5% commission and 5% allowance(dis.)"。信用证要求的商品是女式衬衫，单价为每件 2.80 美元，CIF London，共 2 500 件，我们应怎样缮制出口发票金额？

　　【分析】应首先核对信用证，如果与信用证相符，按商业习惯做法在缮制出口发票时，应在总金额(单价×数量)中先扣除 5% 优惠(折扣)得出一个毛净价，然后在此基础上再扣除 5% 佣金，得出净价。具体制单如下：

Ladies Blouses

2,500 pieces @ USD 2.80 7,000.00

Less 5% allowance 350.00

——————————————

6,650.00

Less 5% commission：332.50

——————————————

CIF London net：USD 6,317.50

　　注意：在既有折扣又有佣金的交易中，我们应掌握先扣除折扣，然后再计扣佣金，因为折扣部分是不应支付佣金的。

　　案例 3：我国某外贸公司与美国"金华企业公司"(KAM WA ENTERPRISES INC. USA)签订了销往香港的花岗石合同，总金额达 1 950 万美元，并通过香港某银行开出了上述合同项下的第一笔信用证，金额 190 万美元，购 5 千立方米花岗石砌石。信用证规定：货物只能待收到开证人指定船名的装运通知后装运，而该装运通知将由开证行以修改方式发出。该外贸公司开立信用证后，将质保金260万元付给了买方的指定代表。该外贸公司的做法对不对？

【分析】不对。因为信用证规定"装运通知由开证行签发和以修改形式进行"，以使该信用证的主动权落在开证申请人手中。如果对方以货物质量不合格为由，拒绝发出"装运通知"，会致使货物滞留产地，中方公司根本无法发货收汇，质保金白白丧失，损失惨重。

【案例4】：我方出口手表到印度，按FCA Shanghai Airport签约，交货期8月。出口企业8月31日将该手表运到上海虹桥机场并由航空公司收货并开具航空运单。我方即电传印度发出装运通知。9月2日手表抵达孟买，将到货通知连同发票和航空运单送交孟买××银行。该银行即通知印商提货、付款，但印商以延迟交货为由拒绝。

问：根据案例，分析最后结果。

【分析】FCA（FREE CARRIER）"货交承运人（……指定地点）"是指卖方只要将货物在指定的地点交给买方指定的承运人，并办理了出口清关手续，即完成交货。此案例中没有指明承运货物的航空公司是否为买方所指定的，但即便买方没有指定，卖方也可按惯例指定航空公司运输（费用到付，即买方承担），只要卖方在约定的时间内（8月31日前，包括8月31日）将货交予承运人，卖方即完成交货，买方需按约付费，所谓的延迟交货不成立，卖方应立即支付所有款项。

【课堂讨论】上海某公司与美国某公司达成一项出口交易。我方收到美国商业银行开来的信用证，证上最大金额为30 000美元，但我方在装运出口时，实装不同规格、不同单价的货品的总金额为30 098美元，超出了信用证允许的最大金额，议付行不同意接受，而我经办人员以该外商资信较好为由，认为区区小数不会计较，结果遭到开证行的拒付。请问，在本项交易中我方应吸取什么教训？

【参考答案】：我方对此应吸取的教训之一就是必须对信用证业务下"单证相符"有足够认识。《统一惯例》中对开证行的责任有如下规定：开证行必须合理谨慎地审核一切有关单据，并从表面上确定其是否与信用证条款相符，以决定是否承担付款的责任。因此，银行付款的依据只是看单据表面是否相符，而不管客户如何表态之类事宜。不论我方所提交发票金额比信用证金额多出多少，都以单证不符论处而拒付。

【课堂讨论】我某公司与法国某公司按CIF条件签订一笔大宗商品出口合同，合同规定装运期为6月份，但未规定具体开证日期。法国公司拖延开证，我方见装运期快到，从5月月底开始，连续多次电催外商开证。6月5日，收到开证行的简电通知，我方因怕耽误装运期，即按简电办理装运。6月28日，我方才收到信用证证实书，该证实书对有关单据作了与合同不符的规定。经办人审证时未予注意，交银行议付时，银行也未发现，开证行即以单证不符为由，拒付货款。你认为，我方应从此事件中吸取哪些教训？

【参考答案】：

(1)在签订合同时，不仅要规定装运日期，还必须规定好信用证的开证日期。信用证下，出口方先备货，等进口方开来信用证并审核无误时才发货，所以如果不规定开证日期，进口方拖延开证，甚至超过合同的装运日期，出口方只会处于被动地位。

(2)信用证是一项纯单据业务，审核信用证时要做到"单单一致，单证一致"。我方收到信用证证实书，该证实书对有关单据作了与合同不符的规定。但经办人审证时未予注意，交银行议付时，议付行也未发现。业务员在审证时应做到"单单一致，单证一致"。

Exercises 练习

一、选择题

1. 一份于 5 月 20 日开立的信用证，规定最迟装运期为 7 月 31 日，信用证有效期为 8 月 15 日，受益人于 8 月 10 日持全套单据向银行交单议付，则下列日期签发的提单中，（　　）将被银行接受。

　　A. 5 月 10 日　　　　B. 8 月 1 日　　　　C. 7 月 21 日　　　　D. 7 月 19 日

2. 信用证的"BENEFICIARY"一般是指（　　）。

　　A. 合同的买方　　　B. 合同的卖方　　　C. 开证申请人　　　D. 通知行

3. 下列有关信用证的描述中，正确的是（　　）。

　　A. 信用证若未注明是否可撤销，则认为它是可撤销的

　　B. 即使是资信高的大银行开出的信用证，金额较高的还须保兑

　　C. 受益人只有收到开证行通过通知行转递的修改通知后，对信用证的修改才有效

　　D. 不能接受到期地点规定为国外的信用证

4. 信用证的受益人，一般应该填（　　）。

　　A. 进口商的名称和地址　　　　　　　B. 出口商的名称和地址

　　C. 汇票的付款人　　　　　　　　　　D. 托收行

5. 下列说法，错误的是（　　）。

　　A. 对同一信用证修改书的内容，必须全部接受，部分接受无效

　　B. 在受益人告知通知行他接受修改前，原信用证对受益人仍有效

　　C. 不能接受信用证的到期地点在开证人所在地的信用证

　　D. 信用证下汇票的付款人是开证行，否则汇票将被视作附属单据

6. 在审核和修改信用证中，只有（　　）有权决定是否接受修改信用证。

　　A. 开证申请人　　　B. 受益人　　　　C. 开证行　　　　D. 议付行

7. 信用证当事人中，（　　）在收到开证行通过通知行转递的修改通知后，对信用证进行修改才有效。

　　A. 开证申请人　　　B. 受益人　　　　C. 偿付行　　　　D. 议付行

二、简答题

1. 我国某外贸公司与澳大利亚某商达成一项皮手套出口合同，价格条款为 CIF 悉尼，支付方式为不可撤销的即期信用证，投保中国保险条款一切险。生产厂家在生产的最后一道工序时，降低了湿度标准，使得产品的湿度增大，然后将产品装入集装箱。货物到港后，检验结果表明，产品全部霉变，损失达八万美元。调查后发现，该货物出口地不异常热，进口地不异常冷，运输途中无异常，属于正常运输。

　　请问：（1）保险公司对该批货物是否负责赔偿？为什么？

　　　　　（2）进口商是否该支付货款？为什么？

2. 我某进出口公司出口一批轻纺织品，合同规定以不可撤销的即期信用证为付款方式。买方在合同规定的开证时间内将信用证开抵通知银行，并立即转交给了我进出口公司。我进出口公司审核后发现，有关条款与合同不一致。为争取时间、尽快将信用证修改完毕，以便办理货物的装运，我方立即电告开证银行修改信用证，并要求将信用证修改书直接寄交我公司。

请问：（1）我方的做法可能会产生什么后果？

（2）正确的信用证修改渠道是怎样的？

3. 中方某公司与美国某公司达成一项出口交易，我方收到美国花旗银行开来的信用证，证上最大金额为 15 000 美元，但我方在装运出口时，实装不同规格、不同单价的货品的总金额为 15 042 美元，超出了信用证允许的最大金额，议付行不同意接受，而我经办人员以该外商资信较好为由，认为区区小数不会计较，请银行寄单，后果由出口人负责。结果遭到开证行的拒付。

请问：在本项交易中我方应吸取什么教训？

4. 我方某公司与美国某公司达成一项出口交易，合同规定以不可撤销的即期信用证为付款方式。买方在合同规定的开证时间内将信用证开抵通知银行，并立即转交给了我进出口公司。我方公司审核后发现，有关条款与合同不一致。为争取时间、尽快将信用证修改完毕，以便办理货物的装运，我方立即电告开证银行修改信用证，并要求将信用证修改书直接寄交我公司。

请问：（1）我方的做法可能会产生什么后果？

（2）正确的信用证修改渠道是怎样的？

三、审核信用证并修改

根据以下的销售合同审核国外开来的信用证，请指出信用证中存在的 10 个问题并进行修改。

Sales Confirmation

No：0003916

Date：Sep. 30, 2022

Seller：Ningbo Fadu Textile International Trade Corp.

Buyer：Sunny Men Corporation, P. O. Box No. 6789 Toronto, Canada.

Commodity and Specifications：Polo brand full cotton men's shirt 15,000 pcs, 5% more or less at seller's option

Packing：In cartons of 20 pcs each, containerized

Unit Price：US $ 1. 20 Per Piece CFR Toronto

Total value：US $ 18,000. 00(U. S. Dollars Eighteen Thousand only)

Time of shipment：During Nov. /Dec. 2022 in two equal monthly lots, from China to Toronto, allowing transshipment.

Insurance：To be covered by the Buyer

Terms of Payment：By Irrevocable Sight Letter of Credit to reach the Seller 15 days before the month of shipment and remained valid for negotiation in China until the 15th days after date of shipment.

IRREVOCABLE DOCUMENTARY CREDIT

NO. 051086

Oct. 12, 2022

FROM：THE ROYAL BANK OF CANADA

TO：BANK OF CHINA, NINGBO, CHINA

WE OPEN IRREVOCABLE DOCUMENTARY CREDIT NO. 051086

BENEFICIARY：NINGBO FADU TEXTILE IMP. AND EXP. CO. LTD. （1）JIEFANG SOUTH ROAD 111, NINGBO, CHINA

APPLICANT：SUNNY MEN CORPORATION   P. O. BOX NO. 6789 TORONTO, CANADA

AMOUNT：US＄18,000.00(US DOLLARS EIGHTEEN THOUSAND ONLY)

THIS CREDIT IS AVAILABLE BY BENEFICIARY'S DRAFT AT 30 DAYS AFTER SIGHT (2)FOR 100% OF INVOICE VALUE DRAWN ON THE ROYAL BANK OF CANADA

ACCOMPANIED BY THE FOLLOWING DOCUMENTS：

1. SIGNED COMMERCIAL INVOICE IN 3 COPIES.

2. FULL SET OF CLEAN ON BOARD BILL OF LADING MADE OUT TO ORDER AND BLANK ENDORSED MARKED FREIGHT PREPAID AND NOTIFY APPLICANT.

3. INSURANCE POLICY IN DUPLICATE COPIES FOR 110% OF INVOICE VALUE. （3）COVERING ALL RISKS AND WAR RISK SUBJECT TO CIC DATED JAN. 1ST, 2022.

4. CERTIFICATE OF ORIGIN IN DUPLICATE ISSUED BY CHINA INTERNATIONAL CHAMBER OF COMMERCE OR OTHER GOVERNMENT AUTHORITIES.

5. INSPECTION CERTIFICATE OF QUALITY ISSUED BY APPLICANT COVERING：（4）

POLO BRAND FULL COTTON MEN'S SHIRT 15,000PCS（5）AT US＄1.20 PER PIECE CFRC3%（6）TORONTO AS PER S/C NO. 0003916 DATED SEP. 30, 2022.

LATEST SHIPMENT：（   ）NOV. 30,2022 FROM NINGBO（8）TO TORONTO.

PARTIAL SHIPMENTS：ALLOWED

TRANSHIPMENT：PROHIBITED

（9）THE GOODS SHALL BE CONTAINERIZED. DOCUMENTS MUST BE PRESENTED WITHIN 8 DAYS（10）AFTER THE DATE OF THE B/L, BUT WITHIN THE VALIDITY OF THE CREDIT.

THE ROYAL BANK OF CANADA

练习答案

一、选择题

1. C 2. B 3. C 4. B 5. C 6. A 7. B

二、简答题

1. (1)保险公司对该批货物不负责赔偿。根据中国保险条款，货物本身内在的缺陷或特征所造成的损失或费用，属于保险除外责任。这批皮手套的霉变，是由于工厂降低了湿度标准后，货物本身内在的缺陷或特征所致的，所以保险公司是不会负责赔偿的。

(2)进口商必须支付货款。因为 CIF 是象征性交货，交单即是交货。只要单证相符、单单相符，开证银行必须付款。

2. (1)我方的做法可能会产生：①因开证银行不同意修改信用证或拖延修改信用证，导致我方无法单证一致而安全收汇；②我方无法辨别信用证修改书的真伪就办理装运，可能会货款两空。

（2）正确的信用证修改渠道：受益人与开证申请人联系修改信用证，开证申请人到开证银行修改信用证，开证银行将信用证修改送达通知银行，通知银行审核修改的真伪性后将修改送达受益人。

3. 我方对此应吸取的教训之一就是必须对信用证业务下"单证相符"有足够认识。《统一惯例》中对开证行的责任有如下规定：开证行必须合理谨慎地审核一切有关单据，并从表面上确定其是否与信用证条款相符，以决定是否承担付款的责任。因此，银行付款的依据只是看单据表面是否相符，而不管客户如何表态之类事宜。不论我方所提交发票金额比信用证金额多出多少，都以单证不符论处而拒付。在此项交易中，我方可在发票中加"quote：written off USD 42"作内部注销，使发票金额与信用证金额相符，从而保证基本货款顺利结汇。

4. （1）我方的做法可能会产生：①因开证银行不同意修改信用证或拖延修改信用证，导致我方无法单证一致而安全收汇。②我方无法辨别信用证修改书的真伪就办理装运，可能会货款两空。

（2）正确的信用证修改渠道：受益人与开证申请人联系修改信用证，开证申请人到开证银行修改信用证，开证银行将信用证修改送达通知银行，通知银行审核修改的真伪性后将修改送达受益人。

三、审证信用证并修改，参考答案

1. "NINGBO FADU TEXTILE IMP. AND EXP. CO. LTD."

AMENDS TO "NINGBO HUADU TEXTILE INTERNATIONAL TRADE CORP."

2. THE TENOR OF DRAFT IS "AT SIGHT" **INSTEAD OF** "AT 30 DAYS AFTER SIGHT"

3. "INSURANCE POLICY IN DUPLICATE COPIES FOR 110% OF INVOICE VALUE. COVERING ALL RISKS AND WAR RISK SUBJECT TO CIC DATED JAN. 1ST, 1981" SHOULD BE **DELETED**

4. "INSPECTION CERTIFICATE OF QUALITY ISSUED BY APPLICANT COVERING"

AMENDS TO "INSPECTION CERTIFICATE OF QUALITY ISSUED BY GOVERNMENT AUTHORITIES OR SELLER."

5. "POLO BRAND FULL COTTON MEN'S SHIRT 15,000 PCS AT US $ 1. 20 PER PIECE"

AMENDS TO "POLO BRAND FULL COTTON MEN'S SHIRT 15,000 PCS, 5% MORE OR LESS AT SELLER'S OPTION AT US $ 1. 20 PER PIECE"

6. "CFRC 3% TORONTO" **AMENDS TO** "CFR TORONTO"

7. "LATEST SHIPMENT：NOV. 30, 2022"

AMENDS TO "LATEST SHIPMENT：DEC. 31, 2022

8. "FROM NINGBO TO TORONTO."

AMENDS TO "FROM ANY PORT OF CHINA TO TORONTO."

9. "TRANSHIPMENT：PROHIBITED"

AMENDS TO "TRANSHIPMENT：ALLOWED"

10. THE PERIOD OF PRESENTATION

AMENDS TO "WITHIN 15 DAYS AFTER THE DATE OF THE B/L".

Chapter 3 Commercial Invoice 商业发票

Key Points and Difficulties

- To Understand the Use of Commercial Documents
- To Know the Elements and the Contents of Commercial Invoice and Packing Documents
- To Make out the Above Documents

Learning Objectives

- The Contents of Commercial Invoice and Packing Documents
- Making out Commercial Invoice and Packing Documents

Section One   Commercial Documents 商业单据

Commercial documents are generally issued by importer, exporter or some relevant non-governmental business organizations. They aim to ensure smooth transaction. Commercial documents usually include: Commercial invoice, Pro-forma Invoice and Packing Documents.

商业单据通常由出口方、进口方和一些相关的非政府商业组织开具，目的是保证交易顺利进行。商业单据通常包含商业发票、形式发票和包装单据。

1. Commercial Invoice 商业发票

Commercial invoice is a price list issued by the seller(exporter), which contains the name, quantity, price and other contents of the goods. It serves as the central document for the delivery of goods and settlement of payment between the buyer and the seller. It is also a necessary document for import and export inspection, certificate of origin, license, and insurance claim and settlement, and export documents.

商业发票是卖方(出口商)开立的载有货物名称、数量、价格等内容的价目清单，作为买卖双方交接货物和结算货款的中心单据，也是进出口报检，办理产地证、许可证，办理保险索赔与理赔以及出口交单的必备单据。

2. The Structure of Commercial Invoice 商业发票的结构

A commercial invoice is mainly made up of three parts: the heading, the body, and the complementary close.

商业发票主要由三部分组成：开头、主体和结尾部分。

Heading 开头

The contents in the heading include the term "Commercial Invoice" or "Invoice", the date and number of the invoice, details of the buyer and the seller, the sales contract number, the name of vessel, the port of loading and discharge or transhipment, the L/C number, the name of the issuing bank, the date of shipment, etc. All the items must be in compliance with the stipulations of the credit.

开头部分的内容包括：专业术语"商业发票"或"发票"、日期、发票号、买卖双方的详细信息、销售合同的编码、货轮名称、装卸港口和转运港口、信用证号、开证行名称、装船期等。所有的项目必须符合信用证的规定。

Body 主体

The body of a commercial invoice consists of items, such as the name and description of goods, shipping mark, quantity, price and invoice amount, packing, gross and net weight, etc.

According to the UCP 600, if there is the term "about" or "approximately", the quantity is allowed to be 10% more or 10% less than that stipulated in the credit. Sometimes, the credit itself contains a more or less clause, say "more or less 5%", the quantity indicated in the invoice should comply with the stipulations. In the case that the credit contains no "more or less" clause, if the quantity is measured in weight such as kilogram, ounce, yard, etc., it allows more or less 5% leeway, while if the quantity is measured in numbers such as parcel, barrel, piece, etc., it allows no leeway. In both cases, if the quantity or number is less than the stipulation, it is considered partial shipment.

In a commercial invoice, the unit price is expressed as "$1.80 per yard CIF Liverpool", including the price term. Besides, the total amount of the invoice should not be more than that of the credit.

商业发票的主体部分包括以下项目：货物名称和货物品名、装运唛头、数量、价格和发票金额、包装、毛重和净重等。

根据 UCP 600，如果有"大约"这样的字眼，数量可以是信用证所规定的 10% 的溢短。有时，信用证本身包含溢短条款，如"5%溢短"，信用证所标注的数量应与规定相符。当信用证没有包含溢短条款时，数量以千克、盎司和码等作为计量单位，允许有 5% 溢短；数量以袋、桶、件等作为计量单位，不允许有任何溢短。在上述两种情况下，数量如比规定的少，则视为分批装运。

在商业发票中，单价表示为"$1.80 每码利物浦到岸价"，包括价格条款。此外，发票的总金额不应多于信用证总金额。

Complementary Close 结尾

A complementary close of a commercial invoice includes import or export license numbers, if any, the special statement, and the signature of the exporter, if required. According to the UCP 600 Article 18, commercial invoices must appear on their face to be issued by the beneficiary as provided in Article 38, and it need not be signed. But whether the commercial invoices need to be signed or not depends on the stipulations of the credit.

商业发票的结尾包括进出口许可证编号，如有需要还包括特别说明和出口商签名。根据 UCP 600 第 18 条款，商业发票表面如第 38 条款必须说明信用证由受益人开具，但不需要由受益人签名。商业发票是否需要署名根据信用证条文规定而定。

3. Notes 注意

In transaction involving a documentary credit, it is vitally important that the description of the goods in the commercial invoice correspond precisely to the description of goods in the documentary credit. The invoice amount should match exactly (or at least should not exceed) the amount specified in the credit. Banks have the right to refuse invoices issued for amounts in excess of the amount stated in the credit. For this, as well as other reasons, the invoice should be made out in the same currency as the credit amount.

Unless otherwise stipulated in the documentary credit, the commercial invoice must be made out in the name of the applicant (buyer). However, in a transferable documentary credit, the invoice may be made out to the intermediary. The buyer, seller, and the bank should all carefully check for discrepancies in the invoice. The details specified therein should not be inconsistent with those of any other documents, and should exactly conform to the specifications of the documentary credit.

在涉及跟单信用证的交易中，商业发票中的货物描述与跟单信用证中的货物描述完全一致是至关重要的。发票金额应与信用证规定的金额完全一致（或至少不应超过）。银行有权拒绝开具超过信用证规定金额的发票。因此，发票的货币也必须与信用证货币一致。

除非跟单信用证另有规定，商业发票必须以申请人（买方）的名义开具。然而，在可转让跟单信用证中，发票可以开具给中间人。买方、卖方和银行都应仔细检查发票中的差异。其中规定的细节不应与任何其他单据的细节不一致，并应完全符合跟单信用证的规定。

4. The Function of Commercial Invoice 商业发票的作用

(1) The invoice is the legal proof of the transaction, the center of the shipping document and the general description of the shipped goods.

发票是交易的合法证明文件，是货运单据的中心，也是装运货物的总说明。

(2) The invoice is the basis for the buyer and the seller to receive and pay the payment for goods and keep accounts.

发票是买卖双方收付货款和记账的依据。

(3) The invoice is the calculation basis for the buyer and the seller to handle customs declaration and tax payment.

发票是买卖双方办理报关、纳税的计算依据。

（4）Where the credit does not require a draft, the invoice replaces the draft as the basis for payment.

在信用证不要求提供汇票的情况下，发票代替了汇票作为付款依据。

（5）The invoice is the basis for the exporter to prepare other export documents.

发票是出口人缮制其他出口单据的依据。

5. Specimen of Commercial Invoice 商业发票的样单

COMMERCIAL INVOICE

（1）Exporter					
（2）To:					
		（3）Invoice No. （4）Date： （5）S/C No. （6）L/C No.			
（7）From		to			
（8）Marks & Nos	（9）Description of Goods	（10）Number of Cargo	（11）Unit Price （USD）	（12）QTY （PCS）	（13）Amount （USD）
（14）Total					
SAY _____ ONLY.					
（15）Declaration & Statement and Other Contents					
					（16）The Seller：_____

6. The Contents and Key points of Commercial Invoice 样单拆解：商业发票的内容及缮制要点

（1）Name of the issuer：Generally the issuer of the invoice is the exporter. It is usually printed in advance. The name and address of the invoice issuer shall be consistent with the name and address of the beneficiary of the Letter of Credit, and the English name and address of the drawer shall be filled in.

出票人的名称和地址：此项应填写出口商的名称和地址，该栏通常是预先印好的。发票出票人的名称和地址应与信用证受益人的名称和地址相一致。

（2）Consignee：Usually it is the name and address of the buyer. They should be strictly in accordance with the stipulations of L/C.

收货人：此页即发票接受方的名称和地址，多数情况下填写进口商的名称，并与信用证开证申请人的名称和地址一致。

（3）Invoice No.：The number is given by Export Company itself.

发票号：此项由出口公司出具。

（4）Date：The date of invoice should be earlier than the date of shipment, and no later than the date of draft and the validity of L/C. If the L/C requires original invoice, "original" should be printed on the top of the invoice.

发票日期：发票日期应该早于装运期，并且不得晚于汇票日期和信用证有效期。如果信用证要求正本发票，在发票上应该打上"original"。

（5）S/C No.：The number of Sale conformation.

销售确认书的号码。

（6）L/C No.：When using a letter of credit to pay for goods, the letter of credit is the basis for issuing the invoice. Therefore, the invoice under the letter of credit must be filled in with the letter of credit number.

信用证号码：当采用信用证支付货款时，信用证是出具发票的依据，因此信用证项下的发票需填写信用证号码。

（7）Transport Details：The port of loading, port of destination, and ship by …

运输信息：此项应与货物的实际起运港（地）、目的港（地）以及运输方式一致，如果货物需转运，应把转运港的名称打上。如：Shipment from Shanghai to Hamburg with transhipment at Hong Kong by vessel（装运自上海到汉堡，在香港转运），"From Dalian to Helsinki W/T（with transhipment）Hong Kong"（从大连到赫尔基辛，在香港转运），有时，还会填上运输方式，如有需要，还要填写装运时间和转运船名。

（8）Shipping Marks & Nos.：Usually it is the package number, shipper's company name, country of origin, port of destination, package weight, specification, and the number of shipper. If there is no mark, "N/M" is printed.

装运唛头和编号：此项又称装运标志和编号。唛头的内容包括包装号码、船运公司名称、原产地国家、最终目的港、包装重量、规格和发货人的编号。若没有唛头则写"N/M"。

（9）Description of Goods：The name of goods and description of the goods, usually including shipping terms, types of container, gross weight, quantity, and the measurement of each container.

商品名称及货物描述：此项包括装运条件、集装箱的类型、每个集装箱的毛重、货物的数量、货物的尺码。

（10）Number of Cargo.

货号。

（11）Unit Price：It consists of currency, measurement unit, and sum and trade terms. These four parts should strictly keep in accordance with L/C.

单价：在国际贸易中，单价包括四部分：货币名称、计价单位、单价金额和贸易术语。这四部分必须完全符合信用证。

（12）Quantity.

数量。

（13）Amount：The total amount is consistent with the amount in figures, expressed in English capital letters.

总额与小写金额一致，用英文大写表述。

（14）Total：It includes the total quantity, total weight（inclusive of net and gross weight）if it is required in the L/C, and total value in words.

总计：如果信用证有要求，那么总计应包括总数量、总重量（净重和总重），总计金额应用大写。

（15）Declaration & Statement and Other Contents：It includes some special issues according to requirements of buyers and L/C. For example, it states reference No., license No., and the name of manufacturer. It certifies realness and accuracy of the invoice, and origin of the goods.

声明及其他内容：主要是根据买方和信用证的要求，对一些特殊事项加以注明，如加注某些参考号、许可证号、生产厂家名称，以此证明发票的真实性和准确性，以及货物的原产地。

（16）Signature and Others：The invoice will take effect after signed by the beneficiary. Signatures on documents are classified into the followings：handwriting, facsimile signature, perforated signature, stamp, symbol and mechanical or electronic method of authentication.

签章及其他：发票的签章应该与受益人名字一致。单据上的签字可以手签，也可以传真签名、穿孔签字、盖章、符号，以及以任何机械或电子正式的方法处理。

7. Case Study 案例实训

FROM：INDUSTRIAL BANK OF KOREA SEOUL

CONTRACT NO. AB2101/008.

L/C NO.：TZ6680897

BENEFICIAL：CHINA JIANGSU INTERNATIONAL ECONOMIC-TECHNICAL CO-OPERATION WEST BEIJING ROAD, NANJING 210008 P. R. CHINA

APPLICANT：DAYU ART CO. LTD., NO. 500 SEOCHO-DONG SEOCHO-GU, SEOUL, KOREA

OPENING BANK：INDUSTRIAL BANK OF KOREA SEOUL

THE LATEST SHIPMENT DATE：SEPTEMBER 10, 2021

EXPIRY DATE：OCTOBER 1, 2021.

：32B/AMOUNT   USD 4,200

：44A/LOADING ON BOARD /DISPATCH/ ANY POET IN CHINA

：44B/FOR TRANSPORTATION TO BUSAN PORT, KOREA

：45/DESCRIPTION OF GOODS/SERVICES：

GLASSWARE AS PER SALES CONFIRMATION NO. AB1101/008

DATE 7-1-2021   CIF BUSAN PORT, KOREA

：46/DOCUMENTS REQUIRED

DOCUMENT IN TRIPLICATE（UNLESS OTHERWISE SPECIFIED）

+ PACKLISNG LIST

卖方于9月1日装完船，取得提单。货物明细如下：

品名：GLASSWARE

货号	单价	数量	箱号	尺码	毛重（KG）	净重（KG）
06-21-11	USD10	200	1-21	55×45×60	643	537
06-21-22	USD11	200	2-11	35×65×43	432	401

唛头；无

船名：EASTWIND　　　航次：V.001X　　　装运港：上海

由 Ala Yang 开具发票.（外贸业务员）

ORIGINAL

COMMERCIAL INVOICE

中国江苏国际经济技术合作公司

CHINA JIANGSU INTERNATIONAL ECONOMIC-TECHNICAL CO-OPERATION

ADD：WEST BEIJING ROAD, NANJING 210008 P. R. CHINA

TEL：86 25 231 0938, 331-0892　　FAX：86 25 331-0081

TO：DAYU ART CO. LTD., NO.500 SEOCHO-DONG SEOCHO-GU, SEOUL, KOREA	INVOICE NO.：JS123456 DATE：Aug. 28, 2021

L/C NUMBER：TZ6680897

ISSUED BY：INDUSTRIAL BANK OF KOREA SEOUL

SHIPPED PER：EASTWIND V.001X　FROM　SHANGHAI, CHINA

　　　　　　　　　　　　TO　BUSAN PORT, KOREA

MARKS&NO.	DESCRIPTION OF GOODS			AMOUNT
N/M	GLASSWARE AS PER SALES CONFIRMATION NO. AB1101/008 CIF-BUSAN PORT, KOREA			USD 4, 200
	Number of Cargo.	**UNIT PRICE**	**QTY**	
	06-21-11	USD10	200	
	06-21-22	USD11	200	

Total value in words：SAY US DOLLAR FOUR THOUSAND TWO HUNDRED ONLY

DECLARATION：

SIGNATURE：Ala Yang

CHINA JIANGSU INTERNATIONAL ECONOMIC-TECHNICAL CO-OPERATION

Section Two Other Invoices 其他发票

In order to abide by regulations of control on foreign trade and foreign exchange, importers of some countries probably call for other forms of invoice as follows:

为了符合国际贸易和国际交易管理条例,一些国家的进口商可能需要以下发票形式:

- Customs Invoice 海关发票
- Consular Invoice 领事发票
- Certificate Invoice 证书发票
- Pro-forma Invoice 形式发票

1. Customs Invoice 海关发票

Customs invoice is made by the exporter by filling out a given invoice form specified by the customs of importing country, which is a necessary evidence for the goods entry with a levy of lower import duty or even free of duty. The same as the consular document, it determines the basis of calculating import duty and serves to prevent dumping of imports at low prices (lower than its domestic price). The custom of importing country uses it also for statistical purposes and checking origin of goods.

在缮制海关发票时,出口方需要填写由进口方国家海关出具的发票形式。这是一个很有必要的证明,它证明货物可以以低关税或者免关税进口。领事单据同样具有这样的功能,它是计算进口关税的基础,也能够阻止低价位的(低于国内价格)进口倾销。进口国家海关利用它进行数据统计和货物原产地的核查。

2. Consular Invoice 领事发票

Consular invoices are ones attested, in the country of dispatch, by the consulate of the importing country. Such invoices, mostly required by the Latin American countries, are used by customs official of the entry country to verify the value, quantity, the country of origin, and the nature of merchandise. The certification and legalization of such invoices made by the consulate take more time than the normal commercial invoice. Accordingly, seller and buyer have to think over whether such invoices are really needed or not.

领事发票是指在发货国,由进口方所在国家的领事馆证实后开具的发票。这类发票通常在拉美国家使用广泛,在拉美,进口国家的海关机构使用该发票证明商品的价值、数量、原产地和性质。这类发票的认证和合法化都由领事馆负责,其过程比商业发票花费的时间更长。因此,买卖双方必须考虑是否开立此类发票。

3. Certificate Invoice 证书发票

Certificate invoice is sealed by a Chamber of Commerce of Chamber of Manufacturers on the commercial invoice. This kind of special invoice is normally asked for by the customs or laws of the trading nations. Forms and contents of such invoices vary from country to country, and even from product to product.

证书发票由生产商的商会盖印。这类特殊的发票通常由贸易国的海关和依法律规定出

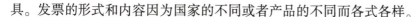

具。发票的形式和内容因为国家的不同或者产品的不同而各式各样。

4. Pro-forma Invoice 形式发票

Pro-forma invoice is made by the exporter prior to shipment of goods and marked the wording "Pro-forma" on the invoice. Actually, it is a form of "offer" or "quotation" to the buyer which shows the intention of the exporter to conclude the contract with the buyer. Meanwhile, pro-forma invoice is often used for application of import license or foreign exchange. Once the pro-forma invoice is accepted by the buyer wholly, it will become a formal contract between the buyer and the seller. In such case, a commercial invoice will be made out for payment.

形式发票由出口方在货物装运之前出具，并且在发票上注明"形式"字样。事实上，这也是给买方发盘和报价的形式，它表示出口方愿意与进口方订立合同。同时，形式发票通常用作进口证书或者国际汇兑。一旦买方接受商业发票，那么此发票就成为买卖双方的正式合同。在这种情况下，出口方缮制商业发票以便进行支付。

Section Three   Customs Invoice 海关发票

Customs Invoice: The customs invoice is a document issued by the exporter at the request of the customs of the importing country. Its basic content is similar to the ordinary commercial invoice, and its format is generally formulated and provided by the customs of the importing country. It is mainly used for the customs of the importing country to make statistics, verify the origin, and check the composition of the price of imported goods.

海关发票：海关发票是出口商应进口国海关要求出具的一种单据，基本内容同普通的商业发票类似，其格式一般由进口国海关统一制定并提供，主要用于进口国海关统计、核实原产地、查核进口商品价格的构成等。

The following is a case study of the main columns and preparation methods of the customs invoice, using the invoice from Canadian Customs as an example. 下面用加拿大海关发票作为案例说明海关发票的主要栏目及缮制方法。

（1）VENDOR NAME AND ADDRESS：Fill in the exporter's name and address, including city and country names. Fill in the beneficiary's name and address in this column under the payment terms of the letter of credit. 卖方的名称与地址：填写出口商的名称及地址，包括城市和国家名称。信用证支付条件下此栏填写受益人名址。

（2）DATE OF DIRECT SHIPMENT TO CANADA：Fill in the shipping date for direct shipment to Canada, which should be consistent with the bill of lading date. If the documents are sent to the bank for preliminary review, the bank can also be asked to annotate them according to the original bill of lading date. 直接运往加拿大的装运日期：填写直接运往加拿大的装运日期，此日期应与提单日期相一致。如单据送银行预审，也可请银行按正本提单日期代为加注。

（3）ORDER REFERENCE, INCLUDE PURCHASER'S ORDER NUMBER：Fill in the relevant contract, order or commercial invoice number. 其他参考事项，包括买方订单号码：填写有关合同、订单或商业发票号码。

(4)CONSIGNEE, NAME AND ADDRESS: Fill in the name and detailed address of the Canadian consignee. Under a letter of credit, it is generally the issuer of the letter of credit. 收货人名称及地址：填写加拿大收货人的名称与详细地址。信用证项下一般为信用证的开证人。

(5)PURCHASER'S NAME AND ADDRESS: Fill in the name and address of the actual purchaser. If the consignee in the fourth column is the same, then this column can be marked with "SAME AS CONSIGNEE". 买方：填写实际购货人的名称及地址。如与第四栏的收货人相同，则此栏可打上"SAME AS CONSIGNEE"。

(6)COUNTRY OF TRANSHIPMENT: Fill in the name of the transhipment location. If transhipment occurs in Hong Kong, you can fill in the form: "FROM SHANGHAI TO VANCOUVER WITH TRANSHIPMENT AT HONG KONG BY VESSEL". If there is no transhipment, N/A (i. e. NOT APPLICABLE)can be filled in. 转运国家：应填写转船地点的名称。如在香港转船，可填写："FROM SHANGHAI TO VANCOUVER WITH TRANSHIPMENT AT HONG KONG BY VESSEL"。如不转船，可填 N/A(即 NOT APPLICCABLE)。

(7)COUNTRY OF ORIGIN OF GOODS: Fill in "CHINA". If it is not a single domestic product, the names of the respective countries of origin should be listed in detail in column 12. 生产国别：填写 CHINA。若非单一的国产货物，则应在 12 栏中详细逐项列明各自的原产地国名。

(8)TRANSPORTATION, GIVE MODE AND PLACE OF DIRECT SHIPMENT TO CANADA: As long as the goods are not processed abroad, regardless of whether they are transhipped, the name of the place of origin and destination, as well as the means of transportation used, should be filled in. e. g. From SHANGHAI to MONTREAL BY VESSEL. 运输方式及直接运往加拿大的起运地点。只要货物不在国外加工，不论是否转船，均填写起运地和目的地名称以及所用运载工具。如：FROM SHANGHAI TO MONTREAL BY VESSEL。

(9)CONDITION OF SALES AND TERMS OF PAYMENT, I. E. SALE, CONSIGNMENT, SHIPMENT, LEASED GOODS, ETC: Fill in according to the price terms and payment method of Commercial invoice. e. g. CIF VANCOUVER D/P AT SIGHT OR C AND F MONTREAL BY L/C AT SIGHT. 价格条件及支付方式，如销售、委托发运、租赁商品等：按商业发票的价格术语及支付方式填写。如 CIF VANCOUVER D/P AT SIGHT 或 C AND F MONTREAL BY L/C AT SIGHT。

(10)CURRENCY OF SETTLEMENT: The name of the currency required by the seller shall be consistent with the currency used in the commercial invoice. e. g. CAD. 货币名称：卖方要求买方支付货币的名称，须与商业发票使用的货币相一致，如 CAD。

(11)NUMBER OF PACKAGE: Fill in the total number of packages of the goods. e. g. 600 CARTONS. 件数：填写该批商品的总包装件数，如 600 CARTONS。

(12)SPECIFICATION OF COMMODITIES, KIND OF PACKAGES, MARKS AND NUMBERS, GENERAL DESCRIPTION AND CHARACTERISTICS, I. E. GRADE, QUALITY: Fill in the commercial invoice and the project description, and fill in the packaging status and shipping mark. 商品详细描述(包括种类、唛头、品名和特性，即等级、品质)：应按商业发票和项目描述填写，并将包装情况及唛头填入此栏。

(13)QUANTITY, STATE UNIT: Fill in the specific quantity of the goods, not the number of the packages. 数量：应填写商品的具体数量，而不是包装的件数。

（14）UNIT PRICE：Fill in each unit price recorded in the commercial invoice, and the currency used shall be consistent with the letter of credit and the commercial invoice. 单价：应按商业发票记载的每项单价填写，使用的货币应与信用证和商业发票一致。

（15）TOTAL：Should be filled in according to the total amount of the commercial invoice. 总值：应按商业发票的总金额填写。

（16）TOTAL WEIGHT：Fill in the total gross weight and total net weight, which should be consistent with the total gross weight and total net weight of other documents. 净重及毛重的总数：填写总毛重和总净重，应与其他单据的总毛重和总净重相一致。

（17）TOTAL INVOICE VALUE：Fill the total amount of commercial invoice. 发票总金额：按商业发票的总金额填写。

（18）IF ANY OF FIELDS 1 TO 17 ARE INCLUDED ON AN ATTACHED COMMERCIAL INVOICE, CHECK THIS BOX. 如果1—17栏的任何栏的内容均已包括在所随附的商业发票内，则在方框内填一个"√"记号，并将有关商业发票号填写在横线上。

（19）EXPORTERS NAME AND ADDRESS, IF OTHER THAN VENDOR：If the exporter is not the same name as the seller in column 1, the actual exporter name shall be included; if the exporter is the seller in the first column, mark "THE SAME AS VENDOR" in this column. 出口商名称及地址，如并非买方：如出口商与第1栏的卖方不是同一名称，则列入实际出口商名称；而若出口商与第一栏卖方为同一者，则在本栏打上"THE SAME AS VENDOR"。

（20）ORIGINATOR, NAME AND ADDRESS. 负责人的姓名及地址。

（21）DEPARTMENTAL RULING, IF ANY：Means the relevant provisions of the customs and tax authorities of the Canadian party on the import of the goods. If so, please fill, if not, "N/A"(i. e. NOT APPLICABLE). 主管当局现行管理条例，如适用者：指加方海关和税务机关对该货进口的有关规定。如有，则要求填写，如无，则填"N/A"（即 NOT APPLICABLE）。

（22）IF FIELDS 23 TO 25 ARE NOT APPLICABLE CHECK THIS BOX：if columns 23-25 are not applicable, a "√" mark can be placed in the box. 如果23—25这三个栏目均不适用：如果23—25栏不适用，可在方框内打"√"记号。

（23）IF INCLUDED IN FIELD 17 INDICATE AMOUNT：Freight and insurance fees from the place of origin to Canada：The total of the freight and insurance fees can be filled in, and can be filled in the original currency of payment. If not applicable, fill in "N/A". The cost incurred for the construction, installation, and assembly of goods imported into Canada shall be filled in according to the actual situation; If not applicable, N/A can be marked. Ⅲ. Export packaging fees can be calculated based on the actual situation. If there are no packaging fees, fill in "N/A". 如果以下金额已包括在第17栏内：自起运地至加拿大的运费和保险费：可填运费和保险费的总额，并且可以用原始支付货币填写，若不适用则填"N/A"。货物进口到加拿大后进行建造、安装及组装而发生的成本费用，按实际情况填列；若不适用，可打上"N/A"。Ⅲ. 出口包装费用可按实际情况将包装费用金额打上，如无，则填"N/A"。

（24）IF NOT INCLUDED IN FIELD 17 INDICATE AMOUNT：If column 17 is not included, indicate the amount as follows：items Ⅰ, Ⅱ, and Ⅲ, usually filled with "N/A". If, under FOB and other price conditions, the seller hires a ship for the buyer to book the space, and the freight is paid upon arrival of the goods, the actual freight amount can be filled in column I. 如果以下金额不包括在第 17 栏内：若 17 栏不包括，则注明金额：Ⅰ、Ⅱ、Ⅲ 三项，一般填"N/A"。如果在 FOB 等价格条件下，卖方又替买方租船订舱时，其运费于货到时支付，则在 I 栏可填实际运费额。

（25）CHECK（IF APPLICABLE）：This column is used for compensation trade, incoming parts, processing and assembly; general trade is not applicable, "N/A" can be filled in the box. 若适用，在方格内打"√"记号。本栏系补偿贸易、来件、来料加工、装配等贸易方式专用；一般贸易不适用，可在方格内填"N/A"。

CANADA CUSTOMS INVOICE

		Page	
			of
1. Vendor(name and address)	2. Date of direct shipment to Canada		
	3. Other references(include purchaser's order No.)		
4. Consignee(name and address)	5. Purchaser's name and address(if other than consignee)		
	6. Country of transhipment		
	7. Country of origin of goods	IF SHIPMENT INCLUDES GOODS OF DIFFERENT ORIGINS ENTER ORIGINS AGAINST ITEMS IN 12	
8. Transportation: Give mode and place of direct shipment to Canada	9. Conditions of sale and terms of payment (sale, consignment shipment, leased goods, etc)		
	10. Currency of settlement		

11. Number of packages	12. Specification of commodities(kind of packages, marks and numbers, general description and characteristics.)	13. Quantify (state unit)	Selling price	
			14. Unit price	15. Total
18. If any of fields 1 to 17 are included on an attached commercial invoice, check this box ☐ Commercial Invoice No. _____		16. Total weight		17. Invoice total
		Net	Gross	
19. Exporter's name and address (if other than vendor)	20. Originator(name and address)		
21. CCRA ruling(if applicable)	22. If fields 23 to 25 are not applicable, check this box ☐		

续表

23. If included in field 17 indicate amount： （i）Transportation charges. Expenses and insurance from the place of direct shipment to Canada _____ （ii）Costs for construction, erection and assembly incurred after importation into Canada _____ （iii）Export packing _____	24. If not included in field 17 indicate amount： （i）Transportation charges. Expenses and insurance from the place of direct shipment to Canada _____ （ii）Amounts for commissions other than buying commissions _____ （iii）Export packing _____	25. Check（if applicable）： （i）Royalty payments or subsequent proceeds are paid or payable by the purchaser ☐ （ii）The purchaser has supplied goods or services for use in the production of these goods ☐

Section Four   Packing Documents 包装单据

一、Packing Documents 包装单据

Packing Documents are those documents which provide a full description of the packing condition of the goods; they are some kind of additional documents of commercial invoice, and key documents in transportation as well. There are some categories of packing documents as follows：

包装单据是指对货物包装状况进行全面说明的单据；它们是商业发票的附加单据，也是运输中的关键单据。包装单据分为以下几类：

- Packing list/Packing Slip 装箱单
- Packing Specification 包装说明
- Detail Packing List 详细装箱单
- Packing Summary 包装提要
- Weight List/Weight Note 重量单
- Weight Certificate/Certificate of Weight 重量证书
- Weight Memo 磅码单
- Measurement List 体积/尺码单
- Assortment List 花色搭配单
- The Function of packing documents 包装单据的作用

（1）Packaging documents are the basic data for measurement and pricing when exporters prepare commercial invoices and other documents.

包装单据是出口商缮制商业发票及其他单据时计量、计价的基础资料。

（2）The packing document is the basis for the importer to count the quantity or weight and sell the goods.

包装单据是进口商清点数量或重量以及销售货物的依据。

（3）The packing document is the certificate for the customs to inspect the goods.

包装单据是海关查验货物的凭证。

（4）Packing documents are the reference materials for notarization or commodity inspection authorities to inspect the goods.

包装单据是公证或商检机构查验货物的参考资料。

二、Packing List 装箱单

Packing List is an independent document. It is usually requested by the importer to confirm the name of commodity, specification, quantity, marks, number of carton and the packing conditions. Usually issued by the exporter, packing list doesn't show the value of the goods, shipment and consignee, while weight memo shows something about the weight emphatically, such as gross weight, net weight and so on. Measurement list shows something about each individual lot's length, width, height and total volume on the basis of packing list.

装箱单是独立单据。通常由买方要求出具，证明商品的名称、规格、数量唛头、箱号和包装条件。出口方出具此单据时，不需要注明货物价值、装运和收件人；而重量单主要注明关于重量的事宜，如毛重、净重等；体积单在装箱单的基础上注明每批货物的长度、宽度、高度和总体积。

A packing list is a document prepared by the shipper listing the kinds and quantities of merchandise in a particular shipment. Packing list is also a type of certificate of fulfillment, presenting that the shipper has packed the goods in accordance with the terms of contract or the goods are suitable for some transport mode, so that the goods can reach the destination with perfect condition. On the other hand, packing list is necessary for carrier to arrange loading, unloading and transhipment during transportation.

装箱单是由运输方所准备的单据，并注明某一批商品的种类和数量。装箱单也是运输方履行合同的证明。它证明运输方已经按照合同的条款包装货物，也证明货物适合某种运输方式，以便货物能够完好无缺地抵达目的地。而且，装箱单是运输方安排货物装卸以及转运的重要依据。

1. The Contents of Packing List 样单拆解：装箱单的制作要点及内容

- Number and Date 装箱单的号码和日期
- Contract Number or L/C Number 合同号码或信用证号码
- Shipping Marks 唛头

（1）Description of goods：You can only fill in the general name of the goods, but it must not conflict with the description of the goods specified in the letter of credit. 货物描述：可以只填写货物的统称，但不得与信用证规定的货物描述相抵触。

（2）Quantity：Fill in the actual quantity of the goods. If there are different quality specifications, they should be listed separately and the total number should be accumulated. Due to the importer not wanting the actual buyer to know the detailed cost and price of the goods, the packaging documents generally do not record the unit price and total price of the goods. 数量：填写货物的实际数量，如品质规格不同，应分别列出并累计总数。由于进口商不想让实际买主了解货物的详细成本价格情况，包装单据一般不记载货物的单价和总价。

（3）Packaging: Generally, the maximum packaging quantity should be filled in. If there are different types or specifications of goods, the maximum packaging quantity for each type or specification of goods should be listed separately, and the total number should be accumulated. 包装：一般填写最大包装数量，如货物种类或规格不同，应分别列出每种或每规格货物的最大包装数量，并累计其总数。

（4）Gross weight, Net weight, Measurement: Fill in the unit gross weight, net weight, measurement, and calculate the total gross weight, net weight, and volume. If there are goods of different specifications or types, they should be listed separately and the total number should be accumulated. 货物的毛重、净重、体积：填写每件货物的单位毛重、净重和体积，并计算出总的毛重、净重和体积，如有不同规格或种类的货物，应分别列出并最后累计其总数。

（5）Total: This column represents the total of columns 8, 9, and 10. 合计：此栏对8、9、10栏合计。

（6）Free Processing Area: Declaration Sentence. 自由处理区：声明文句。

（7）Signature: The signature of the export enterprise shall be consistent with the commercial invoice. If the letter of credit stipulates neutral packaging, this column may not be filled. 签章：出口企业的签章应与商业发票相符，如果信用证规定中性包装，此栏可不填。

2. Specimen of Packing List 装箱单样单

装箱单
PACKING LIST

No.：   Date

Contract No. _____   Page：_____ 页

Seller：

To：

Shipped by   to

标志及箱号 Mark & Nos	品名及规格 Article and specification	数量 Quantity	件数 Package	毛重 Gross Weight （KGS）	净重 Net Weight （KGS）	尺码 Measurement （CM）

3. Case Study 案例实训

请根据所给信用证内容和补充资料缮制装箱单

FORM OF DOC. CREDIT   *40 A：IRREVOCABLE

DOC. CREDIT NUMBER   *20：LRT 0402457

DATE OF ISSUE   *31 C：221125

EXPIRY   *31 D：230110

APPLICANT   *50：A. B. C. CORP. AKEKSANTERINK AUTO P. O. BOX 9, FINLAND

BENEFICIARY   *59：JIANGSU FASHION INTERNATIONAL TRADE CORPORATION

#358 ZHUSHAN ROAD, JIANGNING DISTRICT, NANJING, CHINA

AMOUNT   *32 B：AMOUNT USD 67,500.00

POS./NEG. TOL. (%)   *39 A：05/05

AVAILABLE WITH/BY   *41 A：BANK OF CHINA

DRAFT AT …   *42 C：AT SIGHT

DRAWEE   *42 A：MERITA BANK LTD., FINLAND

PARTIAL SHIPMENTS   *43 P：ALLOWED

TRANSHIPMENT   *43 T：ALLOWED

LOADING IN CHARGE   *44 A：SHANGHAI

FOR TRANSPORT TO …   *44 B：HELSINKI

SHIPMENT PERIOD   *44 C：LATEST DEC 26TH, 2022

DESCRIPT. OF GOODS   *45 A：TRANGLE BRAND 3U-SHAPE ELECTRONIC

ENERGY SAVING LAMP,

TR-3U-A 110V 5W E27/B22 5,000PCS USD2.50/PC

TR-3U-A 110V 7W E27/B22 5,000PCS USD3.00/PC

TR-3U-A 110V 22W E27/B22 5,000PCS USD3.80/PC

TR-3U-A 110V 26W E27/B22 5,000PCS USD4.20/PC

CIF HELSINKI AS PER S/C 22SGQ468001

DOCUMENTS REQUIRED 46 A：   + PACKING LIST IN 5 COPIES

补充资料：

(1)SHIPPING MARK：   ABC

      HELSINKI

      NO. 1400

(2)2022 年 12 月 3 日开出装箱单；12 月 13 日装船，船名 SUNV. 03

(3)C. W. 3,600 KGS, N. C. 3,500 KGS

(4)尺码：(50×50×28)CM3/CTN

装箱单
PACKING LIST

No.： LRT 0402457   Date   171125

Contract No. 22SGQ468001   Page：   1   页

Seller：JIANGSU FASHION INTERNATIONAL TRADE CORPORATION

#358 ZHUSHAN ROAD，JIANGNING DISTRICT，NANJING，CHINA

To：A. B. C. CORP. AKEKSANTERINK AUTO P. O. BOX 9，FINLAND

Shipped by：SUNV. 03 From SHANGHAI CHINA to HELSINKI，FINLAND

Mark & Nos.	Article and Specification	Quantity PCS	Package	Gross Weight (KGS)	Net Weight (KGS)	Measurement (CM)
ABC HELSINKI No. 1400	TRANGLE BRAND 3U – SHAPE ELECTRONIC ENERGY SAVING LAMP TR–3U–A 110V 5W E27/B22	5,000		3,600	3,500	50×50×28
ABC HELSINKI No. 1400	TRANGLE BRAND 3U – SHAPE ELECTRONIC ENERGY SAVING LAMP TR–3U–A 110V 7W E27/B22	5,000		3,600	3,500	50×50×28
ABC HELSINKI No. 1400	TRANGLE BRAND 3U – SHAPE ELECTRONIC ENERGY SAVING LAMP TR–3U–A 110V 22W E27/B22	5,000		3,600	3,500	50×50×28
ABC HELSINKI No. 1400	TRANGLE BRAND 3U – SHAPE ELECTRONIC ENERGY SAVING LAMP TR–3U–A 110V 26W E27/B22	5,000		3,600	3,500	50×50×28

4. Notes 注意

The Packing list is more a detailed version of the commercial invoice but without price information. The type of each container is identified，as well as its individual weight and measurements. The packing list is attached to the outside of its respective container in a waterproof envelope marked "packing list enclosed" and is immediately available to authorities in both the countries of export and import.

Although packing list may not be required in some specific transactions，it is required by most countries and buyers. Bear in mind, the contents of packing list should be consistent with those stated in other documents, especially with the related invoice as well as with the actual packing conditions. So pay attention to：

（1）The name of packing documents must confirm with the name in the L/C. 注意包装单据名称，名称应与信用证内规定一致。

（2）The gross weight and net weight per unit must list, the total of gross weight and net weight must confirm with the figure of Invoice and transport documents, Certificate of origin, export licenses, especially the weight and figure for account must be carefully. 单位毛重和净重必须列出，毛重和净重的总和必须与发票和运输单据、原产地证书、出口许可证的数字确认，特别是重量和数字必须仔细核算。

（3）If the letter of credit stipulates to show Inner Packing, the document must be demonstrated fully. 如果信用证规定显示内包装，则该单据必须充分证明。

（4）If the weight cover with "Certificate of Weight", you would better add the word "We certificate that the weight is true and correct". 如果重量上有"重量证明"，你最好加上"我们证明重量是真实和正确的"。

（5）In generally, packing documents does not list the unit and total price of the goods. 一般来说，包装单据上没有列出货物的单价和总价。

（6）In order to confirm the requirement of the L/C not accept combined document, we can use the single-weight packing lists add the weight document and the size document, make out once time, in accordance with the provisions of the letter credit present to the bank. 为了确认信用证不接受组合单据的要求，我们可以使用单重装箱单加上重量单据和尺寸单据，一次开出，按照信用证的规定提交给银行。

Exercises 练习

一、Useful Words and Expressions 常用词语和搭配

1. commercial documents 商业单据

2. commercial invoice 商业发票

3. packing list 装箱单

4. order 订单

5. contract number 合同号码

6. description of the goods 商品描述

7. unit price and total price 单价和总价

8. currency 货币

9. weight of goods 商品重量

10. shipping marks 装运唛头

11. terms of delivery and payment 装运和支付条款

12. the port of loading and discharge 装卸码头

14. transhipment 转运

15. issuing bank 开证行

16. gross and net weight 总重和净重

17. consignor/consignee 发货人/收货人

18. custom invoice 海关发票

19. consular invoice 领事发票

20. pro-forma invoice 形式发票

21. packing list/packing slip 装箱单

22. packing specification 装箱规格

23. weight list/weight note 重量单

24. weight certificate/certificate of weight 重量证明书

25. measurement list 尺码单

26. assortment list 分类列表

27. case 箱

28. carton 纸箱

29. wooden case 木箱

30. to be packed in bag 装在袋子里

31. to be packed in paper bag 装在纸袋子里

32. gunny bag 麻袋

33. plastic bag 塑料袋

34. foam plastic bag 泡沫塑料袋

35. indicative mark 指示性标志

36. warning mark 警示标志

二、Useful Sentences 常用语句

1. signed commercial invoice 已签署的发票

（in duplicate 一式两份, in triplicate 一式三份, in quadruplicate 一式四份, in quintuplicate 一式五份, in sextuplicate 一式六份, in septuplicate 一式七份, in octuplicate 一式八份, in nonuplicate 一式九份, induplicate 一式十份。一式四份及以上也常说 in four copies, in five copies, in six copies）

2. Beneficiary's original signed commercial invoices at least 8 copies issued in the name of the buyer indicating（showing/evidencing/specifying/declaration of）the merchandise, country of origin and any other relevant information. 以买方的名义开具，注明商品名称、原产国、其他有关资料以及经签署的受益人的商业发票，至少一式八份。

3. Signed attested invoice combined with certificate of origin and value in 6 copies as required for imports into Nigeria. 已签署的，连同产地证明和货物价值，输入尼日利亚的联合发票，一式六份。

4. Signed Commercial Invoice, one original and two copies 已签署商业发票，一份原件两份复印件。

5. Beneficiary must certify on the invoice … Have been sent to the issuer. 受益人须在发票上证明，已将……寄交开证人。

6. 4% discount should be deducted from total amount of the commercial invoice. 商业发票的总金额须扣除4%折扣。

7. Invoice must be showed：under A/P No. … date of expiry 19 Jan. 2011 发票须标明：根据第＊＊＊委托购买证，有效期为2011年1月19日

8. Documents in combited form are not acceptable. 不接受联合单据。

9. Combined invoice is not acceptable. 不接受联合发票。

10. We hereby certify that the above-mentioned particulars and figures are true and correct. 我们仅此证明发票所述详细内容真实无误。

11. We hereby certify that we are the actual manufacturer of the goods invoiced. 兹证明发票所述产品确为本厂制造。

12. It is hereby certified that this invoice shows the actual price of the goods described，that no other invoice has been or will be issued and that all particulars are true and correct. 兹证明发票的价格系所述商品的正式价格，并未签发其他发票，所述详细内容真实无误。

13. Sighed commercial invoice in quintuplicate indicating contract No.，marks and as well as the credit No. 经签署的一式五份的商业发票上标有合同号、唛头和信用证号。

14. The description of the goods in the commercial invoice must correspond with the description in the Credit. 商业发票中的货物描述，必须与信用证规定的相符。

15. Commercial invoice refers to a list issued by the seller containing the name，quantity，price，and other contents of the goods. 商业发票是指卖方开立的载有货物名称、数量、价格等内容的清单。

16. Original commercial invoice covering 20% of the total contract price in 5 copies. 开票金额为合同总价20%的正本商业发票，一式五份。

17. Your signed commercial invoice in octuplicate certifying merchandise to be of China origin. 你方签署的商业发票一式八份，在发票上证明货物原产国是中国。

18. With the adventage of the internet Era，the traditional paper-based commercial paper has been unable to meet market demand. 随着互联网时代的到来，传统纸质票据已不能满足市场的需求。

三、Making out a Commercial Invoices According to the Following Information. 根据所给信息缮制一份商业发票

发票号码：99GD04-017F01，发票日期：2021年3月22日

提单号码：CAN-598024，提单日期：2021年4月5日，船名：TIAN LI 3/DSR

货物装箱情况：25DOZ/CTN,2×20'CY/CY，CYLU2215087，SEAL0958801

外汇核销单编号：8765681，出口许可证号：7680532

运费率：3%，杂费：USD158.00

Manufacturer：广州东升服装厂

GW：18.00KGS/CTN，NW：15.00KGS/CTN，MEAS：50×20×10CM/CTN

唛头：SB TRADING

VIA TRADVERSA DI

本批货由中外运广东分公司于2021年4月3日向广州海关申报。

信用证如下：

TO BANK OF CHINA, BEIJING, ISSUED ON MARCH 04, 2011

WE HEREBY ISSUE OUR IRREVOCABLE DOCUMENTARY CREDIT NO. 9107164 AS FOLLOWS：

APPLICANT：S. B. TRADING SAS DI BERTINT STEFAND E. C. VIA TRAVERSA DI IOLO 50 50044 IOLO DI PRATO(PO)ITALY

BENEFICIARY：GUANGDONG FOREIGN TRADE IMP. AND EXP. CORP.

351 TIANHE ROAD GUANGZHOU CHINA

FOR THE **AMOUNT** OF USD 36,480.00

VALID UNTILL APRIL 26, 2021 IN CHINA

AVAILABLE WITH BANK OF CHINA GUANGDONG BRANCH PAYMENT AT SIGHT A-GAINST PRESENTATION OF THE FOLLOWING DOCUMENTS：

SIGNED COMMERCIAL INVOICE NINE COPIES

FULL SET CLEAN ON BOARD OCEAN BILL OF LADING, MADE OUT TO THE ORDER AND BLANK ENDORSED, EVIDENCING SHIPMENT FROM GUANGZHOU TO LASPEZIA(意大利拉西皮西亚港)PORT NOT LATER THAN APRIL 05, 2011 MARKED "FREIGHT PRE-PAID" AND NOTIFY TO THE APPLICANT.

COVERING(as per contract no. 99ns 061)：

7 PANEL CAP IN COTTON TWILL(斜纹棉布七片帽)

108×58 WITH 4 METAL EYELRTS AND PLASTIC CLOSURE AT BACK

N. BLUE	2,800 DOZ.
RED	1,100 DOZ.
WHITE	1,200 DOZ.
R. BLUR	500 DOZ.
YELLOW	500 DOZ.
GREEN	1,500 DOZ.
TOTAL	7,600 DOZ. AT USD 4.80/DOZ.

AS PER PRO-FORMA INVOICE NO. 08GD04-017 DATED FEBRUARY 25,2021

TERMS OF PAYMENT：	CFR LASPEZIA
PARTIAL SHIPMENTS：	NOT ALLOWED
TRANSHIPMENT：	ALLOWED

SPECIAL CONDITIONS：

5 % MORE OR LESS IN QUANTITY AND AMOUNT IS ACCEPTABLE

DOCUMENTS MUST BE PRESENTED WITHIN 21 DAYS AFTER SHIPMENT DATE BUT WITHIN THE VALIDITY OF THIS DOC. CREDIT.

INSTRUCTIONS TO THE ADVISING BANK：

ALL BANK CHARGES OUTSIDE ITALY ARE FOR BENEFICIARY'S ACCOUNT.

Issuer：		商业发票 COMMERCIAL INVOICE		
To：		No：		Date：
Transport details：		S/C No：		L/C No：
		Terms of payment：		
Marks and numbers	Description of goods	Quantity	Unit price	Amount
See Total				

CONTRACT

Seller
XIAMEN FOOD COMPANY 26 FLOOR，
Greater China International Exchange plaza
Buyer
Pepper. 3 Columbus Circle，MenSi，Japan

Contract No. XMCYD211008
Date Oct. 8，2021
Signed At _____
L/C No. _____

The undersigned Seller and Buyer have agreed to close the following transactions according to the terms and conditions stipulated below：

Shipping Marks	Item No.	Description	QTY	Unit	Unit Price	Amount
N/M	SSS-333	Devil Pepper	4，000	KG	USD 8.00	USD 32，000.00
Total			4，000	KG		USD 32，000.00

Price Term：　　　　　　　CIF MOJI

Total Amount：　SAY US DOLLARS THIRTY TWO THOUSAND ONLY

Percentage of allowance for amount and quantity：　0　% **More or Less**

Payment Term：　　　　　D/P at sight

Time of Shipment：　　　Not later than Nov. 15, 2021

Packing：　　　Pack into carton, 2 pcs/carton, total 300 cartons

Pot of Loading：　　　　SHENZHEN, CHINA

Port of Destination：　　MENSI, JAPAN

Partial Shipment：　　　Not Allowed

Transhipment：　　　　　Allowed

Insurance：**voice value against W. PA. and TP. N. D. as per Ocean Marine Cargo Clauses(1/1/1981)of T**

Special Clause：

Remark：

1. QUALITY/QUANTITY DISCREPANCY：In case of quality discrepancy, claim should be filed by the Buyer within 3 months after the arrival of the goods at port of destination, while of quantity discrepancy, claim should be filed by the Buyer within 15 days after the arrival of the goods at port of destination. It is understood that the Seller shall not be liable for any discrepancy of the goods shipped due to causes for which the Insurance Company, Shipping company, other transportation, organization/or Post Office are liable.

2. The Seller shall not be held liable for failure or delay in delivery of the entire lot or a portion of the goods under this Sales Contract on consequence of any Force Majeure incidents.

3. Arbitration：All disputes in connection with this Contract or the execution thereof shall be settled by negotiation between two paties. If no settlement can be reached, the case in dispute shall then be submitted for arbitration in the country of defendant in accordance with the arbitration regulations of the arbitratian organization of the defendant country. The decision made by the arbitration organization shall be taken as final and binding upon both parties. The arbitration expenses shall be borne by the losing party unless otherwise awarded by the arbitration organization.

4. The Buyer are requested to sign and return one copy of this Sales Contract immediately after receipt of the same. Objection, if any, should be raised by the Buyer within five days after the receipt of this Sales Contract, in the absence of which it is understood that the Buyer has accepted the terms and conditions of the Sales Contract.

This Contract shall come into effect after signature by both parties. This Contract is made in two originals with same effects. Each party holds one.

THE SELLER：　　　　　　　　　**THE BUYER**：

XIAMEN　FOOD　COMPANY　　　　　Pepper. 3 Columbus Circle

参考答案：

ISSUER XIAMEN FOOD COMPANY 26 Floor, Greater China International Exchange Plaza, 1 Fuhua Road, XiaMen, China				COMMERCIAL INVOICE	
TO Pepper. 3 Columbus Circle, MenSi, Japan					
NOTIFY ADDRESS				INVOICE NO.	XME2021/008
				INVOICE DATE	NOV. 15, 2021
				S/C NO.	XMCYD211008
				S/C DATE	OCT. 8, 2021
TRANSPORT DETAILS				TERMS OF PAYMENT	D/P AT SIGHT
FROM XIAMEN TO MENSI			VIA **BY** SEA		
MARKS	DESCRIPTION OF GOODS	QTY	UNIT	UNIT PRICE	AMOUNT
N/M	Devil Pepper.	4, 000	KG	USD 8. 00	USD 32, 000. 00
TOTAL		4, 000	KG	CIF MOJI	USD 32, 000. 00
TOTAL PACKAGES(IN WORDS):					
				ISSUED BY: XIAMEN FOOD COMPANY SIGNATURE ZHANGSAN	

四、Making out a Packing List According to the Following Information. 根据所给信息缮制一份装箱单

FORM OF DOC. CREDIT：IRREVOCABLE

DOC. CREDIT NUMBER：0119008701

DATE OF ISSUE：110213

EXPIRY：DATE 110421 PLACE CHINA

APPLICANT：ABC CORPORATION, OSAKA, JAPAN

BENEFICIARY：GUANGDONG TEXTILES IMP. AND EXP. COMPANY LTD.

168 XIAOBEI ROAD GUANGZHOU 510045 CHINA

AMOUNT：CURRENCY USD AMOUNT 39,800.00

PARTIAL SHIPMENTS：PERMITTED

TRANSHIPMENT：PERMITTED

LOADING IN CHARGE：GUANGZHOU VIA HONG KONG

FOR TRANSPORT TO：OSAKA, JAPAN

LATEST DATE OF SHIP：110331

DESCRIPT. OF GOODS：LADIES GARMENTS

STYLE NO. AH-04B	3,000PCS	USD5.20
STYLE NO. ROCOCO	2,000PCS	USD5.00
STYLE NO. FLORES	1,600PCS	USD4.5
STYLE NO. ROMANTICO	1,000PCS	USD7.00

GUANGZHOU

ADDITIONAL COND.：1. T. T. REIMBURSEMENT IS PROHIBITED

2. SHIPPING MARKS：ABC

OSAKA

NO. 1-380

PRESENTATION PERIOD：DOCUMENTS TO BE PRESENTED WITHIN 15 DAYS AFTER THE DATE OF SHIPMENT, BUT WITHIN THE VALIDITY OF THE CREDIT.

发票号码	2021090/94 WBS	发票日期	MAR. 18, 2021	FORM A 号码	GZ7/80088/5225
提单日期	MAR. 25, 2021	原材料情况	完全自产品	集装箱号码	KOMU1003745/20
提单号码	KFT2582588	船名	BATONG 03/METE MAERSK V. 0304		

DESCRIPTION OF GOODS	G. W.	N. W.	MEASUREMENT
LADIES GARMENTS	12KGS	10KGS	50×30×40CM
STYLE NO. AH-04B			
STYLE NO. ROCOCO	15KGS	12KGS	65×40×40CM
STYLE NO. FLORES	13KGS	11KGS	60×35×35CM
STYLE NO. ROMANTICO	15KGS	12KGS	65×40×40CM

PACKING LIST

No.: _____   Date _____

Contract No. _____   Page：_____ 1 _____ 页

Seller：_____

To：_____

Shipped by：_____ from _____ to _____

Mark & Nos.	Article and Specification	Quantity	Package	Gross Weight (KGS)	Net Weight (KGS)	Measurement (CM)

Chapter 4 Transport Documents 运输单据

Key Points and Difficulties

- To Understand What is a Transport Documents
- What's an Ocean Bill of Lading
- To Know the Kinds and Characters of Bill of Lading, Airway Bill and Other Transport Documents
- To Make out Bill of Lading and Other Transport Documents

Learning Objectives

- Understanding the Contents of Different Kinds of Transport Documents
- Making out a Bill of Lading

Transport Documents 运输单据

Transport documents refer to the certification signed by the carrier to the exporter when he receives the shipped goods. They are important in the process of delivering and receiving the goods, lodging claims, international settlement and negotiation. 运输单据是承运人收到承运货物签发给出口商的证明文件，它是交接货物、处理索赔与理赔以及向银行结算货款或进行议付的重要单据。

Section One　Bill of Lading 海运提单

A Ocean Bill of Lading, also named Marine Bill of Lading sometimes or Port-to-Port Bill of Lading, is a document issued by a carrier or its authorized agents, to a shipper. 海运提单，亦名港口至港口提单，是由运输方或运输方授权的代理人向货主开具的单据。

Its importance lies in three characteristics. First, it is a contract of carriage. Second, it is a receipt for goods and, third, it is a transferable document of title. Just this third characteristic makes the exporters be willing to ship goods before receiving payment, because they can continually control goods through holding the bill of lading until payment is received or a promise to pay is received.

海运提单有三大功能。第一，它是运输合同。第二，它是货物收据。第三，它是可转移的所有权凭证。通过这三个功能，出口方愿意在收款之前运输货物。通过持有海运提单，出口方能够不间断地监管货物直到收到付款或者收到承付。

Only against original bills of lading, as a document of title to the goods, the merchandise after arrival can be released and can be transferred from one person to another. Bill of lading normally is issued in three or more originals to avoid missing through mail or courier services. One of the full set of original bills of lading is used for picking up the goods; the other will be automatically null and void.

作为货物的所有权凭证，在出具原始提单的情况下，货物抵达后便可出货并且能够移交另一方。通常，为了避免在邮递过程中丢失单据，提单开具时应有三份以上的原始单。一整套原始单据用于装载货物，那么，另一套原始单据便会自动失效。

1. Basic Parties of Bill of Lading 海运提单的当事人

（1）Carrier（承运人）. It is the party that issues the contract of transport and is responsible for transporting the goods to the destination. It may be the owner of the vessel, or the chartered party who rents the vessel. 承运人是签发运输合同并负责将货物运输到目的地的一方。其可能是船主，也可能是租用船只的租船方。

（2）Shipper/Consignor（托运人，贷方）. It is the party who consigns the goods to the carrier. The shipper is usually the seller under the sales contract, but sometimes the credit requires the buyer as shipper. The reason may be that the buyer is not the final buyer but a middleman. 托运人指将货物托运给承运人的当事人。发货人通常是销售合同中的卖方，但有时信用证要求买方作为发货人，原因可能是买家不是最终买家，而是中间人。

（3）Consignee（收货人）. It is the party who has the right to pick up the goods from the carrier against bills of lading at the port of destination, usually the buyer under the sales contract. In practice, however, the consignee may be the shipper(seller), the negotiating bank, or the issuing bank. When the bills of lading are made out "to the order of shipper", the shipper(i. e. the se-ller) must endorse them blankly before submitting them to the negotiating bank. 收货人指有权在目的港凭提单向承运人提货的当事人，通常是销售合同中的买方。然而，在实践中，收货人可以是托运人(卖方)、押汇银行或开证银行。如果提单是"按照托运人的指示"开具的，托运人(即卖方)在将其提交给押汇银行之前必须空白背书。

(4)Notify party(被通知方). It is the party whom the carrier will notify of the arrival of the goods. It may be the applicant of the credit, the party nominated in the credit, or simply left blank if there is no requirement in the credit. 被通知方是承运人将通知货物到达的一方。它可以是信用证的申请人，信用证中指定的当事人，或者如果信用证中没有要求，则简单地留空。

(5)Transferee/Holder(受让人或持票人). A bill of lading is a negotiable instrument, that is, it may be transferred with endorsement and delivery. The person to whom a bill of lading is transferred is called the transferee. Against the bill of lading, the transferee is entitled to obtain the goods from the carrier. The holder may be the consignee or the transferee. 提单是一种流通票据，也就是说，它可以通过背书和交付进行转让。提单转让给的人被称为受让人。根据提单，受让人有权从承运人处获得货物。持有人可以是收货人，也可以是受让人。

2. The Types of Bill of Lading 海运提单的种类

- Shipped on Board B/L and Received for Shipment B/L 已装船提单和收妥备运提单
- Clean B/L and Unclean B/L 清洁提单和不清洁提单
- Named B/L, Blank B/L, and Order B/L 记名提单、不记名提单和指示提单
- Direct B/L, Transhipment B/L, and Through B/L 直达提单、转运提单和联运提单
- Long Form B/L and Short Form B/L 全式提单和简式提单
- Liner B/L and Charter Party B/L 班轮提单和租船提单
- Container B/L 集装箱提单
- On Deck B/L 货装舱面提单
- Advanced B/L and Ante-Date B/L 预借提单和倒签提单

3. The Specimen of Bill of Lading 海运提单的样单

BILL OF LADING

SHIPPER (2)		B/L NO.　　　　(1) 中国远洋运输(集团)总公司 CHINA OCEAN SHIPPING(GROUP)CO. CABLE：COSCO BEIJING SHIPPER
CONSIGNEE (3)		TLX： ORIGINAL COMBINED TRANSPORT BILL OF LADING RECEIVED IN APPARENT GOOD ORDER AND CONDITION EXCEPT AS OTHERWISE NOTED THE TOTAL NUMBER OF CONTAINER OR OTHER PACKAGES OR UNITS ENUMERATE BELOW FOR TRANSPORTATION FROM THE PLACE OF RECEIPT TO THE PLACE OF DELIVERY SUBJECT TO THE TERMS HEREOF. ONE OF THE SIGNED BILL OF LADING MUST BE SURRENDERED DULY ENDORSED IN EXCHANGE FOR THE GOODS OR DELIVERY ORDER. ON PRESENTATION OF THIS DOCUMENT DULY ENDORSED TO THE CARRIER BY OR ON BEHALF THE HOLDER OF THE BILL OF LADING, THE RIGHTS AND LIABILITIES ARISING IN ACCORDANCE WITH THE TERMS AND CONDITIONS HEREOF SHALL (WITHOUT PREJUDICE TO ANY RULE OF COMMON LAW OF STATUTE RENDERING THEM BINDING ON THE MERCHANT) BECOME BINDING IN ALL RESPECTS BETWEEN THE CARRIER AND THE HOLDER AS THOUGH THE CONTRACT EVIDENCED HEREBY HAD BEEN MADE BETWEEN THEM. THE NUMBER OF ORIGINAL BILLS OF LADING STATED UNDER HAVE BEEN SIGNED. ALL OF THIS TENOR AND DATE. ONE OF WHICH BEING ACCOMPLISHED, THE OTHER(S) TO BE VOID.
NOTIFY PARTY (4)		
PRE-CARRIAGE BY(5)	PLACE OF RECEIPT(6)	
OCEAN VESSEL Voy. No. (7)	PORT OF LOADING(8)	
PORT OF DISCHARGE (9)	PLACE OF DELIVERY(10)	

MARKS (11)	NOS. &KINDS OF PKGS (12)	DESCRIPTION OF GOODS (13)	G. W. (kg) (14)	MEAS(m³) (15)

TOTAL NO. OF CONTAINERS OR PACKAGES(IN WORDS)　　　(16)

FREIGHT & CHARGES	REVENUE TONS	RATE	PER	PREPAID (17)	COLLECT
PREPAID AT (18)	PAYABLE AT	PLACE AND DATE OF ISSUE(19)			
TOTAL PREPAID	NUMBER OF ORIGINALS B/L(20)				

4. The Content and Key Points of Ocean Bill of Lading 样单拆解：海运提单的主要内容及缮制要点

（1）B/L No.：The carrier or the agent gives the Number of B/L according to the serial number of bill of lading. Consignor also lists the ship's name and number of the bill of lading when he informs the SHIPMENT ADVICE to the consignee.

提单号码：由承运人或其代理人按该航次所属的提单套数顺序编号。当承运人向收货人发出装船通知时，也注明船名及提单号。

（2）Shipper or Consignor：Usually it is exporter' name and address, the beneficiary of L/C.

托运人或发货人：通常是出口商的地址和姓名，也是信用证上的受益人。

（3）Consignee：If it is a straight B/L, the exact name of company or the consignee should be filled; if it is an order bill of lading, ORDER or TO ORDER is filled. If it is required to issue the order, TO ORDER OF SHIPPER or TO ORDER OF CONSIGNEE or TO ORDER OF ×× BANK is filled accordingly.

收货人：如要求记名提单，则可填上具体的收货公司或收货人名称；如属指示提单，则填为"指示"（ORDER）或"凭指示"（TO ORDER）；如需在提单上列明指示人，则可根据不同要求，做成"凭托运人指示"（TO ORDER OF SHIPPER），凭"收货人指示"（TO ORDER OF CONSIGNEE）或"凭银行指示"。

For example：

①"Full set of B/L consigned to A. B. C. Co"——记名收货人

②"Full set of B/L made out to order"——凭指示

③"B/L issued to order of ×××"——记名指示

（4）Notify party：It is the party whom the carrier will notify; the party will inform that the goods have arrived at the port of destination, sometimes the party is the importer. If the B/L is under L/C, the notify party should strictly comply with the L/C; if it is a straight B/L or order B/L, and there is the details of the name and address of notify party, it is usually left blank.

被通知人：这是船公司在货物到达目的港时发送到货通知的收件人，有时即为进口人。在信用证项下的提单，则必须严格按信用证要求填写。如果是记名提单或收货人指示提单，且收货人又有详细地址的，则此栏可以不填。

（5）Pre-carriage by：The first ship's name is filled in if transhipment is allowed.

首程运输：如需转运，填写第一程船的船名，否则留空。

（6）Place of receipt：The first place of the goods has been received in the first transhipment.

收货地点：这里填写第一次转运货物到达的第一个地点。

（7）Ocean vessel voy. No.：If the transhipment is allowed, the second ship's name is filled in here; if the transhipment is not allowed, the first ship's name is filled in.

船名船次：如允许转运，须填写第二程船的船名。否则，只填写第一程船的船名。

（8）Port of loading. e. g. "Tianjin," "Qingdao", it cannot be written as "Chinese Port".

装货港：例如"天津""青岛"，此处不可写成"中国港口"。

（9）The port of discharge：It should be the port where the cargo is actually delivered. If transhipment is allowed, the first port of discharge should be the transhipment port, consignee should be the shipping companies; the port of loading of second voyage should be the above tran-shipment port, the port of discharge should be the final port. If the through bill of lading is used by the first voyage shipping company, then the port of discharge is the delivery port, and first and second line should be filled in the bill of lading. If the goods are transhipped at a certain port, "VIA ××" must be used. When a container transportation is used, the "combined transport B/L" should list: the port of loading, the port of discharge, place of receipt, place of delivery and pre-carriage by, ocean vessel, voy. No. and the port of discharge.

卸货港：填列货物实际卸下的港口名称。如属转船，第一程提单上的卸货港填转船港，收货人为船运公司；第二程提单装货港应为上述转船港，卸货港应为最后目的港。如果由第一程船公司出具联运提单，则卸货港即可填装运港，提单上列明第一和第二程船的船名。如经某港转运，要显示"VIA ××"字样。在运用集装箱运输方式时，目前使用"联合运输提单"，提单上除列明装货港、卸货港外，还要列明"收货地""交货地"以及"第一程运输工具""海运船名和航次"。

(10) Place of delivery: It should be in conformity with the stipulations of the L/C or the requirement of the contract and the invoice.

交货地点：应该与信用证、合同、发票的要求一致。

(11) Shipping mark: It should comply with the requirements of L/C, otherwise shipping marks should be filled according to the Invoice. If there are no marks, fill in "N/M".

装运唛头：应该与信用证、合同、发票的要求一致，假如没有唛头填上"N/M"。

(12) No. and kind of packages: The number of package should be written in figures. The number must comply with the actual packing situation.

包装号码和种类：此处包装号码须用小写。号码必须与包装的实际情况相符。

(13) Description of goods: Fill in the name of commodity. The description of goods under L/C should strictly comply with that in L/C.

品名：本栏的货物品名必须要与信用证规定的货名以及其他单据货名一致。

(14) Gross weight: Fill in gross weight in kilogram as calculating weight unit. If there is no package or in bulk, you can write "Gross for Net" or "Net weight".

毛重：毛重以公斤作为计量单位。如货物没有包装或散装，应填写为"毛净重"或者"净重"。

(15) Measurement: Fill in the cargo's volume, keep three decimal fraction.

尺寸：此处填写货物的体积，并保留至小数点三位。

(16) Total No. of containers or packages: If there are more than two containers, the number of containers must be listed separately and written in words.

集装箱号：如果货物装两个或两个以上集装箱，则分行列出各集装箱号。

(17) Prepaid: Generally the freight is prepaid or freight collect. If the term CIF or the CFR is used, "freight prepaid" should be marked, don't keep in blank, otherwise the consignee cannot receive the goods because of the transport charges, although investigation may be made, it will cause late delivery of goods. If the term FOB is used, then "freight collect" is marked.

预付：一般为预付或到付。如 CIF 或 CFR 出口，一般均填上"运费预付"字样，千万不可漏列，否则收货人会因运费问题提不到货，虽可查清情况，但拖延提货时间，也将造成损失。如系 FOB 出口，则运费可制作"运费到付"字样。

（18）Prepaid at：The place where the freight is prepaid or freight is collect.

预付地点：运费预付或者运费到付的地方。

（19）Place and date of issue：The place and date must be issued by the carrier, master or their agent(s), and signature's name and job title should be explicitly marked, such as CARRIER, CAPTAIN, or "AS AGENT FOR THE CARRIER：×××". And the date of bill of lading must be in compliance with the final shipping date of L/C or contract.

提单签发的日期和地点：提单签发的日期和地点必须由承运人或船长或他们的代理签发，并应明确表明签发人身份。一般表示方法有：CARRIER, CAPTAIN 或 AS AGENT FOR THE CARRIER ×××。提单上所签的日期必须与信用证或合同上所要求的最后装船期一致。

（20）Nos. of Bill of Lading：The copies of bill of lading are generally made out according to L/C. For example, "FULL SET OF" generally refers to three original B/Ls and a couple of copies. When the original B/L is presented for delivering goods, the other copies are null and avoid.

提单份数：提单的副本一般按信用证要求出具。例如，"全套提单"通常指三份正本提单和两份副本提单。当正本提单被出示用于交货时，其他副本无效。

Notes：Some Discrepancies Found in a Bill of Lading

注意：海运提单中一些常见不符点

- Consignee's name is not as per L/C. 收货人的名称与信用证不符。
- Notify party differs from that of L/C. 通知方与信用证的通知方不同。
- Description of goods is not consistent with L/C. 货物描述与信用证不一致。
- Unclean B/L is submitted. 提交了不清洁提单。
- Port of lading/discharge is not as per L/C. 提货港/卸货港不符合信用证规定。
- Less than full set of B/Ls. 少于全套提单。
- No evidence that freight has been paid, and the amount of freight paid is not listed when required by L/C.
- 没有证据表明运费已经支付，并且运费金额没有在信用证要求时列出。
- No "on Board" notation. 没有标识放置"船上"符号。
- "On Board" notation is dated after the latest shipment date on L/C. "已装船"批注的日期在信用证上的最后装运日期之后。
- Marked "on Deck". 标记为"甲板上"。
- Chartered party B/L submitted. 已提交租船方提单。
- No endorsement, when required. 无需背书。
- Mark, number of packages, gross weight, net weight conflict with those on other documents. 标记、包装数量、毛重、净重与其他文件上的内容相冲突。
- The issuer is not a carrier or an agent of a carrier. 发行人不是承运人或承运人的代理人。

5. Case Study 案例实训

Making out a Bill of Lading according to the following information 根据下面的信息缮制海运

提单

(1) THE INFORMATION OF L/C 信用证的信息:

FROM: UNITED OVERSEAS BANK LIMITED SINGAPORE

DATE: 28/07/2021(DD/MM/YY)

S/C No. HL2022

IRREVOCABLE LETTER OF CREDIT NO.: LCMLC459886

ADVISING BANK: BANK OF CHINA, NANJING JIANGSU, CHINA

BENEFICIARY: XINFA IMPORT AND EXPORT TRADE CO., LTD., #86 RENMIN STREET, NANJING CITY, JIANGSU, CHINA.

APPLICANT: LF IMPORT AND EXPORT TRADE CO., LTD., 2ND FLOOR, 4 BEACH ROAD HEX 01-4983 SINGAPORE 190004

AMOUNT: USD69,726.00

EXPIRATION DATE: Oct. 15, 2022

SHIPMENT FROM: SHANGHAI, EUROPEAN EXPRESS   TO: SINGAPORE

: 44A/ON BOARD/DISP/TAKING CHARGE CHINA

: 44B/FOR TRANSPORTATION TO SINGAPORE

: 44C/LATEST DAY OF SHIPMENT: 2022-09-30

: 45A/ DESCRIPTION OF GOODS AND /OR SERVICES FOB SHANGHAI BATH AND FACE TOWELS AS PER SALES CONTRACT NO. HL2011 DATED 28/7/2022

ART NO. 108: 100%COTTON STRIPE FACE TOWEL

ART NO. 218: 100% COTTON TEA TOWEL

ART NO. 75: 100%COTTON PRINTED FACE TOWEL

ART NO. 318: 100% COTTON TEA TOWEL

ART NO. WN167: 100%COTTON SQUARE TOWEL

: 46A/DOCUMENTS REQUIRED

DOCUMENT IN TRIPLICAT UNLESS OTHERWISE STIPULATES

+FULL SET CLEAN ON BOARD OCEAN BILLS OF LADING MADE OUT TO THE ORDER OF UNITED OVERSEAS BANK LTD. NOTIFY APPICANT AND MARKED FREIGHT PREPAID

(2) OTHER INFORMATION 相关资料:

唛头: 无

船名: EUROPEAN EXPRESS   航次: V. W003   装运港: 上海

货名	NO. 1 08	NO. 2 18	NO. 75	NO. 318	NO. WN167
总数量(PCS)			169		
总毛重(KGS)			5,529.00		
总尺码(CM)			20.800		

BILL OF LADING

SHIPPER：（2） XINFA IMPORT AND EXPORT TRADE CO., LTD., #86 RENMIN STREET, NANJING CITY, JIANGSU, CHINA		B/L NO.（1）SSHSINO227637 中国远洋运输(集团)总公司 CHINA OCEAN SHIPPING(GROUP)CO. CABLE：COSCO BEIJING TLX：
CONSIGNEE(3) TO THE ORDER OF UNITED OVERSEAS BANK LIMITED SINGAPORE		**ORIGINAL**
NOTIFY PARTY(4) LF IMPORT AND EXPORT TRADE CO., LTD., 2ND FLOOR, 4 BEACH ROAD HEX 01-4983 SINGAPORE 190004		COMBINED TRANPORT BILL OF LADING RECEIVED IN APPARENT GOOD ORDER AND CONDITION EXCEPT AN OTHERWISE NOTED THE TOTAL NUMBER OF CONTAINERS OR OTHER PACLAGES OR UNITS ENUMERATE BELOW FOR TRANSPORTATION TIAM THE
PRE – CARRIAGE BY(5)	PLACE OF RECEIPT (6)	PALCE BILLS OF LADING MUST BE SURRENDERED DULY ENDORSED IN EXCHANGE FOR THE GLLDS OF DELIVERY ORDER. ON PRESENTATION OF THEIS DOCUMENT DULY ENDORSED TO THE CARRIER BY OR ON BEHALF THE HOLDER OF THE BILL OF LADING, THE
OCEAN VESSEL Voy. No.（7） EUROPEAN EXPRESS V. W003	PORT OF LOADING （8） SHANGHAI, CHINA	RIGHTS AND LIABILITIES ARISING IN ACCORDANCE WITH THE TERMS AND CONDITIONS HERE OF SHALL. WITHOUT PREJUDICE TO ANY RULE OF COMMON LAW OF STATRTE ERNDERING THEM OF THE BILL OF LADING AS THOUGH THE CONTRACT EVIDENCED HEREBY
PORT OF DISCHARGE(9) SINGAPORE	PLACE OF DELIVERY （10） SINGAPORE	TAB BEEN MADE BETWEEN THEM. IN WITNESS WHERE LOF THE NUMBER OF ORIGINAL BILLS OF LADING STATED UNDER HAVE BEEN SIGNED. ALL OF THIS TENOR AND DATE. ONE OF WHICH BEING ACCOMPLISHED. THE OTHER(S)TO BE VOID.

MARKS （11）	NOS. &KINDS OF PKGS （12）	DESCRIPTION OF GOODS （13）	G. W.（kg） （14）	MEAS(m³) （15）
N/M	169	ART NO. 108：100%COTTON STRIPE FACE TOWEL ART NO. 218：100% COTTON TEA TOWEL ART NO. 75：100%COTTON PRINTED FACE TOWEL ART NO. 318：100% COTTON TEA TOWEL ART NO. WN167：100%COTTON SQUARE TOWEL	5,529. 00	20. 800

TOTAL NO. OF CONTAINERS OR PACKAGES(IN WORDS)　　　　（16） ONE HUNDRED AND SIXTY NINE					
FREIGHT & CHARGES	REVENUE TONS	RATE	PER	PREPAID （17）	COLLECT

PREPAID AT (18) SHANGHAI	PAYABLE AT	PLACE AND DATE OF ISSUE(19) AS AGENT FOR THE CARRIER ××× 2022/14/09			
TOTAL PREPAID	NUMBER OF ORIGINALS B/L(20)				

Notes：注意

1. Consignee shall fill in strictly in accordance with the requirements of the letter of credit. 收货人严格按照信用证要求填写。

Registered Bill of Lading. 记名提单。例如：ABC CO

Indicative Bill of Lading：指示提单。例如：TO ORDER，TO ORDER OF SHIPPER，TO ORDER OF ABC BANK

Bearer Bill of Lading：不记名提单。例如：TO BEARER

2. Description of Goods 货物描述

★ If the transaction price is CIF or CFR, fill in FREIGHT PREPAID in this column. 成交价格为 CIF 或 CFR，这一栏里填写 FREIGHT PREPAID.

★ The transaction price is FOB, fill in FREIGHT COLLECT in this column. 成交价格为 FOB，这一栏里填写 FREIGHT COLLECT。

★ The additional information required by the letter of credit to be displayed in the bill of lading can be filled in this column. 信用证要求在提单里显示的附加信息可以填写在本栏。

3. Place and Date of Issue of Bill of Lading：The location should be the shipping location, and the date should generally be the shipping date. 提单的签发地点和日期：地点应为装运地点，日期一般为装运日期。

4. Laden on Board the Vessel Date：No later than the latest shipment date specified in the letter of credit or contract. 装船日期：不得迟于信用证或合同所规定的最迟装运日期。

Section Two　Shipping Note 托运单

Shipping note is a document that the consignor addresses to the carrier when transacting the consignment in terms of the contract and letters of credit. According to the details of booking note, the carrier accepts the consignment after consideration of the shipping route, port of call, sailing schedule and shipping space, etc.

运单是发货人在根据合同和信用证进行托运时向承运人发出的文件。根据预订单的详细信息，承运人在考虑了航线、停靠港、航行时间表和舱位等因素后接受托运。

1. The Specimen of a Shipping Note 托运单样单

Shipping Note 托运单

Shipper(发货人) (1)				D/R NO.(编号)(4)		
Consignee(收货人) (2)				集装箱货物托运单 船代留底 第一联		
Notify Party(通知人) (3)						
Pre-Carriage By(前程运输) (5)		Place of Receipt(收货地点) (6)				
Ocean Vessel(船名) Voy. No. (船次)(7)		Port of Loading(装货港) (8)				
Port of Discharge(卸货港) (9)		Place of Delivery(交货地点) (10)		Final Destination for the Merchant's Reference(目的地)		
Container No. (集装箱号)(11)	Seal No.(封志号)(12)	Marks & Nos. (标记与号码)(13)	No. of Containers or PKgs(箱数或件数)(14)	Kind of Packages: Description of Good(包装种类与货名)(15)	Gross Weight 毛重(公斤)(16)	Measurement(尺码立方米)(17)
TOTAL NUMBER OF CONTAINERS OR PACKAGES(IN WORDS)集装箱数或件数合计(大写)(18)						
FREIGHT& CHARGES(运费与附加费)(19)	Revenue Tons(运费吨)	Rate(运费率)	Per(每)	Prepaid(运费预付)	Collect(运费到付)	
Ex Rate(兑换率)　　Prepaid At(预付地点)　　Payable At(到付地点)　　Place of Issue(签发地点)(20)						
Transhipment Permitted/Prohibited 可否转船(22)			Partial shipment Permitted/Prohibited 可否分批			
装船期		Date of Validity 有效期(23)		The number of B/L 提单张数(21)		
Total Value 金额	(24)					
Date of Shipping Note 制单日期(25)						

2. The Contents of a Shipping Note 样单拆解：托运单的主要内容及缮制方法

（1）Shipper：The exporter's detailed address is asked to make out including street, doorplate number, city and country.

托运人：填写出口公司的详细名称和地址。

（2）Consignee：The shipping note under L/C, there are two ways of expressing the consignee. "Consigned to ×××(Consignee)" or "To order of ×××(Consignee)".

收货人：在信用证支付的条件下，对收货人的规定常有两种表示方法：A. 记名收货人；B. 指示收货人。

（3）Notify Party：The notify party stipulated in the L/C is usually in this blank. The notify party assumes the responsibility of receiving the shipper's notice that the goods has reached the port of destination. He has no right to take delivery of goods.

被通知人：此栏填写信用证中规定的被通知人。被通知人的职责是及时接受船方发出的到货通知并将该通知转告真实收货人，但是，被通知人无权提货。

（4）D/R No.

托运单编号：一般填写商业发票的号码。

（5）Pre-Carriage By：Usually it is the name of the transportation tool before sea transportation.

前程运输：本栏填海运前一段的运输工具名称。

（6）Place of Receipt：Namely it is the place where the carrier receives the goods from the consignor.

收货地点：指前段运输的承运人从发货人手中接收货物的地点。

（7）Ocean Vessel, Voy. No.：It is the name of steam ship and the voyage number.

船名，船次。

（8）Port of Loading：It is the port of shipment of combined transport bill of lading.

装货港：联合运输中海运段的装货港名称。

（9）Port of Discharge：It is the final destination port, and it must comply with the stipulations of L/C or the contract.

卸货港：本栏所填的卸货港就是最终的目的港，并须与信用证及合同规定一致。

（10）Place of Delivery：The name of the final destination should be put in this column. Otherwise this column is blank.

交货地点：本栏填最终目的地的名称，否则本栏留空不填。

（11）Container No.：If there are more than two or more containers, the container number must be listed separately.

集装箱号：如果货物装两个或两个以上集装箱，则分行列出各集装箱号。

（12）Seal No.

封志号是海关对货物查验后所加施的封条号。

（13）Marks & Nos.

唛头与号码：根据买卖合同或者信用证的规定来写，如无唛头，则表明"N/M"。

（14）No. of Containers or Pieces of Packing.

件数或集装箱数。

（15）Kind of Packages and Description of Goods：The Number of containers, kind of packages should be marked here.

包装种类与货名：本栏主要填写提单项下商品外包装的合计件数和包装种类。

(16)Gross Weight：Fill in the gross weight in kilogram. If there is only net weight in the naked goods，"N/M" is added before net weight.

毛重：本栏为该货的毛重，并以公斤表示。若裸装货物没有毛重只有净重时，在净重前加注"N/M"。

(17)Measurement：It refers to the volume，the actual size of goods. It is measured in cubic meter.

尺码：货物的体积、实际尺码，以立方米为单位。

(18)Total Number of Containers or Packages.

集装箱数或件数合计(大写)。

(19)Freight & Charges.

运费与附加费。

(20)Ex Rate，Prepaid At，Payable At，Place of Issue. 兑换率，预付地点，到付地点，签发地点。

(21)The number of B/L.

提单张数。

(22)Transhipment Permitted/Prohibited.

可否转船。

　　Partial shipment Permitted/Prohibited

可否分批。

(23)Date of Validity.

有效期。

(24)Total Value.

金额。

(25)Date of Shipping Note.

制单日期。

Section Three   Combined Transport Bill of Lading
联合运输提单

In practice of international trade，the marine B/L is often combined with the multimodal transport bill of lading or combined transport bill of lading，which covers at least two different modes of transport of goods from the point of departure to the point of final destination by sea，inland waterway，air，rail or road.

在国际贸易实践中，海运提单通常与多式联运提单或联运提单相结合，多式联运提单涵盖了从出发点到最终目的地的至少两种不同的货物运输方式，包括海运、内河、空运、铁路或公路。

1. The Specimen of Combined Transport Bill of Lading 联合运输提单样单

Combined Transport Bill of Lading

Shipper(2)	BILL OF LADING B/L No.（1）
Consignee(3)	COSCO 中国远洋运输公司 （5） CHINA OCEAN SHIPPING COMPANY Cable： Telex：
Notify Party(4)	COSCO PEKING 22264 CPCPK CN COSCO CANTON 44080 COSCA CN

Pre-carriage by （6）	Place of Receipt by Pre-carrier（7）	COSCO SHANGHAI 33057 COSCO CN COSCO TSINGTAO 32037 OCSQD CN
Ocean Vessel Voy. No. （8）	Port of Loading （9）	COSCO TIENTSIN 23221 TOSCO CN COSCO DAIREN 86162 DOSCO CN

Port of discharge （10）	Final Destination （11）	Freight Payable at （12）	Number of Original Bs/L （20）

Container No. （13）	Seal No. Marks & No. （14）	Number of kind of Packages； Description of goods（15，16）	Gross Weight（kgs） （17）	Measurement （m³）（18）

TOTAL PACKAGES(IN WORDS)SAY _____ ONLY   （19）

Freight and Charges （21）	Shipped on board the vessel named above in apparent good order and condition(unless otherwise indicated)the goods or packages specified herein and to be discharged at the above mentioned port of discharge or as near thereto as the vessel may safely get and be always afloat. The weight, measure, marks, numbers, quality, contents and value being particulars furnished by the Shipper, are not checked by the Carrier on loading. 　　In witness whereof, the Carrier or his Agents has signed Bills of Lading all of this tenor and date, one of which being accomplished, the others to stand void. 　　Shippers are requested to note particularly the exceptions and conditions of this Bill of Lading with reference to the validity of the insurance upon their goods.
	Place and Date of Issue： （22）
	Signed for the Carrier(SIGNATURE) （23） （24）

2. The Contents of Combined Transport Bill of Lading 样单拆解：联合运输提单的主要内容及缮制要点

（1）B/L No.：The carrier or the agent gives the Number of B/L according to the serial number of bill of lading.

提单号码：由承运人或其代理人按该航次所属的提单套数顺序编号。

（2）Shipper or Consignor：The consignor of bill of lading under letter of credit must be the beneficiary of letter of credit.

发货人或托运人：信用证下的提单发货人必须与信用证的受益人名称一致。

(3)Consignee：The bill of lading under the collection can be generally made out "TO OR-DER" or "TO ORDER OF SHIPPER", etc.

收货人：托收方式下的提单，一般可填"TO ORDER"或"TO ORDER OF SHIPPER"等。

(4)Notify party：The notify party of bill of lading under the collection must be the buyer according to the contract. The detailed address is required in this column, even if there isn't any stipulation in the originals or the copies of L/C.

被通知人：托收方式下的提单被通知人可按合同的买方名称填入。本栏要求填详细地址，即使信用证没有规定地址，虽正本不表示，但副本也要表示。

(5)Carrier：Though the forms of the bill of lading of each shipping company are different, the name of carrier's shipping company is usually printed in the middle of B/L since it is very important in transaction.

承运人：虽然各船公司提单的格式不同，但在提单的上端均印有作为承运人的船公司名称。提单上的承运人名称是非常重要的项目。

(6)Pre-carriage by：Usually it is the name of the traffic before sea transportation.

前程运输：本栏填海运前一段运输工具名称。

(7)Place of Receipt by Pre-carrier：It is the place where the carrier receives the goods from consignor.

收货地点：前段运输的承运人从发货人手中接收货物的地点。

(8)Ocean Vessel, Voy. No.：It is the name of steam ship and the voyage number, it is not necessary to mark voyage number, if there is no voyage number.

海运船名、航次号：此为船名和航次号，如无航次号可不填航次号。

(9)Port of loading：It is the port of shipment of combined transport bill of lading.

装货港：联合运输中海运段的装货港名称。

(10)Port of Discharge：If sea transportation is the last means of transportation in the combined transportation, Port of Discharge is the final destination port; it must comply with that in letter of credit or the contract.

卸货港：如果海运是全程运输最后一种运输方式时，则本栏所填的卸货港就是最终的目的港，并须与信用证及合同规定一致。

(11)Final Destination. If the port of discharge in the 10th column is not the final destination, the final destination is the place where the goods are actually delivered by the other means of transportation after sea transporting; the final destination should be marked in this column. Otherwise this column keeps in blank.

交货地点：如果第10栏所填的卸货港并非最终目的地，在海运方式后仍需以其他运输方式接着继续运输才能到达最终目的地，则本栏填最终目的地的名称。否则本栏留空不填。

(12)Freight Payable at：Freight Clause should be marked according to the stipulations of the letter of credit. If there is no stipulation, it should be the price terms "Freight prepaid," "Freight to collect" under FOB.

运费条款：应按信用证规定填写。若信用证未具体规定，应按价格条款如 FOB 条件下应填"Freight prepaid""Freight to collect"（运费预付、运费到付）等。

（13）Container No.：If there are more than two containers, the number of containers must be marked separately and written in words.

集装箱号：如果货物装两个或两个以上集装箱，则分别用大写列出各集装箱号。

（14）Seal No., Shipping Marks & Nos.：Shipping Marks and Numbers should be in Conformity with that in letter of credit. Usually the goods in Combined Transport Bill of Lading is container goods, so this column always fill "Container Number and Seal Number", if there are more than two containers, the container number and seal number must be listed separately, and the pieces, gross weight, size of container should appear as well.

封志号、唛头和号码：本栏中的唛头、号码则应与信用证要求的原型一致。联合运输提单多数系集装箱货物，所以本栏填上"集装箱号和封志号"，如果货物由两个或两个以上集装箱装运，则分别列出各集装箱号和封志号，而且还要列出集装箱各自不同的件数毛重和尺码。

（15）Number of containers or packages; kind of packages.

件数或集装箱数：本栏目主要填提单项下商品外包装的合计件数和包装种类。

（16）Description of Goods：Fill in the name of commodity. The description of goods under L/C should strictly comply with that in L/C.

品名：本栏的货物品名必须要与信用证规定的货名以及其他单据货名一致。

（17）Gross weight（kgs）：Fill in the gross weight in kilogram as calculating weight unit. If there is no package for the naked goods, then "N/M" is added in front of the net weight.

毛重：本栏填该货的毛重，并以公斤表示。若裸装货物没有毛重只有净重时，在净重前加注"N/M"。

（18）Measurement（cubic meter）：Fill in the cargo's volume, it is the volume of the goods, the actual sizes of the goods, cubic meter is the unit.

尺码：货物的体积、实际尺码，以立方米为单位。

（19）Total No. of Containers or Packages（in words）：Total number of containers or packages is filled out and written in words.

集装箱总箱数或合计数（大写）。

（20）Number of Original B/Ls：The original bill of lading under the letter of credit is signed and issued according to the letter of credit, the copies of original bill of lading under collection are generally two or three. The copies should be written in English.

正本提单份数：信用证项下的正本提单签发的份数要依据信用证规定办理，托收支付方式的正本提单，一般签发两份或三份都可以。在本栏填列的份数用英语标示。

（21）Freight and Charges：Generally it is unnecessary to list out the rate or freight charges, unless letter of credit has specially stipulated. Sometimes "Freight as arranged" is marked, but most of time this column keeps in blank.

运费和费用：一般没有必要将运费具体的费率和运费金额列出，除非信用证有特别规定。有的在本栏填"Freight as arranged"，但本栏多数都是留空。

（22）Place and Date of Issue：The place of issue is generally the place where the carrier delivers the goods. But the issuing places of a combined bill of lading is the place of the carrier's business location, generally, he has his agencies at the port of shipment, so the place of issue is at the port of shipment. If it is a bill of lading on board, the date of issue is the shipping date.

签单地点和日期：签单地点一般是承运人接管货物或装货的地点。但联运提单的签单地点多数是承运人经营业务所在的地点，一般承运人多数在装运港设有代理人，所以签单地点一般都在装运港。如是已装船提单，其签单日期被视为该货装运日期。

（23）Signed for the Carrier：Any kind of transportation document will not come into force unless signed by its carrier; this is a carrier's obligation. Any signature or verification must show "the carrier" or "the captain".

承运人：任何一种运输单据必须由其承运人签章才能生效，这是承运人的义务。承运人或船长的任何签字或证实，必须表明"承运人"或"船长"的身份。

（24）On board notation：Generally this column is called "on board notation". Sometimes it doesn't appear in combined bill of lading, we can mark "on board" or "shipped on board" on the blank space of the bill of lading, and then sign the name of carrier and mark the shipping date. This is called "on board notation".

装船批注：一般将本栏称为"on board notation"（装船批注或装船备忘录）。有些联运提单格式尚未专门设立装船批注栏目，则在提单的空白处另批注"on board"或"shipped on board"，再由承运人签字签章，并加注装船日期。这种批注也叫"on board notation"。

Notes：SOME B/LS IN L/CS 信用证中提单要注意的一些问题

• FULL SET CLEAN ON BOARD OCEAN BILL OF LADING ISSUED TO ORDER, BLANK ENDORSED MARKED FREIGHT PAYABLE AT DESTINATION NOTIFY PARTY AS ABC COMPANY AND SHOWING INVOICE VALUE, UNITE PRICE, TRADE TERMS, CONTRACT NUMBER AND L/C NUMBER UNACCEPTABLE. 根据订单签发的全套清洁已装船海运提单，空白背书注明运费在目的地支付，通知方为 ABC 公司，并显示发票价值、单价、贸易条款、合同号和信用证号，不可接受等内容。

• FULL SET OF CLEAN ON BOARD B/L ISSUED TO OUR ORDER, MARKED NOTIFYING APPLICANT AND FREIGHT PREPAID AND SHOWING FULL NAME AND ADDRESS OF THE RELATIVE SHIPPING AGENT UN EGYPT. 以我方为受益人的全套已装船清洁提单，注明通知申请人并预付运费，并注明相关埃及船运代理的全名和地址。

• FULL SET CLEAN ON BOARD PORT TO PORT BILL OF LADING, MADE TO THE ORDER AND BLANK ENDORSED TO OUR ORDER, MARKED FREIGHT PREPAID DATED NOT LATER THAN THE LATEST DATE OF SHIPMENT NOT PRIOR TO THE DATE OF THIS CREDIT. PLUS THREE NON-NEGOTIABLE COPIES. 全套已装船清洁的港到港提单，以我方为收益人，或以我方为收益人的空白背书，注明运费预付，日期不迟于最晚装运日期，不早于本信用证日期，加上三份不可转让的副本。

3. Case Study 案例实训

信用证条款如下：

FROM：TOKYO COMMERCE BANK OF JAPAN, JAPAN

DATE：20/07/2021（DD/MM/YY）

LETTER OF CREDIT NO. : 3012K10032

ADVISING BANK：BANK OF CHINA, NANJING JIANGSU, CHINA

BENEFICIARY：JIANGSU FASHION INTERNATIONAL TRADE CORPORATION #358 ZHUSHAN ROAD JIAN GNING DISTRICT, NANJING, CHINA.

APPLICANT：POWER PLAY INC. 2ND FLOOR, NO. 137E, 33RD STREET, TOKYO, 90032 JAPAN.

AMOUNT：USD66,726.00

EXPIRATION DATE：Sept. 15, 2022

SHIPMENT FROM：SHANGHAI, M. V. GLORIA SHIPMENT TO：TOKYO, JAPAN.

LATEST SHIPMENT DATE：AUGUST 30, 2022

PARTIAL SHIPMENT ARE ALLOWED,

TRANSHIPMENT IS PROHIBITED.

: 44A/LOADING ON BOARD/DISPATCH/TAKING IN CHARGE AT /FROM … :
SHANGHAI CHINA

: 44B/FOR TRANSPORTATION TO YOKOHAMA, JAPAN

: 44C/LATEST DAY OF SHIPMENT：20220830

: 45/DESCRIPTION OF GOODS/SERVICES：400 CARTONS OF CHINESE LIGHT SPECKLED KIDNEY BEANS AS PER SALES CONFIRMATION NO. HQ（DTR）0321

DATED20/07/2022（DD/MM/YY）

CIF-YOKOHAMA, JAPAN

: 46/DOCUMENTS REQUIRED：

DOCUMENTS IN TRIPLICATE（UNLESS OTHERWISE SPECIFIED）

+FULL SET CLEAN SHIPPED ON BOARD OCEAN BILLS OF LADING MADE OUT TO THE ORDER OF THE JAPAN'S MITSUBISHI BANK NOTIFY APPLICANT MARKED FREIGHT PREPAID

相关资料：

卖方于 8 月 20 日在南京起运，铁路运输，于 8 月 26 日在新港装船完毕，取得联运提单。

车厢号为 Foang No. 322112

唛头：F. C. L

25016

XINGANG

NO. 1—900

船名：M. V. Gloria；航次：V. 008A；装运港：新港

G. W.：25,000KGS；MEASUREMENT：24.750M^3

Container No.：20'DWTU2200129 M7740 CY/CY

Combined Transport Bill of Lading

Shipper JIANGSU FASHION INTERNATIONAL TRADE CORPORATION #358 ZHUSHAN ROADJIANGNING DISTRICT, NANJING, CHINA			**BILL OF LADING** B/L No. 23456 COSCO 中国远洋运输公司 CHINA OCEAN SHIPPING COMPANY Cable： Telex： COSCO PEKING 22264 CPCPK CN COSCO CANTON 44080 COSCA CN COSCO SHANGHAI 33057 COSCO CN COSCO TSINGTAO 32037 OCSQD CN COSCO TIENTSIN 23221 TOSCO CN COSCO DAIREN 86162 DOSCO CN		
Consignee TO THE ORDER OF TOKYO COMMERCE BANK OF JA-PAN, JAPAN					
Notify Party POWER PLAY INC. 2ND FLOOR, NO. 137E, 33RD STREET, TOKYO, 90032 JAPAN.					
Pre-carriage by Foang No. 322112	Place of Receipt by Pre-carrier NanJing				
Ocean Vessel Voy. No.： M. V. Gloria V. 008A	Port of Loading XINGANG, CHINA				
Port of Discharge YOKOHAMA, JAPAN	Final Destination	Freight Payable at FREIGHT PREPAID	Number of Original B/Ls THREE		
Container No. 20'DWTU2200129 M7740 CY/CY	Seal No. Marks & No. F. C. L 25016 XINGANG NO. 1-900	Number of kind of Packages/Description of goods 400CARTONS OF CHINESE LIGHT SPECKLED KIDNEY BEANS	Gross Weight （kgs）25,000		Measurement （m^3）24.750
TOTAL PACKAGES(IN WORDS)SAY FOUR HUNDRED CARTONS ONLY					
Freight and Charges FREIGHT AS ARRANGED	Shipped on board the vessel named above in apparent good order and condition(unless otherwise indicated)the goods or packages specified herein and to be discharged at the above mentioned port of discharge or as near thereto as the vessel may safely get and be always afloat. The weight, measure, marks, numbers, quality, contents and value being particulars furnished by the Shipper, are not checked by the Carrier on loading. 　In witness whereof, the Carrier or his Agents has signed Bills of Lading all of this tenor and date, one of which being accomplished, the others to stand void. 　Shippers are requested to note particularly the exceptions and conditions of this Bill of Lading with reference to the validity of the insurance upon their goods.				
	Place and Date of Issue：XINGANG Aug. 25, 2022				
	Signed for the Carrier　　　　　黎明(SIGNATURE)				

Section Four   Air Waybill 航运提单

In case of an air shipment, an air waybill will be required. Generally, air waybills are issued by the carrier or airline when the goods need to be sent by air freight. There is no such thing as a bill of lading with air transport document. Therefore, air waybill refers to a document issued by carrier or airline acknowledging receipt of the goods.

航空运输需要航运提单。通常，当货物需要航空运输时，运输公司或航空公司开具航运提单。因没有类似提单的航空运输提单，所以航运提单就成为运输公司或者航空公司开具的确认货物已收到的单据。

Similar to a sea waybill, an air waybill does not convey title to the goods; instead, the shipment is consigned to a particular party. The consignee may obtain access to the goods without presentation of an air waybill. Normally, the consignee takes delivery at the port of destination as per the shipment advice issued by destination airport evidencing arrival of goods.

与海运提单类似，航运提单不需要注明货物的所有权。相反，货物装运交予特定一方负责。收货方在不出具航运提单的条件下可以处理货物的相关事宜。通常，收货方在目的港按照目的港机场发布的装运通知提货，这一通知能够证明货物已抵达目的港。

As the shipper cannot control the goods when he hands over them to the airline, even though a bill of exchange is attached to the shipping documents under collections, the exporter still probably suffers from losses of both goods and proceeds. To overcome this, the goods can be consigned by the shipper to a trusted third party(if he agrees)who will release the goods after receiving payment or a promise of payment made by importer. An air waybill usually contains the following items:

当承运方将货物交给航空公司后，承运方便失去对货物的管理权，即使汇票随附托收下的装运单据，出口方还是会在货物本身以及收益上遭受损失。为了尽可能避免这一情况，承运方将货物委托给可信的第三方受理，第三方在收到支付或进口方的支付保证之后发货。空运提单通常包括以下条款：

- Place and date of issue. 签发地点和日期。
- Name of departure and destination airports. 出发地和目的地机场名称。
- Name and address of consignor, consignee and carrier(the airline or shipping company). 发货人、收货人和承运人(航空公司或船运公司)的名称和地址。
- Description of goods. 品名。
- Number of packages with marks, weights, quantity and dimensions. 带有标记、重量、数量和尺寸的包装数量。
- Freight charges prepaid or to collect. 运费预付或待收。

If the document does not contain a flight date, the date of issue will be deemed to be date of shipment. 如果文件不包含航班日期，则签发日期视为装运日期。

- Signature of shipper or his agent. 托运人或其代理人签字。
- Signature of issuing carrier or his agent. 签发承运人或其代理人签字。

1. The Ways of International Air Freight Transportation 航空运输常见方式

（1）Flight transportation 班机运输

（2）Transports by chartered aircraft 包机运输

（3）The centralism consigns for shipment 集中托运

（4）Combined transport way 联运方式

Notes 注意

（1）Air waybill differs from ocean bill of lading to a large extent that it is greatly important to the carrier and his/her agent. Since it is a shipping contract between the consignor and the consignee, the two sides assume legal responsibilities to the contents of the contract. 航空货运单在很大程度上不同于海运提单，因为它对承运人及其代理人非常重要。由于是托运人和收货人之间的运输合同，双方对合同内容承担法律责任。

（2）Air waybill is nottransferrable, therefore, taking air waybill doesn't mean that the goods are owned by the holder of air waybill. 航空货运单是不可转让的，因此，取得航空货运单并不意味着货物归航空货运单持有人所有。

2. The Specimen of Air waybill 航运提单样单

Shipper's name and address 发货人名称和地址				NOT NEGOTIABLE 航空公司的名称 Air Waybill Issued by				
Consignee's name and address 收货人名称和地址				It is agreed that the goods described herein are accepted in apparent good order and condition (except as noted) for carriage SUBJECT TO THE CONDITIONS OF CONTRACT ON THE REVERSE HEREOF, ALL GOODS MAY BE CARRIED BY ANY OTHER MEANS. INCLUDING ROAD OR ANY OTHER CARRIER UNLESS SPECIFIC CONTRARY INSTRUCTIONS ARE GIVEN HEREON BY THE SHIPPER. THE SHIPPER'S ATTENTION IS DRAWN TO THE NOTICE CONCERNING CARRIER'S LIMITATION OF LIABILITY. 　　Shipper may increase such limitation of liability by declaring a higher value of carriage and paying a supplemental charge if required.				
Issuing Carrier's Agent Name and City 承运人代理的名称和地点								
Agents IATA Code		Account No.						
Airport of Departure (Add. of First Carrier) and Requested Routing 起运地				Accounting Information 会计事项				
to	By first carrier 转运地	to	by	to	by	Currency 运费货币及支付方式	Declared Value for Carriage 申报价值	Declared Value for Customs 托运人申明的价值
Airport of Destination 目的地机场		Flight /Date 航班号及起飞日期	Amount of Insurance 保险金额	INSURANCE–If carrier offers insurance and such insurance is requested in accordance with the conditions thereof indicate amount to be insured in figures in box marked "Amount of Insurance"				

No. of Pieces 件数	Gross Weight 毛重	Rate Class 运价等级	Chargeable Weight 计费重量	Rate/ Charge 费率	Total 运费总额	Nature and Quantity of Goods 货物品名及数量
Handling Information 处理情况						

Prepaid Weight Charge Collect 预付运费金额		Other Charges 其他费用
Valuation Charge		
Tax		
Total Other Charges Due Agent		Shipper certifies that the particulars on the face hereof are correct and that insofar as any part of the consignment contains dangerous goods, such part is properly described by name and is in proper condition for carriage by air according to the applicable Dangerous Goods Regulations. (托运人关于所装货物非危险品的保证) Signature of Shipper or his agent
Total Other Charges Due Carrier 由于承运人需要而产生的其他费用		
Total Prepaid 预付费用总额	Total Collect	签发地点和日期 Executed on ____ at Signature of issuing（承运人或其代理人的印章） Carrier or as Agent
Currency Conversion Rates	CC Charges in des. Currency	
For Carrier's Use Only at Destination	Charges at Destination	Total Collect Charges	Air Waybill Number

3. The Contents of Air Waybill 样单拆解：航空运单的主要内容和缮制要点

（1）Airway Bill No：When not preprinted, the Air Waybill number provided by the issuing carrier shall be inserted in the upper left corner, in the upper right corner and in the lower right corner. The Air Waybill number shall have dimensions sufficient to make it readable. The issuing carrier's three-digit IATA airline code number shall be inserted.

航空运单的编号：由航空公司编制，所以从航空运单号可以区别出哪一国的航空公司。例如，编号前三位数"999"系中国国际航空公司的代号；"131"是日本航空公司的代号。

（2）Issuing Carrier's Name and Address：When not preprinted, the issuing carrier's name and head office address corresponding to the airline code number shown in（1）shall be inserted in accordance with the issuing carrier's instructions.

承运人名称：本栏可标明"中国国际航空公司（AIR CHINA）"作为承运人的名称。

（3）Shipper's Name and Address：The name, address and country（or two-letter country code）of the shipper shall be inserted. One or more method of contact（telephone, telex or telefax）and number may be inserted below.

发货人名称及地址：信用证项下必须与收益人名称及地址一致。托收项下按合同的卖方、地址填。要求填托运人的全称、街名、城市名称、国名，以及电话号、电传号或传真号。

（4）Sipper's Account Number：This box shall not be completed unless used by the issuing carrier at its option.

发货人账号：为便利双方结算而提供账号，一般可不填，所以本栏可留空。

（5）Consignee's Name and Address：The name，address and country（or two-letter country code）of the consignee shall be inserted. One or more method of contact（telephone，telex of telefax）and number may be inserted below.

收货人名称及地址：填收货人的全称、街名、城市名称、国名以及电话号、电传号或传真号。航空运单的收货人一般不作指示式，因为航空运单不是物权凭证，只代表承运人已收到货的收据。

（6）Consignee's Account Number：This column shall not be completed unless used by the last carrier at its option.

收货人账号：根据实际需要，在必要时可填入收货人账号。没有特别要求，一般可以不填。

（7）Issuing Carrier's Agent Name and City：When not preprinted，the name and location（airport or city）of the carrier's IATA Cargo Agent entitled to the commission shall be inserted，preceded by the words "Commissionable Agent". When commission is payable to an IATA Cargo Agent in the country of destination，in accordance with the Cargo Agency Administration Rules，the name and location（airport or city）of such IATA Cargo Agent shall be inserted and then preceded by the words "Commissionable Agent".

签发运单的承运人的代理人名称及城市：如果运单系由承运人的代理人签发时，本栏填实际的代理人名称及城市名。如果直接由承运人本人签发，本栏可不填。

（8）Agent's IATA Code：When not preprinted，the IATA code of the Cargo Agent shall be inserted as follows：A：In non-CASS areas，the IATA seven-digit code shall be inserted. B：In CASS areas，the IATA seven-digit code shall be followed by a three-digit CASS address modulus 7 system.

代理人的 IATA 代号：填承运人代理人的国际航空运输协会的代号。一般本栏可不填。IATA 系 "International Air Transport Association"（国际航空运输协会）的简写。

（9）Agent's Account No：This box shall not be completed unless used by the issuing carrier at its option.

代理人账号：如需要时填代理人的账号，供承运人结算使用。

（10）Airport of Departure and Requested Routing.

起航机场和指定航线。

（11）Accounting Information：Only accounting information required by the participating carriers may be inserted，such as：Payment by cash or cheque；when "Payment by credit card" appear，the credit card number shall be shown.

会计结算情况指与费用结算有关的情况。如运费预付、到付或发货人结算使用信用卡号以及其他必要的情况。

（12）Airport of Transhipment（to … by … to … by … ）.

转运地。

（13）Airport of Destination：Here is the airport of destination of the last carrier or the city（when the city is served by more than one airport and the name of the airport is unknown，the name of city shall be inserted）.

目的地机场：此处应为目的地机场或城市（如城市里有两个及两个以上的机场，发货人不知道机场名称，此时应加上城市的名字）。

（14）Flight/Date（for carrier use only）：These are to be completed by the carrier/agent/shipper effecting the booking.

航班号及该飞机实际起飞日期：本栏所填的内容只能供承运人使用，故起飞日期不能视为本货物的装运日期，一般以航空运单的签发日期作为装运日期。

（15）Currency and Charges：The three-letter code "ISO" of the currency is applied in the country of departure for completion of the Air Waybill according to the applicable rating rules. CHARGES CODES, only used when the Air Waybill data is transmitted by electronic means.

费用币制及费用代号：支付费用使用的币制用货币国际标准电码表示，如人民币用"CNY"表示。费用代号（Chgs. code）一般可不填。

（16）WT/VAL and Others.

运费/声明价值费和其他费用：声明价值费是指向承运人声明价值时，必须与运费一起交付声明价值费（Valuation charge）。

（17）Declared Value for Carriage：It shall be inserted as specified by the shipper. Where no value is declared, "NVD" shall be inserted.

供运输使用声明价值：该价值即为承运人负赔偿责任的限额。但如果所交运的货物无声明价值金额，可在本栏内填"NVD"（NO VALUE DECLARED 未声明价值）。

（18）Declared Value for Customs：The shipper or the agent may declare and insert a customs value, which may be NCV, or leave the box blank.

供海关使用声明价值：任何运输方式的国际贸易货物均须受海关监督和检查，本栏所填的价值作为海关征税的依据。目前有的地区以出口货物报关单申报或提供商业发票作为征税依据时，则本栏可不填。

（19）Amount of Insurance：The amount to be insured shall be inserted. When the service is not provided by the issuing carrier or no insurance is requested by the shipper, "×××" shall be inserted.

保险金额：中国民航各空运企业暂未开展国际航空运输代保险业务，本栏可空着不填。

（20）Handling Information.

处理情况。

根据需要填内容，如注明下列内容：

①Name of documents to accompany the AWB, such as the "Shipper's Certification for Live Animals". 货运单所附文件（DOCUMENT TO ACCOMPANY AIRWAY BILL）填随附在货运单上送往目的地的文件，应填上所附文件名称。

②Method of packing. 包装情况。

③Special handling instructions that may be required. 发货人对货物在途中的某些特别指示，或对第二承运人的要求等。

（21）No. of Pieces：The total number of pieces shall be inserted.

件数。

（22）Gross Weight：Fill in the gross weight in kilogram as calculating weight unit. If there is no package for the naked goods, then "N/M" is added in front of the net weight.

净重：计算重量时填入净重（单位公斤）。如果货物裸装，则在净重前加入"N/M"。

（23）Kg. /b.：The unit of weight used（K or L）shall be inserted in the first rating line only. 公斤或磅。

（24）Rate Class.

运价分类代号。

One of the following codes shall be inserted as appropriate：

M——Minimum Charge

N——Normal Rate

Q——Quantity Rate

B——Basic Charge（optional use）

K——Rate per Kilogram（optional use）

C——Specific Commodity Rate

R——Class Rate Reduction

S——Class Rate Surcharge

运价分类代号有"M""N""Q""C""R""S"。

（25）Commodity Item No.

商品编号。

（26）Chargeable Weight：The chargeable weight, calculated according to applicable rating rules.

计费重量。

（27）Rate/Charge：The applicable rate or charge shall be inserted as follows：

a. When a minimum charge applies, this charge shall be inserted on the "M" rate class line.

b. When a normal rate applies, the applicable rate per unit of weight shall be inserted on the "N" rate class line.

c. When a quantity rate applies, the applicable rate per unit of weight shall be inserted on the "Q" rate class line.

费率：按实际计费的费率填入。例如费率是以每公斤 20. 61 元计算的，即填"20. 61"。如果以"M"运价代号（起码费率）计费则列出起码费率。

（28）Total：The total charge of discount for each line entry shall be inserted on the same horizontal line.

运费总额：填计收运费的总额，即计费重量×费率＝运费总额。

（29）Nature and Quantity of Goods（including dimensions or volume）.

货物的品名和数量（包括尺寸或体积）：本栏填货物的品名、数量、体积、尺寸等。

（30）Weight Charge：The weight/volume charge for air carriage shall be inserted and shall correspond to the total shown in 28.

以重量计算的运费额：本栏有两项，预付额（Prepaid）和待付额（Collect）。根据实际情况填制，并与第 28 栏金额相同。

（31）Other Charges：The total of all the prepaid charges, i. e. weight/volume charge, valuation charge, other prepaid charges due carrier and, if applicable, tax and other charges due agent shall be inserted. Other charges incurred at origin shall be inserted at the time of Air Waybill issuance as either wholly prepaid or wholly collect.

其他费用：此处应填写所有的预付费用，例如，重量/体积费、估价费，以及由于承运人需要而产生的其他费用，例如税费。在空运提单的签发中应注明费用来源为"已付"或"预付"。

(32) Total Other Charges Due Carrier.

由于承运人需要而产生的其他费用总额。

(33) Total Prepaid：The total of all the prepaid charges, i. e. weight/volume charge, valuation charge, other prepaid charges due carrier and, if applicable, tax and other charges due agent, shall be inserted.

预付费用总额：此项是预付运费和其他费用总和。

(34) Signature of Shipper or His Agent.

发货人或其代理人签名：发货人或其代理人在本栏签名后表示保证所托运的货物并非危险品。

(35) Executed on(date)at(place), Signature of Issuing Carrier or His Agent.

承运人或其代理人签字及签发运单日期、地点。

(36) Original：Air waybill is made out in 3 copies. One is marked "original 1(for issuing carrier)" for air line's file, the other is "original 2(for consignee)" for consignee, and another is "original 3(for shipper)" for shipper. There are 9 copies of air waybill, which shall be distributed according to air line's stipulations.

正本：航空运单正本按国际习惯一式三份。第一份"ORIGINAL 1(FOR ISSUING CARRIER)"，由航空公司留存；第二份"ORIGINAL 2(FOR CONSIGNEE)"，随机转给收货人；第三份"ORIGINAL 3(FOR SHIPPER)"，交给发货人。虽然正本签发三份，但银行允许只交一份正本。副本共九份，由航空公司根据规定和需要分发。

Section Five　Railway Bill 铁路运单

Rail waybill is transport document covering transport of cargo from named points via rail modals of transport. Its contents are similar to an inland bill of lading, such as freight and other charges, and routing. The contents of a rail waybill are as follows：

铁路运单是指货物通过铁路运输方式运输时出具的单据。其内容与陆路运输单据类似，如运费、其他费用以及运输路线。铁路运单的内容如下：

- Name of carrier with a signature or authentication identified as that of carrier or its authorized agent.
- Name and address of sender and consignee.
- An indication of the place of shipment and place of destination.
- Ordinary description of goods including item name, weight, packing, quantity(if any)like air waybill and sea waybill, road waybill and rail waybill are not title documents either.

1. Specimen of Railway Bill 铁路运单样单

Railway Bill

中国对外贸易运输公司上海分公司

承运货物收据　　　　　　　运输编号 NO. _____

CARGO RECEIPT　　　　　　发票 NO. _____

第一联(凭提货物)　　　　　　合约 NO. _____

委托人： Shipper	收货人： Consignee 通知： Notify

From Shanghai Via SHENZHEN To HONG KONG

发运装车　　日期：　　　　　车号：Car No.

标记 Marks & Nos	件数 Packages	货物名称 Description of Goods	附记 Remarks

请向下列地点接洽提货

For Delivery Apply to:

香港中国旅行社有限公司

CHINA TRAVEL SERVICE(HK)LTD.

全程运费在上海付讫

FREIGHT PREPAID AT SHANGHAI

押汇银行签收　　　　　　　　　　　　　收货人签收

Bank's Endorsement　　　　　　　　　　Consignee's Signature

2. The Contents of Rail Waybill 样单拆解：铁路运单的主要内容和缮制要点

(1) CONSIGNOR'S NAME AND ADDRESS 发货人及地址

(2) CONTRACT NO. 合同号码

(3) POINT MADE 发站

(4) CONSINOR'S DECLARED VALUE 发货人的特别声明

(5) CONSIGNEE'S NAME AND ADDRESS 收货人名称及地址

(6) THE RECORDS ARE NOT BINDING ON THE RAILWAYS 对铁路无约束力的记载

(7) THROUGH THE BORDER STATION 通过的国境站

(8) ARRIVED AT THE BORDER STATION 到达的国境站

(9) MARKS AND NUMBERS 标记/号码

(10) METHOD OF PACKING 包装方式

(11) NATURE OF GOODS 货物名称

(12) NO. OF PACKAGES 件数

(13) DETERMINE THE NUMBER OF THE CONSIGNOR 发货人确定的数量

(14) A TOTAL NUMBER OF REPORTERS(CAPITAL)共计件数(大写)

(15) TOTAL WEIGHT(CAPITAL)共计重量(大写)

(16) CARRIER SIGNATURE 承运人签字

(17) CONSIGNOR BURDEN FOLLOWING TRANSIT COSTS 发货人负担下列过境费用

(18) LOADING FROM 由何方装车

(19) THE STATEMENT GOODS PRICES 货物的声明价格

(20) IMPARTING THE DOCUMENT SENDER 发货人添附的文件

(21) DATE TIME STATION DEVELOPMENT 发站日期戳

(22) DETERMINE THE NUMBER OF RAIL 铁路确定的数量

(23) DETERMINE THE WEIGHT SIDE 确定重量方

(24) WEIGHT STATION SIGNATURE 过磅站戳记、签字

(25) SELF 自重

(26) FOR CUSTOMS 海关记载

(27) MARK ARRIVAL DATE 到站日期戳

Exercises 练习

一、Useful Words and Expressions 常用词语和表达

1. goods/freight/cargo 货物

2. transportation business/forwarding business/carrying trade 运输业

3. transportation company(corporation)运输公司

4. transportation by land 陆上运输

5. transportation by sea 海上运输

6. goods traffic/freight traffic/carriage of freights/carriage of goods 货物运输

7. freight/freight rates/goods rate 运费率

8. carriage charges/shipping expenses/express charges 运费

9. carriage prepaid/carriage paid 运费预付

10. carriage forward/freight collect 运费到付

11. mode of transportation 运输方式

12. shipping invoice 装运单/载货单

13. shipping documents 装运单据

14. mate's receipt 大副收据

15. shipping order 装船单

16. delivery order 提货单

17. shipping advice 装船通知

18. parcel receipt 包裹收据

19. shipping permit 准装货单

20. charter party 租船契约

21. named port of shipment 指定的装运港

22. named port of destination 指定的目的港

23. sea and inland waterway transport 海运和内陆河运

24. container traffic 集装箱运输

25. arrange the charter party or rent the ship space 租船订舱

26. bear the risk and cost 承担风险和费用

27. shipping weight/in-take-weight 装运重量

28. unloading/discharging/landing 卸货

29. dead freight 空舱费

30. short shipment/goods short shipped/goods shut out/shut-outs 退关

二、Useful Sentences 常用语句

1. loading port and destination

(1) dispatch/shipment from Chinese port to … 从中国港口发送/装运往

(2) evidencing shipment from China to … CFR by steamer in transit Saudi Arabia not later than 15 July, 2011 of the goods specified below 列明下面的货物按照成本加运费价格用轮船不得迟于 2011 年 7 月 15 日从中国通过沙特阿拉伯装运到……

2. date of shipment 装船日期

(1) bills of lading must be dated not later than August 15, 2011

提单日期不迟于 2011 年 8 月 15 日

(2) shipment must be effected not later than July 30, 2010

货物不得迟于 2010 年 7 月 30 日装运

(3) shipment latest date … 最迟装运日期

(4) Evidencing shipment/dispatch on or before …

列明货物在某年某月某日或在该日以前装运

(5) From China port to … not later than 31 August 2011

不迟于 2011 年 8 月 31 日从中国港口至……

3. partial shipment and transhipment 部分装船及允许转船

(1) partial shipment are(not) permitted/allowed 允许(不允许)分装

(2) partial shipment are prohibited 不允许分装

(3) without transhipment 不允许转运

(4) transhipment at HK allowed 只允许在香港转运

(5) partial shipments are permissible, transhipment is allowed except at…

允许分批装船，除在……外，允许转运。

(6) partial/prorate shipments are permitted 允许分装/按比例装运

(7) transhipment are permitted ay any port, through B/L 凭提单允许在任何港口转运

4. available against surrender of the following documents bearing our credit number and the

full name and address of the opener 凭交出下列注明本证号码和开证人的全称及地址的单据付款

5. documents to be presented to negotiation bank within 15 days after shipment 单据需在装船后 15 天内交给议付行

6. Documents must be presented for negotiation within … days after the on board date of bill of lading/after the date of issuance of forwarding agents' cargo receipts 单据需在已装船提单/运输行签发之货物承运收据日期后……天内提示议付……

7. Time of Shipment：Within 15 days after the payment, not be allowing transhipment and partial shipment 装运期限：收到货款后 15 天内装出，不可转船及分批装运

8. When shipping company accepts space booking you will receive in due time a Container Load Plan 假如船公司接受了订舱，到时候你就会收到装货单

9. Our customer requests the shipment to be made in five equal lots, each every three months 我们的客户要求按相等数量分 5 批装船，每 3 个月装一船

10. Time of shipment：Within×days after receipt of deposit not allowing transhipment and partial shipments 装运期限：收到可以转船分批装运之信用证×天内装出。

三、Making out a Bill of Lading according to the following information 根据所给信息缮制海洋提单

L/C NO. , A-12B-34C DATED JAN. 11, 2011

APPLICANT：SUMITOMO CORPORATION, OSAKA

BENEFICIARY：ZHENJIANG ZHONGDA IMPORT & EXPORT GROUP COMPANY, LTD.

CURRENCY：USD AMOUNT：28000. 00

PARTIAL SHIPMENT：ALLOWED

TRANSHIPMENT：ALLOWED

LOADING IN CHARGE：SHIPMENT FROM CHINESE MAIN PORT

FOR TRANSPORT TO：OSAKA, JAPAN

DESCRIPTION OF GOODS：HALF DRIED APPLE PRUNE

    DETAILS AS PER ASLES CONTRACT NO. : FJE2145

    CFR OSAKA

PACKING：IN WOODEN CASES, 12 KGS PER CASE

DOCUMENTS REQUIRED：

……

+2/3 SET OF CLEAN ON BOARD OCEAN BILLS OF LADING MADE OUT TO ORDER AND BLANK ENDORSED MARKED "FREIGHT PREPAID" AND NOTIFY "SUMITOMO CORPORATION OSAKA". COMBINED TRANSPORT BILL OF LADING ACCEPTABLE

……

+1/3 ORIGINAL B/L AND OTHER SHIPPING DOCUMENTS MUST BE SENT DIRECTLY TO APPLICANT SUMITOMO CORPORATION IN 3 DAYS AFTER B/L DATE, AND SENT BY FAX ALL DOCUMENTS MUST BEAR THIS L/C NO.

B/L NO. ：GSO456

DATE OF B/L：FEB. 18, 2011

OCEAN VESSEL VOY. NO.：CHANG GANG V. 203984

TOTAL QUANTITY OF GOODS：16,800 KGS

GROSS WEIGHT：15 KGS/CASE

MEASUREMENT：@（20×10×10）CM/CASE

CONTAINER NO.：2×20'FCL CY/CY（TRIU 3682886，KHLU 3792838）

SHIPPING MARK：SC

NOSI-1500

OSAKA

MADE IN CHINA

BILL OF LADING

SHIPPER		B/L NO. 中国远洋运输（集团）总公司 CHINA OCEAN SHIPPING（GROUP）CO. CABLE：COSCO BEIJING
CONSIGNEE		SHIPPER TLX： ORIGINAL COMBINED TRANSPORT BILL OF LADING RECEIVED IN APPARENT GOOD ORDER AND CONDITION EXCEPT AS OTHERWISE NOTED THE TOTAL NUMBER OF CONTAINER OR OTHER PACKAGES OR UNITS ENUMERATE BELOW FOR TRANSPORTATION FROM THE PLACE OF RECEIPT TO THE PLACE OF DELIVERY SUBJECT TO THE TERMS HEREOF. ONE OF THE SIGNED BILL OF LADING MUST BE SURRENDERED DULY ENDORSED IN EXCHANGE FOR THE GOODS OR DELIVERY ORDER. ON PRESENTATION OF THIS DOCUMENT DULY ENDORSED TO THE CARRIER BY OR ON BEHALF THE HOLDER OF THE BILL OF LADING, THE RIGHTS AND LIABILITIES ARISING IN ACCORDANCE WITH THE TERMS AND CONDITIONS HEREOF SHALL（WITHOUT PREJUDICE TO ANY RULE OF COMMON LAW OF STATUTE RENDERING THEM BINDING ON THE MERCHANT）
NOTIFY PARTY		
PRE – CARRIAGE BY	PLACE OF RECEIPT	
OCEAN VESSEL Voy. No.	PORT OF LOADING	BECOME BINDING IN ALL RESPECTS BETWEEN THE CARRIER AND THE HOLDER AS THOUGH THE CONTRACT EVIDENCED HEREBY HAD BEEN MADE BETWEEN THEM. THE NUMBER OF ORIGINAL BILLS OF LADING STATED UNDER HAVE BEEN SIGNED. ALL OF THIS TENOR AND DATE. ONE OF WHICH BEING ACCOMPLISHED, THE OTHER（S）TO BE VOID.
PORT OF DISCHARGE	PLACE OF DELIVERY	
MARKS　　　　NOS. &KINDS OF PKGS MEAS(m³)	DESCRIPTION OF GOODS　　　G. W.（kg）	
TOTAL No. OF CONTAINERS OR PACKAGES(IN WORDS)		

FREIGHT & CHARGES	REVENUE TONS	RATE	PER	PREPAID	COLLECT

PREPAID AT	PAYABLE AT	PLACE AND DATE OF ISSUE	

TOTAL PREPAID	NUMBER OF ORIGINALS B/L		

LOADING ON BOARD THE VESSEL DATE	BY (SIGNATURE)

四. **Making out a Shipping Note according to the following information** 根据所给资料缮制托运单

APPLICANT: CHANG LIN HAI COMPANY LTD. SINGAPORE

BENEFICIARY: ZHEJIANG TEXTILE IMPORT AND EXPORT CORPORATION

PORT OF SHIPMENT: SHANGHAI

PORT OF DISCHARGE: SINGAPORE

PARTIAL SHIPMENT: NOT ALLOWED; TRANSHIPMENT: ALLOWED

L/C NO. ZJ278, DATED MAY 5, 2011

EXPIRY DATE: JUN 25, 2011

LATEST DATE OF SHIPMENT: JUN 20, 2011

DESCRIPTION OF GOODS: 100% COTTON SHIRTS

DOCUMENT REQUIRED:

FULL SET OF CLEAN ON BOARD OCEAN BILLS OF LADING MADE OUT TO ORDER OF SHIPPER, MARKED "FREIGHT PREPAID" AND NOTIFY APPLICANT.

QUANTITY OF GOODS: 1,000 DOZS

PACKAGES: 30 PCS/CTN

GROSS WEIGHT: @14KGS/CTN; NET WEIGHT: @12KGS/CTN

MEASUREMENT: @ (50×30×20) CM/CTN

Shipping Note 托运单

Shipper(发货人) (1)				D/R NO.(编号)(4)		
Consignee(收货人) (2)				集装箱货物托运单 船代留底 第一联		
Notify Party(通知人) (3)						
Pre-Carriage By(前程运输) (5)		Place of Receipt(收货地点) (6)				
Ocean Vessel(船名) Voy. No.(船次)(7)		Port of Loading(装货港) (8)				
Port of Discharge(卸货港) (9)		Place of Delivery(交货地点) (10)		Final Destination for the Merchant's Reference(目的地)		
Container No.(集装箱号)(11)	Seal No.(封志号)(12)	Marks & Nos.(标记与号码)(13)	No. of Containers or PKgs(箱数或件数)(14)	Kind of Packages: Description of Goods(包装种类与货名)(15)	Gross Weight 毛重(公斤)(16)	Measurement(尺码立方米)(17)
TOTAL NUMBER OF CONTAINERS OR PACKAGES(IN WORDS)集装箱数或件数合计(大写)(18)						
FREIGHT& CHARGES(运费与附加费)(19)	Revenue Tons(运费吨)	Rate(运费率)	Per(每)	Prepaid(运费预付)	Collect(运费到付)	
Ex Rate(兑换率) Prepaid At(预付地点) Payable At(到付地点) Place of Issue(签发地点) (20)						
Transhipment Permitted/Prohibited 可否转船(22)			Partial shipment Permitted/Prohibited 可否分批			
装船期		Date of Validity 有效期(23)		The number of B/L 提单张数(21)		
Total Value 金额	(24)					
Date of Shipping Note 制单日期(25)						

五、Making out an Air Waybill according to the following information 根据所给材料缮制一份航空单

CHINA NATIONAL FOODSTUFFS IMPORT & EXPORT CORPORATION, LIAONING BRANCH 144 RENMIN ROAD, DALIAN, CHINA 与 UNIVERSAL TRADING CO., LTD TEL: ××× FAX: ××× 签订一份出口 EDIBLE PIGMENT 的合同，开来信用证，号码是: TF003M057678。与航空运单有关的信用证条款如下:

44A/LOADING ON BOARD/DISPATCH/TAKING IN CHARGE AT/FROM … :

DALIAN, CHINA

44B/FOR TRANSPORTATION TO:

NEW YORK, USA

45/DESCRIPTION OF GOODS/SERVICES:

5 DRUMS OF EDIBLE PIGMENT

46/DOCUMENTS REQUIRED:

+AIRWAY BILL EVIDENCING UNIVERSAL TRADING CO., LTD.

TEL: ××× FAX: ××× AS CONSIGNEE AND MARKED FREIGHT PREPAID.

卖方于 2011 年 11 月 8 日在大连起运，取得航空运单。该批货物的重量是 230 公斤。

Marks: 无

AIRWAY BILL

Shipper's name and address	NOT NEGOTIABLE Air Waybill Issued by
	Copies 1, 2 and 3 of this Air Waybill are originals and have the same validity
Consignee's name and address	It is agreed that the goods described herein are accepted in apparent good order and condition (except as noted) for carriage SUBJECT TO THE CONDITIONS OF CONTRACT ON THE REVERSE HEREOF, ALL GOODS MAY BE CARRIED BY ANY OTHER MEANS. INCLUDING ROAD OR ANY OTHER CARRIER UNLESS SPECIFIC CONTRARY INSTRUCTIONS ARE GIVEN HEREON BY THE SHIPPER. THE SHIPPER'S ATTENTION IS DRAWN TO THE NOTICE CONCERNING CARRIER'S LIMITATION OF LIABILITY. Shipper may increase such limitation of liability by declaring a higher value of carriage and paying a supplemental charge if required.
Issuing Carrier's Agent Name and City	
Agents IATA Code | Account No.	
Airport of Departure (Add. of First Carrier) and Requested Routing	Accounting Information

续表

to	By first carrier	to	by	to	by	Currency		Declared Value for Carriage	Declared Value for Customs
Airport of Destination		Flight/Date		Amount of Insurance		INSURANCE—If carrier offers insurance and such insurance is requested in accordance with the conditions thereof indicate amount to be insured in figures in box marked "Amount of Insurance"			

Handling Information
"NOTIFY PARTY—SAME AS CONSIGNEE"

No. of Pieces	Gross Weight	Rate Class	Chargeable Weight	Rate/ Charge	Total	Nature and Quantity of Goods
				Other Charges		
Valuation Charge						
Tax						
Total Other Charges Due Agent				Shipper certifies that the particulars on the face hereof are correct and that insofar as any part of the consignment contains dangerous goods, such part is properly described by name and is in proper condition for carriage by air according to the applicable Dangerous Goods Regulations.		
Total Other Charges Due Carrier						
				_____ Signature of Shipper or his agent		
Total Prepaid		Total Collect		Executed on (date) _____ at (place) _____ Signature of issuing Carrier or as Agent		
Currency Conversion Rates		CC Charges in des. Currency				
For Carrier's Use Only at Destination		Charges at Destination		Total Collect Charges	Air waybill number	

Chapter 5 Insurance Documents 保险单

Key Points and Difficulties

- To Understand the Definition of Insurance Documents
- To Know the Types of Insurance Documents
- To Make out Insurance Documents

Learning Objectives

- The Meanings of Insurance Documents
- Making out Insurance Documents

Section One   Understanding Insurance Document 认识保险单

1. Insurance Documents 保险单

Owing to long-distance transportation, goods under international trade could be damaged by various accidents. Additionally, by loading and warehousing there are also some risks. In order to be indemnified in even of damage, seller or buyer, depending on the trade terms, effects insurance prior to the shipment. Insurance documents are ones, issued by insurance companies, indicating the type and amount of insurance is provided to cover loss of or damage to cargo while in transit.

在长途运输中，国际贸易下的货物会由于各种原因受到损害。而且，在货物仓储和转运中也存在很多风险。保险单是由保险公司开具的单据之一，它表明险别和保额并且在交易过程中用来进行损失和损害的赔偿。

As a title document, insurance document can be transferred. The same as the bill of lading transfer can be made by endorsing and delivering the full set of originals. Under the term of CIF, the seller effects the insurance or the risk. However, it will be undertaken by the buyer as soon as the goods cross the rail of ship. Accordingly, the seller should transfer insurance document together with the bills of lading, i. e. the right of indemnity will be also transferred. Insurance documents are the evidence of insurance contract signed between the insurer and the insured.

保险单作为产权凭证，是可以进行转让的。与提单相同，可以通过背书和交付全套正本进行转让。根据到岸价格（CIF）条款，卖方承担保险或风险。但是，一旦货物越过船舷，将由买方承担。因此，卖方应将保险单与提单一并转让，即赔偿权也将随之转让。保险凭证是保险人与被保险人签订保险合同的凭证。

There are two types of endorsement by transferring insurance documents, i. e. blank and named. Most of endorsements are made in blank. Insurance documents made of in the name of exporter have to be sealed by the exporting company and be signed by the authorized person through endorsing.

转让保险单的背书分为空白背书和记名背书两种。大多数背书都是空白的。以出口商名义制作的保险单必须由出口公司盖章，并由授权人背书签字。

2. The Parties of Insurance 保险当事人

The parties to be involved are as simple as only two. One is the insurer, the other is the insured. In some cases, there may be an insurance broker in between. Once damages occur, the party who suffers will lodge a claim against the insurance policy. The party is called the claimant.

保险中主要涉及两方，一个是承保人，另一个是被保险人。某些情况下，在承保人和被保险人之间，可能还有保险经纪人。一旦风险发生，遭受损害的一方根据保险单的有关规定向保险公司提出索赔，那么这方称为索赔人。

Notes：保险单的相关专业名词

- insurer 保险人
- insurant 被保险人
- insurance brokers 保险经纪人
- insurance agents 保险代理人
- transcripts 勘验人
- paid agents 赔付代理人
- claimant 提出索赔人
- Insurance Policy/Policy 保险单
- Insurance Certificate 保险凭证
- Combined Insurance Certificate 联合凭证
- Open Policy 预约保单
- Cover Note 暂保单
- Endorsement 批单

3. Specimen of Insurance Policy 保险单的样本

中国人民保险公司
大连分公司

The People's Insurance Company of China
DALIAN BRANCH

总公司设于北京一九四九年创立

HEAD OFFICE：BEIJING ESTABLISHED IN 1949

地址：中国大连中山路 141 号   CABLE：42001 DALIAN
ADDRESS：141 ZHONGSHAN ROAD DALIAN CHINA   FAX：336650 804558
                                                                 TLX：86215 PICC CN

发票号次（1）   保险单号次（2）
INVOICE NO.   POLICY NO.

中国人民保险公司（以下简称本公司）

THIS POLICY OF INSURANCE WITNESSES THAT THE PEOPLE'S INSURANCE COMPANY OF CHINA（HEREINAFTER CALLED）

"THE COMPANY"，AT THE REQUEST OF _____（3）_____

根据（以下简称被保险人）的要求，由被保险人向本公司缴付约（HEREINAFTER CALLED THE "INSURED"）AND IN CONSIDERATION OF THE AGREED PREMIUM PAYING TO THE COMPANY BY THE INSURED.

一定的保险费，按照保险单承保险别和背书所载条款与下列

UNDERTAKES TO INSURE THE UNDERMENTIONED GOODS IN TRANSPORTATION SUBJECT TO THE CONDITIONS OF THIS POLICY

条款承保下述货物运输保险，特立保险单。

AS PER THE CLAUSES PRINTED OVERLEAF AND SPECIAL CLAUSES ATTACHED HEREON.

标记 MARKS & NOS.	包装及数量 PACKAGE & QUANTITY	保险货物项目 DESCRIPTION OF GOODS	保险金额 AMOUNT INSURED
（4）	（5）	（6）	（7）

总保险金额：

TOTAL AMOUNT INSURE：_____（8）_____

保费   费率   装载运输工具
PREMIUM ____（9）____ RATE _____ PER ____（10）____

开航日期   自   至
SLG. ON OR ABT. ____（11）____ FROM ____（12）____ TO ____

承保险别 ALL RISKS AND WAR RISKS AS PER OCEAN MARINE CARGO CLAUSES

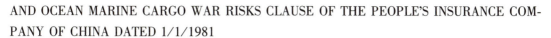

AND OCEAN MARINE CARGO WAR RISKS CLAUSE OF THE PEOPLE'S INSURANCE COM-PANY OF CHINA DATED 1/1/1981

CONDITIONS(13)

所保货物，如遇出险，本公司凭本保险单及其他有关证件给付赔款。CLAIMS, IF ANY, PAYABLE ON SURRENDER OF THIS POLICY TOGETHER WITH OTHER RELEVANT DOCUMENTS,

所保货物，如发生本保险单项下负责赔偿的损失或事故，

IN THE EVENT OF ACCIDENT WHEREBY LOSS OR DAMAGE MAY RESULT IN A CLAIM UNDER THIS POLICY IMMEDIATE NOTICE

应立即通知本公司下述代理人查勘。(14)

APPLYING FOR SURVEY MUST BE GIVEN TO THE COMPANY's AGENT AS MEN-TIONED HEREUNDER.

(NAME OF AGENCIES ...)

中国人民保险公司大连分公司

赔款偿付地点　　　　　　　　　　THE PEOPLE'S INSURANCE CO. OF CHINA

CLAIM PAYABLE AT ____(15)____　　　At: _____(17)

日期　　　　DATE ____(16)____

Agent of the insurance(18)　　　　　　　　Authorized Signature(19)

4. The Contents of Insurance Policy 样单拆解：保险单的主要内容及缮制要点

(1)Invoice No.：The Number of the invoice.

发票号码：根据发票号填入。

(2)Policy No.：The number should be given by insurance company.

保险单号码：通常由保险公司编制。

(3)Insured：Unless stated in L/C, under terms of CIF and CIP, insurance should be co-vered by exporters, so the insured should be the beneficiary in the L/C. Some fixed patterns are used here, such as,

被保险人：除非 L/C 有规定，在 CIF 或 CIP 贸易条件下，投保人就是卖方，所以被保险人栏填写卖方名称。常见的表达方式如下：

a. Insurance policy to order of whom it may concern ...

b. Insurance policy/certificate insured party as the beneficiary ...

c. Insurance policy issued to order of ABC Co. ...

d. Insurance policy in favor of the beneficiary ...

(4)Mark & Nos：

唛头和号码：有唛头，填唛头；若无唛头，则填 "N/M"；或者可填写 "AS" PER INVOICE NO. ×××.

(5)Package & Quantity：It is the number of the biggest packages(or "In Bulk"), and quantity(gross or net weight)

包装和数量：它是最大包裹的数量(或"散装")和数量(毛重或净重)。

(6) Description of Goods: Marks, packaging and the number of goods should be consistent with L/C and the Bill of Lading.

保险货物描述：装运唛头、包装和货物编号应与信用证和提单一致。

(7) Amount Insured: Amount Insured of cargo loss occurred when insurance companies are the maximum compensation limit. Generally 110% of the insured amount of the invoices by DEQ, if it exceeds 10%, excess is at the buyer's account, the policy must confirm with the stipulation of L/C. Moreover, currency in amount insured should be consistent with that in L/C, and written out in full name, such as "USD" should be written as "U. S. DOLLARS". Amount in words should be followed with "ONLY" in case of being altering.

保险金额：保险公司发生货物损失时的保险金额为最高赔偿限额。DEQ 通常为发票保险金额的 110%，如果超过 10%，超出部分由买方承担，保单必须按照信用证的规定进行确认。此外，保险金额中的货币应与信用证中的货币一致，并以全名填写，如"美元"应写为"U. S. DOLLARS"。如有更改，大写金额后应加"ONLY"，以防涂改。

(8) Total Amount Insured: Insurance amount, insurance amount is the maximum amount of compensation paid by an insurance company, which is the basis for calculating insurance premiums.

总保险金额：保险金额、投保金额是保险公司支付的最高赔偿金额，是计算保险费的依据。

币种：除非 L/C 另有规定，投保币种与 L/C 的币种一致。

金额：L/C 有规定的，按 L/C 规定填。

... for 110% invoice value ...

For USD 1,567. 34

L/C 无规定的，按 CIF 或 CIP 发票价格的 110%填

L/C 未对投保比例做任何规定，发票显示货物 CIF 总价为 USD100,000.00，则投保金额为 USD 110,000.00

L/C 中若有"... for 120% invoice value ..."，发票显示为：

CIF	USD 100,000. 00
LESS 1% COMM.	USD 1,000. 00
TOTAL	USD 99,000. 00

那么，投保金额为 USD120,000.00

L/C 未对投保比例做任何规定，发票显示为：

TOTAL MERCHANDISE VALUE	USD 1,100,000. 00
LESS ADVANCE PAYMENT	USD 550,000. 00
NET DUE UNDER THE L/C	USD 550,000. 00

那么投保金额为 USD1,210,000.00

(9) Premium & Rate: Premium and rate is often pre-printed on "As Arranged" unless otherwise provided in the L/C.

保费和费率：通常事先印就"As Arranged"（按约定）字样，除非 L/C 另有规定。

(10) Per Conveyance S. S: The name of the vessel and the second ship (in case of transhipment) will be specified. "As per B/L" can be also filled in.

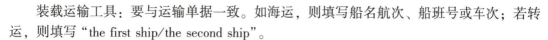

装载运输工具：要与运输单据一致。如海运，则填写船名航次、船班号或车次；若转运，则填写 "the first ship/the second ship"。

(11)Sig. or Abt … Sailing dates usually can be filled, "As Per L/C" or "As per Transportation Documents", departure, destination, loading tool(Per Conveyance) should be the same with bill of lading.

开航日期：通常填提单上的装运日，或填"As Per B/L"或"As per Transportation Documents"，起运地、目的地、装载工具(Per Conveyance)的填写与提单上的操作相同。

(12)From … to …：Direct shipment from loading port to destination port; Transfer from loading port to destination port W/T transit port; If the destination port is A and insurance is required to be covered to B, then it is from the loading port to the destination port and then to the insured destination.

起讫地点：直运从装运港到目的港；转运从装运港到目的港 W/T 中转港；如目的港为甲，要求投保至乙，那么则为从装运港到目的港，然后到投保到达地。

(13) Conditions：It should be consistent with L/C, such as AS PER MARINE CARGO CLAUSES OF THE PICC.

承保险别：条件与合同或者信用证一致，例如按照中国人民保险公司的海运条款。

(14)Surveying agent and Claim Setting Agents.

货损检验与理赔代理人。

(15)Claim Payable at …：According to the stipulation of contract or L/C, the port of destination is usually the payable place, such as AT HONG KONG IN USD.

赔付地点：赔付地点根据合同或信用证的规定来填，通常目的港是赔付地点。

(16)Date & Place：It refers to the date and place of the policy. Unless otherwise specified, the date of issuance policies must be issued before the date of transport documents.

日期及地点：除另有规定，保单的签发日期必须在运输单据的签发日期之前。

(17)AT：It should be the place of beneficiary.

出单地点。

(18)Agent of the insurance. The name and address of an agent of the insurance company at port of destination should be mentioned here for the sake of insured.

保险代理人：为了被保险人的利益，此处应提及目的港保险公司代理人的姓名和地址。

(19)Authorized Signature：It is formally signed or stamped to show effect by the insurance companies.

签章：由保险公司签字或盖章以示保险单正式生效。

(20)Endorsement(on the overleaf of the policy)：The consignor should make an endorsement on the overleaf of the policy so as to transfer all rights of it to the consignee. The endorsement is always to be made in blank except otherwise required by the consignee.

背书：发货人应当在保险单的背面做好背书。这样便于把所有权利移交给收货人。若收货人无额外要求，背书通常为空白背书。

5. Case Study 案例实训

Marine insurance policy in duplicate endorsed in blank for 110 percent of the invoice value against all risks & war risk, subject to CIC dated 1. 1 2021, claims to be payable in Denmark, in currency of the draft.

最后装运期限：May 31, 2021

受益人：SILVER SAND TRADING CORP. 6TH FLOOR, JINDU BUILDING, 135 WUXING ROAD, GUANGZHOU, P. R. CHINA

开证人：F. L. SMIDTH & CO. A/ S77, VIGERSLEV ALLE, DK-2600 VALBY, COPENHAGEN, DENMARK

起运港：GUANGZHOU, P. R. CHINA

目的港：COPENHAGEN, DENMARK

币种：USD

贸易术语：CIF C5 COPENHAGEN

合同号：JH-FLSSC11

发票号码：JH-FLSINV11

付款方式：L/C

保险加成率：10PCT

投保险别：ALL RISKS AND WAR RISKS AS PER PICC

理赔地点、币种：COPENHAGEN, DENMARK' IN THE CURRENCY OF DRAFT

唛头：FLS/ 9711/ COPENHAGEN/ CARTON 1-1,200

船名、航次：YIXIANG, V703

数量、包装：EACH 600 SETS, ALTOGETHER 1,200 SETS IN 1,200 CARTONS

品名规格、单价：FOREVER BRAND BICYCLE YE803 26'

　　　　　　　　600 SETS USD66. 00/SET

　　　　　　　　FOREVER BRAND BICYCLE TE600 24'

　　　　　　　　600 SETS USD71. 00/SET

中国人民保险公司

THE PEOPLE'S INSURANCE COMPANY OF CHINA

Head Office Beijing 总公司设立于北京

Established in 1949 一九四九年创立

保　险　单

INSURANCE POLICY

发票号码：　　　　　　　　　　　　　　　保险单号次：

INVOICE NO.：123　　　　　　　　　　　　POLICY NO.：YCA456

被保险人：

INSURED：SILVER SAND TRADING CORP. 6TH FLOOR, JINDU BUILDING, 135 WU-XING ROAD, GUANGZHOU, P. R. CHINA

中国人民保险公司(以下简称本公司)根据被保险人的要求，由被保险人向本公司缴付约定的保险费，按照本保险单承保险别和背面所载条款与下列条款承保下述货物运输保险，特立本保险单。

THIS POLICY OF INSURANCE WITNESSES THAT THE PEOPLE'S INSURANCE COMPANY OF CHINA(HEREINAFTER CALLED "THE COMPANY") AT THE REQUEST OF THE INSURED AND IN CONSIDERATION OF THE AGREED PREMIUM PAID TO THE COMPANY BY THE INSURED, UNDERTAKES TO INSURE THE UNDERMENTIONED GOODS IN TRANSPORTATION SUBJECT TO THE CONDITIONS OF THIS POLICY AS PER THE CLAUSES PRINTED OVERLEAF AND OTHER SPECIAL CLAUSES ATTACHED HEREON.

标记 MARKS & NOS	包装及数量 QUANTITY	保险货物项目 DESCRIPTION OF GOODS	保险金额 AMOUNT INSURED
FLS 9711 COPENHAGEN CARTON1~1,200	EACH 600 SETS, ALTOGETHER 1,200 SETS, IN 1,200 CARTONS	FOREVER BRAND BICYCLE YE803 26' 600 SETS USD66.00/SET FOREVER BRAND BICYCLE TE600 24' 600 SETS USD71.00/SET	USD90,420.00

总保险金额：

TOTAL AMOUNT INSURED：US DOLLARS NINTY THOUSAND FOUR HUNDRED AND TWENTY ONLY

保费：　　　　　费率：　　　　　装载运输工具：

PREMIUM：AS ARRANGED　RATE：AS ARRANGED　PER S. S.：YIXIANG, V703

开航日期　　　　　　　自　　　　　　　　至

SLG. ON OF ABT. June 1, 2021 FROM GUANGZHOU, CHINA　TO COPENHAGEN, DENMARK

承保险别：

CONDITIONS：ALL RISK AND WAR RISK AS PER OCEAN MARINE CARGO CLAUSES OF THE PEOPLE'S INSURANCE COMPANY OF CHINA,

WITH CLAIMS PAYBLE AT COPENHAGEN

NUMBER OF ORIGIN：THREE

中国人民保险公司北京分公司

THE PEOPLE'S INSURANCE CO. OF CHINA

BEIJING BRANCH

赔款偿付地点：

CLAIM PAYABLE AT/IN：COPENHAGEN

日期：

DATE：May 25, 2021

出单公司地址：　　　　　　　　　Authorized signature：

ADDRESS OF ISSUING OFFICE：GUANGZHOU, CHINA

6. Transportation Insurance 运输保险单

被保险人 Insured's Name:	（请详细填写被保险人公司全称）		报单号 Policy No. 发票号 Invoice No. 合同号 Contract No. 信用单号 L/C No.
兹有下列物品向中国人民保险公司投保 Insurance is required on the following commodities:			
标记 Marks & Nos.	包装及数量 Quantity:	保险货物项目 Description of goods	发票金额 Amount Invoice 加成 Value plus about 保险金额 Amount Insured：（以人民币填写） 费率 Rate 保险费 Premium
装载工具(请以 by air, by sea, by car 字样填写)（如是海运，请用英文写明船名及船期） Per conveyance：			
开航日期以出港日期为准 Slg. On ant.	提单号（真实的运单号） B/L No.		赔付地点(详细地址) Claims Payable At
自 From	经 Via		到 To
承保险别 Conditions &/or Special Coverage：（需要保何种险别，请在此注明） 备注 Remarks：			
			投保人盖章 Applicant's Signature
日期 Date			日期 Date

Section Two　The Other Documents of Insurance 其他保险单

1. Insurance Policy 保险单

An insurance policy is a written legal contract between the insurance company and the party insured, containing all terms and conditions of the agreement (normally preprinted on the back side of the policy). It shows full details of the risks covered, which is also called the formal insurance document.

保险单是保险公司与被保险方之间的书面法律合同，包含协议的所有条款和条件（通常预先印在保单背面）。它显示了所涵盖风险的全部细节，也被称为正式保险文件。

Insurance policy is the official certificate which is used by insurant to claim for compensation or appeal to insurance agent, it is also the main evidence of compensating. Insurance policy is transferable and one of the common certificates that insurant used to negotiate with bank. In CIF contract, insurance policy is the essential certificate that seller needs to provide to buyer.

保险单也是官方凭证。受保人使用它进行索赔或者向保险公司提出索赔。保险单是可转让的常用凭证之一。受保人使用此凭证与银行议付。在 CIF 合同中，保险单是卖方提供给买方的最基本的凭证。

2. Insurance Certificate 保险凭证

An insurance certificate is a document issued to the insured certifying that insurance has been effected. It contains the same details as an insurance policy except that the version of provisions is abbreviated. If a documentary credit calls for insurance policy, the bank will refuse an insurance certificate for payment because the latter relies on other documents, lack of complete independence.

保险单据是给被保险人开立的单据，用来证明保险已办理。除了条例版本是缩写版，其他的内容和保险单类似。如果跟单信用证上要求出具保险单，那么银行就会拒绝支付保险凭证，因为保险凭证只有在出示其他单据的情况下才能支付，它自身并不能完全独立使用。

3. Cover Note 暂保单

Cover note is a document normally issued to give notice that an insurance has been placed pending the making policy or certificate. Such document is normally applied by the buyer before shipment from the seller's country under the term of FOB by which goods would be on the way after the buyer receives the shipment notice, therefore it does not contain full details of the insurance, such as quantities of the goods to be insured amount to be insured, vessel's name, and so on. The insurer shall also make claims payable if the goods were damaged or lost after issuing the cover note and prior to issuing formal policy. Normally, documentary credit will not require a cover note as the insurance documents.

暂保单是保险人签发正式的保险单之前所出具的临时性证明。在 FOB 条件下，保险人在收到被保险人的装船通知后才签发正式保险单，因此它并没有包含完整的保险内容，如：货物数量、保险金额、船名等尚未确定。暂保单用于针对货物起运到签发正式保单这一时段的风险。在暂保单发出之后，如果货物被损坏或丢失，应当由保险人进行索赔。通常情况下，信用证不会要求作为保险文件的暂保单。

4. Open Cover/Open Police 保险合同或预约保单

An open cover is an insurance document by which the underwriter undertakes to issue a specific policy subsequently in conformity to the terms of cover, also called a general insurance for the recurring shipment. The details of the insurance for each shipment may be unknown usually when the insurance is affected. The operation of an open cover for the insured is likewise bound to declare each shipment effected thereunder unless the insurance contract otherwise provided. Upon receipt of declaration, the underwriter issues the policy. Regarding to payment to the seller under an open cover under a credit, UCP 500 states "banks will accept a declaration under an open cover pre-signed by insurance companies or underwriters or their agents".

预约保单是由保险公司开具的特定保险单，它与保单的条款相一致，因此，亦被称为可进行反复装运的一般保险。当投保时，每一次装运的具体保险信息是未知的。对于被保险方，预约保单的实施必须按照保险合同进行。一旦收到此类报单，保险公司开立保单。关于在预约保单下支付的问题，UCP500注明"银行接受保险公司或其代理方预约保单下的申报"。

Among insurance documents stated above, insurance policy is the most formal one, which can substitute others if necessary. Exactly speaking, if a L/C specifically calls for insurance or declaration under an open cover, banks will accept, in lieu thereof, an insurance policy. Under a letter of credit, the minimum amount of an insurance document should be 110 percent of either(1)the CIF or CIP value of shipment, (2)the amount of the payment specified in the L/C, or(3)the gross amount of the commercial document. Banks will not accept an insurance document which bears a date of insurance later than the date of loading on board or dispatch or taking in charge as indicated in the related transport document. It is noted that documentary credit transactions indicating CIF or CIP pricing should list an insurance document in their required documentation. Usually, "cover note" issued by insurance brokers are not accepted in L/C transactions unless authorized specifically by the L/C. 在上述的保险单据中，保险单最为正式。如有需要，可替换其他保单。准确来讲，如果信用证对预约保单下的保险和报单有特殊要求的话，银行可以用保险单来代替。根据信用证，保险单据的最低金额应为(1)CIF或CIP价的110%，(2)信用证中规定的付款额，或(3)商业单据的总金额。银行不会接受保险日期晚于相关运输单据中注明的装船日期、发货日期或接管日期的保险单据。需要注意的是，指示CIF或CIP定价的跟单信用证交易应在其所需文件中列出保险文件。通常，除非信用证特别授权，否则在信用证交易中不接受保险经纪人签发的"保险单"。

5. Combined Certificate 联合凭证

Combined certificate is also named combined invoice, which combines invoice and insurance policy. Though it is simpler than the above-stated insurance documents, its functions are the same as the above.

联合凭证亦为联合发票，这是一种联合发票和保险单的单据。尽管这种保险单比上述的保险单据简洁，但是其功能一样。

6. Endorsement 批单

When the above come into effect, if the contents of insurance contract need altering, the insurant has to make out an endorsement to apply for alteration. However, endorsements shall be made out before the arrival of shipped goods.

当上述的保险已办理，如果保险合同的内容需要修改，受保人必须缮制背书提出修改申请。但是，背书必须在货物到达目的地之前缮制完毕。

7. Claim Against Damage or Loss 保险索赔

The consignee should always note on the delivery document any damage or loss prior to signing for receipt of the goods. The consignee has responsibility to make reasonable efforts to mini-mize loss. This includes steps to prevent further damage to the shipment. Expenses incurred in such efforts are almost universally collectible under the insurance policy. Prompt notice of loss is essential. Copies of documents necessary to support an insurance claim include the insurance poli-cy, bill of lading, invoice, packing list, and a survey report(usually prepared by a claims agent).

　　收货人在签收货物之前，需要注意装运单据上有关损害和损失条款。收货人有责任将损失减少至最小，其中包括防止进一步的装运损害。此过程中产生的费用一般在保险单下进行支付。损失应及时通知。保险理赔所需的单据复印件包括保险单、提单、发票、装运单和检验报告(通常由理赔代理人准备)。

Exercises 练习

一、Useful Words and Expressions 常用词语和表达

1. Insure 保险；投保 e. g. Please insure the goods against all risks and war risk.

Insurance 保险

Insurance agents

Insurance amount

Insurance certificate

Insurance company

Insurance coverage

在表示"投保""办理保险"时，常与 insurance 搭配的动词或动词词组有：

to arrange insurance

to cover insurance

to effect insurance

to provide insurance

to take out insurance

说明保险情况时，insurance 后接介词的一般用法：

表示所保的货物，后接 on，如 insurance on the 100 tons of wool；

表示投保的险别，后接 against，如 insurance against all risks；

表示保额，后接 for，如 insurance for 110% of the invoice value；

表示保险费或保险费率，后接 at，如 insurance at a slightly high premium, insurance at the rate of 50%；

表示向保险公司投保，后接 with，如 insurance with the People's Insurance Company of China.

2. Insurance policy 保险单即大保单

Insurance certificate 保险凭证即小保单

Combined insurance certificate 联合保险凭证即发票

Open cover 预约保险单

Endorsement 保险批单

3. All Risks 全险

4. WPA，with particular average 水渍险

5. General Additional Risk 一般附加险

险种名称	英文
偷窃，提货不着险 Theft, Pilferage and Non-delivery Risk	T. P. N. D.
淡水雨淋险 Fresh Water and rain Damage Risk	F. W. R. D.
渗漏险	Leakage Risk
短量险	Shortage Risk
混杂，玷污险	Intermixture and Contamination Risk
碰损，破碎险	Clash and Breakage Risk
串味险	Taint and Odor Risk
受潮受热险	Sweat and Heating Risk
钩损险	Hook Damage Risk
包装破裂险	Breakage of Packing Risk
锈损险	Rush Risk

6. Special Additional Risk 特殊附加险

险种名称	英文
罢工险	Strikes Risk
战争险	War Risk
舱面险	On Deck Risk
进口关税险	Import Duty Risk
黄曲霉素险	Aflatoxin Risk
拒收险	Rejection Risk
交货不到险	Failure to Deliver Risk

二、Useful Sentences 常用保险句型

1. What kind of insurance are you able to provide for my consignment?

贵公司能为我的货物投保哪种保险？

2. May I ask what exactly insurance covers according to your usual C. I. F terms?

请问根据你们常用的 CIF 价格条件，所投的保险究竟包括哪些险别？

This insurance is classified into the following three Conditions—Free From Particular Average (F. P. A.), With Average(W. A.) and All Risks. Where the goods insured hereunder sustain loss or damage, the Company shall undertake to indemnify therefor according to the insured Condition specified in the Policy and the Provisions of these Clauses。

本保险分为平安险、水渍险及一切险三种。被保险货物遭受损失时，本保险按照保险单上明确的承保险别的条款规定，负赔偿责任。

3. The policy holder shall submit a claim within 30 days of any loss or damage to the property

insured.

保险单持有人应在受保险财产遭到损失或损坏后 30 天内提出索赔。

4. Premium will be added to invoice amount together with freight charges.

保险费将同运费一起并入发票金额。

5. Claims, if, any, payable on surrender of this Policy together with other relevant documents. In the event of accident where by loss or damage may result in a claim under this Policy, immediate notice applying for survey must be given to the company's Agent as mentioned hereunder.

所保货物，如遇出险，本公司凭本保险单或其他有关证件给付赔款。所保货物，如发生本保险单项下负责赔偿的损失或事故，应立即通知本公司下述代理人查勘。

6. Covering W. A. and SRCC including W/W clause as per and subject to the relevant Ocean Marine Cargo Clauses of The People's Insurance Company of China dated 1/1. 1981.

根据中国人民保险公司 1981 年 1 月 1 日海洋货物保险条款投保水渍险和罢工、暴动、民变险，保险期限才用仓至仓条款。

7. Insurance policy(certificate) ... Name of Assured to be showed：ABC Co. Ltd.

保险单或凭证作成以 ABC 有限公司为被保险人。

8. in triplicate covering all risks and war risks including W. A. and breakage in excess of five percent on the whole consignment and including W/W up to buyer's warehouse in Penang.

投保一切险和战争险包括水渍险，破碎损失有 5%绝对免赔率，按全部货物计算，包括仓至仓条款，负责到买方在槟城的仓库为止(的保险单)一式三份。

9. insurance policy or certificate settling agent's name is to be indicated, any additional premium to cover uplift between 10% and 17% may be drawn in excess of the credit value.

保险单或凭证须表明理赔代理人的名称，保险费如增加 10%~17%可在本证金额以外支付。

10. The shipping insurance and freight are being prepared by our forwarding agent, the China Ocean Shipping Company Shenzhen Branch. On whom you can rely export handling. Immediately after receive your shipping advice, we will arrange accordingly and send you the shipping documents.

我方船务代理，即中国远洋运输公司深圳分公司，已经办妥了海上保险和运输事宜。该公司处理出口业务，贵方尽可放心，一经收到贵方的装船通知，我方便即刻指示办理并寄送装船文件。

三、Making out an Insurance Policy According to the Following Information. 根据所给信息缮制一份保险单

Xinhua Trading Co., Ltd. (676 Liaohe East Road, Dalian, China) 与加拿大 Overseas. Co., Ltd ... (address) ... 于 2021 年 7 月 6 日签订一份出口陶瓷餐茶具(Chinese ceramic dinnerware) 的合同，合同号：RS123897。开证行 The Royal Bank of Canada(British Columbia International Centre 1055 West Georgia, Vancouver, B. C., Canada)于 2021 年 7 月 26 日开来信用证，号码是：T38951。信用证的最晚装运日期是 2021 年 9 月 15 日，有效期至 2021 年 9 月 30 日。根据信用证条款缮制保险单。相关的信用证条款如下：

: 32B/AMOUT

: 44A/LOADING ON BOARD/DESPATCH/TAKING IN CHARCE AT/FROM ... :

: 44B/FOR TRANSPORTATION TO VANCOUVER, CANADA

：45/DESCRIPTION OF GOODS/SERVICES：

CHINESE CERAMIC DINNERWARE AS PER SALES CONFIRMATION

NO. RS123897

DATED July 1，2021

CIF-VANCOUVER，CANADA

：46/DOCUMENTS REQUIRED

INSURANCE POLICY OF THE PEOPLE'S INSURANCE COMPANY OF CHINA IN TWO ORIGINALS, BLANK ENDORSED FOR 110% OF FULL CIF INVOICE VALUE COVERING ALL RISKS AND WAR RISKS.

：47/ADDITIONAL CONDITIONS

+THE NUMBER AND DATE OF THE CREDIT AND THE NAME OF OUR BANK MUST BE QUOTED ON ALL DOCUMENTS REQUIRED.

卖方于 8 月 30 日装船完毕，取得提单。货物明细如下：

Art. No.	Commodity	Unit	Quantity	Unit Price (USD)	Amount (USD)
	CHINESE CERAMIC DINNERWARE				46, 980. 00 CIF VANCOUVER
HX1115	35PCS DINNERWARE&TEA SET	SET	542	23. 50	12, 737. 00
HX2012	20PCS DINNERWARE SET	SET	800	20. 40	16, 320. 00
HX4405	47PCS DINNERWARE SET	SET	443	23. 20	10, 277. 60
HX4510	95 PCS DINNERWARE SET	SET	254	30. 10	7, 645. 40

保险单

INSURANCE POLICY

中 国 人 民 保 险 公 司

大 连 分 公 司

The People's Insurance Company of China

DALIAN BRANCH

总公司设于北京 一九四九年创立

HEAD OFFICE：BEIJING ESTABLISHED IN 1949

地址：中国大连中山路 141 号

ADDRESS：141 ZHONGSHAN ROAD DALIAN CHINA

CABLE：42001 DALIAN

FAX：336650 804558

TLX：86215 PICC CN

发票号次

INVOICE NO.

保险单号次

POLICY NO.

中国人民保险公司(以下简称本公司)

THIS POLICY OF INSURANCE WITNESSES THAT THE PEOPLE'S INSURANCE COMPANY OF CHINA(HEREINAFTER CALLED)

根据"THE COMPANY"，AT THE REQUEST OF _____

(以下简称被保险人)的要求，由被保险人向本公司缴付约(HEREINAFTER CALLED THE"INSURED")AND IN CONSIDERATION OF THE AGREED PREMIUM PAYING TO THE COMPANY BY THE INSURED.

一定的保险费，按照保险单承保险别和背书所载条款与下列

UNDERTAKES TO INSURE THE UNDERMENTIONED GOODS IN TRANSPORTATION SUBJECT TO THE CONDITIONS OF THIS POLICY.

条款承保下述货物运输保险，特立保险单。

AS PER THE CLAUSES PRINTED OVERLEAF AND SPECIAL CLAUSES ATTACHED HEREON.

标记 MARKS & NOS.	包装及数量 PACKAGE & QUANTITY	保险货物项目 DESCRIPTION OF GOODS	保险金额 AMOUNT INSURED

总保险金额：

TOTAL AMOUNT INSURE：_____

保费　　　　　　　　费率　　　　　　　　　装载运输工具

PREMIUM _____ RATE _____ PER

开航日期　　　　　　　　自　　　　　　　　至

SLG. ON OR ABT. _____ FROM _____ TO _____

承保险别 ALL RISKS AND WAR RISKS AS PER OCEAN MARINE CARGO CLAUSES AND OCEAN MARINE CARGO WAR RISKS CLAUSE OF THE PEOPLE'S INSURANCE COMPANY OF CHINA DATED 1/1/1981

CONDITIONS

所保货物，如遇出险，本公司凭本保险单及其他有关证件给付赔款。

CLAIMS, IF ANY, PAYABLE ON SURRENDER OF THIS POLICY TOGETHER WITH OTHER RELEVANT DOCUMENTS,

所保货物，如发生本保险单项下负责赔偿的损失或事故，应立即通知本公司下述代理人查勘。

IN THE EVENT OF ACCIDENT WHEREBY LOSS OR DAMAGE MAY RESULT IN A CLAIM UNDER THIS POLICY IMMEDIATE NOTICE APPLYING FOR SURVEY MUST BE GIVEN TO THE COMPANY'S AGENT AS MENTIONED HEREUNDER.

(NAME OF AGENCIES ...)

中国人民保险公司北京分公司

THE PEOPLE'S INSURANCE CO. OF CHINA

BEIJING BRANCH

赔款偿付地点：

CLAIM PAYABLE AT _____

日期

DATE_____

Chapter 6 Certificate of Origin 原产地证书

 Key Points and Difficulties

- To Understand the Define of Certificate of Origin
- To Know the Classifications of Certificate of Origin
- To Understand the Contents of Certificate of Origin
- To Make out Certificate of Origin

 Learning Objectives

- Making out Certificate of Origin
- Making out Certificate of Origin GSP Form A

Section One   Understanding Certificate of Origin
认识原产地证明书

Certificate of Origin is a document issued by an authority, evidencing the goods originated from a particular country in which the product was manufactured, and in certain cases it may include such information as the local material and labor contents of the product. It could be issued by the Inspection Bureau or by the Council of International Trade or by exporter himself. In China a GSP (Generalized System of Preference) certificate of origin is a certificate used to obtain the treatment of preference customs duty imposed by developed countries on the developing countries. China began to use it in 1978.

原产地证书是由管理机构签发的文件，证明货物来自特定国家生产的该产品，并在某些情况下可能包括当地材料和劳动力生产的产品。它可以经检验检疫局签发或国际贸易委员会或出口商自己本身签发。我国普惠制优惠原产地证书是一种证明，在 1978 年开始使用，用于发达国家对发展中国家获取优惠关税待遇。

A Certificate of Origin is an independent document evidencing the origin of the goods or manufacturer. It contains the description of goods, quantity or weight, value of goods shipped (only for applicant, it will not be indicated on the original official certificate) and the producing area. Two kinds of certificate of origin are generally adopted in our country: Certificate of Origin which is issued by CIQ (China Exit and Entry Inspection and Quarantine Bureau) or CCPIT (the China Council for the Promotion of International Trade). Generalized System of Preference certificate of origin Form A (GSP Form A) is issued by CIQ. GSP Form is used to get preferential import duties in many countries, such as New Zealand, Canada, Japan, EU members and so on.

原产地证书是证明货物或制造商原产地的独立文件。它包含货物的描述、数量或重量、装运货物的价值(仅适用于申请人，不会在原始官方证书上注明)和生产地区。我国一般采用两种原产地证书：由中国出入境检验检疫局(CIQ)或中国贸促会(CCPIT)签发的原产地证书。普惠制原产地证书表格 A(GSP 表格 A)由 CIQ 颁发。普惠制形式在许多国家被用来获得优惠的进口关税，如新西兰、加拿大、日本、欧盟成员国等。

1. Kinds of the Certificate of Origin 原产地证书的种类

According to the certificate of origin which is issued by different departments, there are three kinds as follows: 据不同部门颁发的原产地证书，有以下三种：

● The general Certificate of Origin (普通原产地证明书) which is often called Certificate of Origin of the People's Republic of China, and that is issued by the China Council for the Promotion of International Trade or the China Commodity Inspection Bureau. 一般原产地证书(普通原产地证明书)通常被称为中华人民共和国原产地证书，由中国国际贸易促进委员会或中国商检局颁发。

● The GSP FORM A (普惠制产地证格式 A) is a Certificate of Origin, which is required under the Generalized Scheme of Preferences (GSP) program as a valid proof of origin of goods covered by the specific GSP scheme exported to the donor countries from the beneficiary countries. GSP 表格 A(普惠制产地证格式 A)是一份原产地证书，根据普惠制(GSP)计划，它是从受益国出口到捐助国的特定普惠制计划所涵盖货物的有效原产地证明。

● Manufacturer's Certificate of Origin (厂商产地证) issued by the exporter may be self-certified or require certification by a Chamber of Commerce or the government foreign trade office. 制造商原产地证书(厂商产地证)是由出口商签发的，可以自我认证，也可以要求商会或政府外贸办公室认证。

2. Key Elements of Certificate of Origin 原产地证书的一些关键要素

In documentary credit transactions a certificate of origin should include the following elements: 在跟单信贷交易中，原产地证书应包括以下内容：

● Key details (typically consignor, consignee, and description of goods) regarding the shipment, also such details to be in conformity with other documents (e. g. documentary credit, commercial invoice)有关装运的关键细节(通常是发货人、收货人和货物描述),这些细节也应符合其他文件(如跟单信用证、商业发票)

- A statement of origin of the goods. 货物的原产地说明。

- The name, signature and/or stamp or seal of the certifying authority. 认证机构的名称、签名和/或印盖章或印章。

The certificate of origin is typically required by the buyer's country as a requirement for import processing. If you are the buyer, your country requires such documentation(in form content) in the documentary credit as stipulated by related state authority.

买方国家通常要求原产地证书作为进口加工的要求。如果您是买方,您所在的国家要求在相关国家当局规定的跟单信用证中提供文件(形式内容)。

Notes 注意

The certificate of origin can be the key document required for obtaining special(reduced) tariff rates for imports from countries listed as beneficiary to programs such as the GSP. In such a case specific forms(such as the Certificate of Origin Form A—for GSP Certification)must be used.

原产地证书可以是从普惠制等计划的受益国获得特殊(降低)关税所需的关键文件。在这种情况下,必须使用特定的表格(如 GSP 认证的原产地证书表格 A)。

Buyers should avoid use of such terms as "first class," "well-known," "qualified," "independent," "official," "competent," or "local" when referring to the certifying authority. It is preferable to specifically name the required certifying authority.

在涉及检验检疫机构时,买方应避免使用"一流""知名""合格""独立""官方""主管"或"当地"等术语。最好指定所需的检验检疫机构。。

In certain countries the certificate of origin is prepared by the seller(beneficiary to the documentary credit)on a standard form and then certified(with a signature, stamp or seal)by the certifying authority. Certifying authorities most often used are city and regional chambers of commerce and chambers of commerce and industry.

在某些国家,原产地证书由卖方(跟单信用证的受益人)以标准表格编制,然后由检验检疫机构认证(签名、盖章或封章)。最常用的检验检疫认证机构是城市和地区的商会以及工商联合会。

In China, GSP Certificate of Origin Form A is issued by Commodity Inspection Bureau of Import/ Export. However, the ordinary Certificate of Origin is issued by the Council for Promotion of Foreign Trade.

在中国,GSP 原产地证书表格 A 由进出口商品检验局签发。然而,普通的原产地证书是由对外贸易促进委员会颁发的。

3. Specimen Certificate of Origin 原产地证书样单

Certificate of Origin

(2) Exporter	(1) Certificate No. CERTIFICATE OF ORIGIN OF THE PEOPLE'S REPUBLIC OF CHINA
(3) Consignee	
(4) Means of Transport and Route	(6) For Certifying Authority Use Only
(5) Country /Region of Destination	

(7) Marks and Numbers	(8) Number and Kind of Packages; Description of Goods	(9) H. S. Code	(10) Quantity	(11) Number and Date of Invoices

(12) Declaration by the Exporter The undersigned hereby declares that the above details and statements are correct, that all the goods were produced in China and that they comply with the Rules of Origin of the People's Republic of China	(13) Certification It is hereby certified that the declaration by the exporter is correct. (OFFICIAL STAMP) (SIGNATURE)
Place and date, signature and stamp of authorized signatory	Place and date, signature and stamp of certifying authority

4. Contents and Key Points of Certificate of Origin 样单拆解：原产地证书的主要内容及缮制要点

(1) Certificate No.：It is the same number as that issued by the Certifying Authority.

原产地证书的号码：原产地证书号码应与认证机构所签发的号码相同。

(2) Exporter：This column may not be blank. Type the name, address, city and country of the exporter. If the products are transported through other countries, the word "via" must be used and the exporter fill behind via, then fill in the name, address and country of the transit businessman. e. g. SINOCHEM International Engineering & Trading Corp. 40 Fucheng Road, Beijing, China Via Hong Kong Daming Co., Ltd. 656 Guangdong Road, Hong Kong.

出口商：此该栏不得留空，填写出口商名称、详细地址(包括街道、门牌号、城市)及国家(地区)等。若经其他国家则需要填写转口商名称时，在出口商后面加填英文 VIA，然后再填写转口商名称、地址和国家。如：SINOCHEM International Engineering & Trading Corp. 40 Fucheng Road, Beijing, China Via Hong Kong Daming Co., Ltd. 656 Guangdong Road, Hong Kong。

(3) Consignee：The name, address and country of the buyer. If this certificate of origin un-

der the L/C, the credit applicant must be fill in this column, this column allows blank. Usually "To Whom It May Concern" or "To order" is marked here. If the products are transported through other countries, the word "via" must be used and the consignee fill behind via, then fill in the name, address and country of the transit businessman.

  e. g. AL OTHAIANM TRADING CO., LTD

    P. O. BOX 23631

    DUBAI, U. A. E.

    VIA HONG KONG DAMING CO. LTD

    566 GUANGDONG ROAD, HONG KONG

收货人：填写最终收货人的名称、地址及国家(地区)全称。信用证项下的证书，本栏目填的就是信用证的开证申请人，但是由于贸易的需要，信用证规定所有单证的收货人一栏留空不填。通常标"To Whom It May Concern" or "To order"，如需填写转口商名称时，可在收货人后面加填英文 VIA，然后再填写转口商名称、地址和国家。

如：

AL OTHAIANM TRADING CO., LTD.

P. O. BOX 23631

DUBAI, U. A. E.

VIA HONG KONG DAMING CO. LTD.

566 GUANGDONG ROAD, HONG KONG

  (4) Means of Transport and Route：According to the actual situation state in detail the means of transport and route. Maritime transport, land transport fill in the port of shipment, port of destination and the route. Fill in by sea, by air or by truck. If the products are transported through other countries this can be indicated as follows："With transshipment at Hong Kong" or "via Hong Kong".

  运输工具和路线：根据实际情况填写运输方式和路线。海运、陆运填写装运港、目的港和路线；标明海运、空运或卡车运输。如果产品通过其他国家运输，则可注明如下："With transhipment at Hong Kong"或"via Hong Kong"。

  (5) Country/Region of Destination. It refers to the country or region at which the goods is arrived. The consignee, loading port, landing place, and the destination must be indicated on the invoice as a document for authentication. The middle businessman cannot be made out. The sentence "From(place of shipment, country name)to(place of landing, country name)via(name of place)by(name of vessel(plane)of shipment)on or about(date of(due for)sailing or departure)" is used here.

  目的地国家/地区：应填写货物最终运抵国，一般与最终收货人和最终目的国别一致，不得填写中间商国别。通常填写类似的句子："从(装船，国别)到(卸货，国别)途径(地名)由(轮船、飞机名称)×××天离港。

  (6) For Certificate Authority Use Only：This column is blank fill. Reserved for use by the issuing organization(Chamber of Commerce and Industry or the Certificate Authority) according to the concrete condition.

  此栏仅供证书颁发机构使用：本栏应留空不填，由发证机构(商会、行业协会或证书颁发机构)在必要时填用。

（7）Marks and Packing Number：This information should be consistent with the shipping mark and number on the packaging of the goods. You cannot simply fill in "as per invoice No. ×××" or "as per B/L No. ×××"; If there is no transportation mark for this batch of goods, fill in "Unmarked" "No Mark（N/M）" "No Number（N/N）" or "NIL", this column cannot be left blank.

唛头与包装编号：该信息应与货物包装上的唛头及编号一致。不可简单填写"按照发票（as per invoice No. ×××）"或者"按照提单（As per B/L NO. ×××）"；如果本批货物无运输标志，则填"Unmarked" "No Mark（N/M）" "No Number（N/N）"或者"NIL"，此栏不能留空。

（8）Number and Kind of Packages：Description of Goods type clearly the description of the products exported. This should be identical to the description of the products contained in the invoice. An accurate description will help the Customs Authority of the country of destination to clear the products quickly.

商品的名称、包装种类：货物描述明确注明出口产品的货物描述。货物描述应与发票上对出口产品的描述相一致。确切的描述有助于目的国海关当局对产品的快速清关。

This column should include three contents. （1）Maximum number of packages. Including two methods：upper and lower case, such as "ONE HUNDRED（100）PACKAGES"; （2）Product name. Connect the maximum number of packages and product name with "OF", such as "ONE HUNDRED（100）PACKAGES OF DOOR LOCKS"; （3）Fill the next line of the above content with the termination symbol "×××". When there is more than one type of goods in a FORM A, columns 6, 7, and 8 should correspond one-to-one.

For example：

ONE HUNDRED AND FIFTY（150）CARTONS OF MEN'S

T/C PRINTED JACKET

SIXTY-SEVEN（67）CARTONS OF BOY'S T/C PRINTED JACKET OR

150 CARTONS（ONE HUNDRED AND FIFTY CARTONS ONLY）OF MEN'S T/C PRINTED JACKET

67 CARTONS（SIXTY-SEVEN CARTONS ONLY）OF BOY'S T/C PRINTED JACKET

该栏目填写应包括三项内容。（1）最大包装件数。包括大写、小写两种方式，如："ONE HUNDRED（100）PACKAGES"；（2）商品名称。最大包装件数和商品名称用"OF"连接，如"ONE HUNDRED（100）PACKAGES OF DOOR LOCKS"；（3）使用终止符号"×××"将上述内容的下一行填满。当一份 FORM A 的货物不止一种时，第6、7、8栏要做到一一对应。

比如：

ONE HUNDRED AND FIFTY（150）CARTONS OF MEN'S

T/C PRINTED JACKET

SIXTY-SEVEN（67）CARTONS OF BOY'S T/C PRINTED JACKET OR

150 CARTONS（ONE HUNDRED AND FIFTY CARTONS ONLY）OF MEN'S T/C PRINTED JACKET

67 CARTONS（SIXTY-SEVEN CARTONS ONLY）OF BOY'S T/C PRINTED JACKET

- If the goods are in bulk, add "bulk"（IN BULK）after the trade name, for example, 1,000 metric tons of pig iron, fill in as ONE THOUSAND(1,000)M/T OF PIG IRON IN BULK.

如货物系散装, 在商品名称后加注"散装"(IN BULK), 例如, 1 000 公吨生铁, 填写为 ONE THOUSAND(1,000)M/T OF PIG IRON IN BULK;

• If there are more than thousands of packages, then there can be no "AND" conjunction between thousands and 100 units, otherwise the computer is returned. Should be filled in as follows: TWO THOUSAND ONE HUNDRED AND FIFTY(2,150)CARTONS OF GLOVES;

如果包装件数上千以上, 则千与百单位之间不能有"AND"连词, 否则电脑退回。应填写为: TWO THOUSAND ONE HUNDRED AND FIFTY(2,150)CARTONS OF GLOVES;

• Quantity and product name are generally required to be finished within one page. If the content is too long, the number of packaging boxes can be combined, and the product name can be combined. Like: ONE HUNDRED AND FIFTY(150)CARTONS OF GLOVE, SCARF, TIE, CAP;

数量、品名一般要求在一页内打完, 如果内容太长, 则可以合并包装箱数量、品名。如: ONE HUNDRED AND FIFTY(150)CARTONS OF GLOVE, SCARF, TIE, CAP;

• The quantity and type of packaging should be filled in according to the specific requirements, such as: POLYWOVEN BAG, DRUM, PALLET, WOODEN CASE, etc., and cannot only fill in the PACKAGE. If there is no packaging, fill in "NUDE CARGO"(naked), "IN BULK" (bulk), "HANGING GARMENTS"(hang);

包装数量及种类要按照要求具体填写, 如: POLYWOVEN BAG, DRUM, PALLET, WOODEN CASE 等, 不能只填写 PACKAGE。如果没有包装, 应填写"NUDE CARGO"(裸装货), "IN BULK"(散装货), "HANGING GARMENTS"(挂装);

• The specific commodity name should be filled in(where the corresponding 4 is HS code), such as "TENNIS RACKET"(tennis racket); shall not be generalized, such as "SPORTING GOODS"(sports goods), "FABRIC"(fabric);

应填写具体商品名称(具体到能找到相对应的 4 为 HS 编码), 例如"TENNIS RACKET"(网球拍); 不得用概括性表述, 如: "SPORTING GOODS"(运动用品), "FABRIC"(织物)等;

• The trademark, brand name and goods number(ARTICLE NUMBER) of the commodity can generally not be filled in.

商品的商标、牌名及货号一般可以不填。

(9)H. S. Code: H. S. Refers to "The Harmonized Commodity Description and Coding System". Eight digit H. S. Tariff item number is required to fill out in this column, and it should be in conformity with the number of customs declaration. This column may not be blank.

H. S. 编码: H. S. 编码是"商品名称与编码协调制度"的简写, 本栏目要求填写八位数的 H. S. 税目号, 应与报关单一致, 此栏目不得留空。

(10)Quantity. The quantity and measurement are required to print; Quantity of all goods must be stated clearly. If it is calculate by weight, "gross weight" "net weight" should be marked. E. g. 1,000 M/T or 1,000M/T(N. W.).

数量: 填写出口货物的数量并与商品计量单位联用, 表示重量时要注明毛重和净重。如: N. W. 1,000 M/T or 1,000M/T(N. W.)

(11)Number and Date of Invoices: Please enter the number and date of Invoice as a document for authentication. If the date of Invoice is later than the date written in the field "Declaration by Exporter" on the Certificate of Origin, it cannot be accepted. (If the dates are the same, it is acceptable.)

发票的实际号码和日期：该栏目日期早于或同于实际出口日期，假如发票日期晚于原产地证明书"Declaration by Exporter"栏目的日期，该发票被视为无效。

(12) Declaration by the Exporter. The term "Exporter" refers to the shipper who can either be a trader or a manufacturer. Type the name of the producing country and the importing country and the place and date when the declaration is made. The date is not later than the date of B/L and not earlier than the date of invoice. This box must be signed by the Company's authorized signatory. Any declaration by the exporter should be stated here.

出口方声明：包括原产国，出口国(给惠国)国名和出口公司指派的专人签字，注明生产国和进口国国别、申报地点和申请时间。该日不能早于发票的签发日期，由申请单位的法人代表或其指定人在本栏手签字。

(13) Certification, Signature and Official Stamp. Certification, Signature and Official Stamp will certify in this Box. This will be completed by the Chamber of Commerce and Industry. Please be careful to ensure the name of the company and the signature of the applicant.

签证机构证明、签字、盖章栏：该栏由签证当局签署，签发日期不能早于发票日期和申请日期，印章不得与签字重叠。

(14) Origin Criterion. 此项目填写货物原料的成分比例。

"P": completely self-produced, without imported ingredients；

"W": Goods containing imported raw materials, when exported to the European Union, Switzerland and Japan, meet the above processing standards for Hui countries; and add the four-digit HS tax number of the goods below "W"；

"F": When exporting to Canada, the value of imported ingredients accounts for less than 40% of the ex-factory price of the product；

"Y": When sent to Russia, Belarus, Ukraine, Kazakhstan, and Czechoslovakia, the value of the imported components does not exceed 50% of the offshore price of the goods; and the value of the imported components under the alphabet；

Blank: For goods exported to Australia, New Zealand, this column can be left blank.

"P"：完全自产，无进口成分；

"W"：含有进口原料成分的商品，出口至欧盟、瑞士及日本时，符合上述有关给惠国的加工标准；并且在"W"的下方加注该商品的四位数字级的 HS 税目号；

"F"：对加拿大出口时，含进口成分的价值占产品出厂价 40%以内者；

"Y"：发往俄罗斯、白俄罗斯、乌克兰、哈萨克斯坦、捷克斯洛伐克时，进口成分的价值不超过商品离岸价 50%；并且在字母下加注商品进口成分的价值占商品离岸价的百分比；

空白：出口到澳大利亚、新西兰的货物，此栏可留空不填。

5. Case Study 案例实训

Please Making out a General Certificate of Origin Based on the Given Information 请根据所给资料缮制一份一般原产地证。

CREDIT NUMBER: SK/25067/97

DATE OF ISSUE: DEC. 27, 2022

BENEFICIARY: GUANGDONG TANG TEXTILE GARMENT CO., LTD.

7/F GUANGDONG TEXTILES MANSION, NO. 168 XIAOBEI ROAD NANJING, P. R. CHINA

APPLICANT: FASHION FORCE CO., LTD., DUBAI(UAE)P. O. BOX NO, 6093, DUBAI (UAE), FAX NO. 263745

DESCRIPTION OF GOODS: 4,000 DOZEN EMBROIDERED TABLE CLOTH NO. B4010-A502 CIFC2 DUBEI USD25. 5 PER DOZEN

PACKING: 10DOZ/CTN ALL OTHER DETAILS ARE AS PWE S/C NO. 97/2495

SHIPMENT: FROM NANJING PORT, P. R. CHINA TO DUBAI PORT, DUBAI(UAE)BY SEA

PACKING: ABOUT 50KG GUNNY BAGS EACH GROSS FOR NET

SHIPPING MARKS:

    264553

    DUBAI

    NO. 1-400

DOCUMENTS REQUIRED:

+CERTIFICATE OF ORIGIN ISSUED BY COMPETENT AUTHORITY IN ONE ORIGINAL PLUS TWO COPIES.

发票号码: CD-TX-9057

发票日期: JAN. 02, 2023

商品编码: 62041300

产地证号码: CZC1/12002/56494

产地证申请时间: JAN. 15, 2023

Certificate of Origin

(2) Exporter	(1) Certificate No. CZC1/12002/56494
GUANGDONG TANG TEXTILE GARMENT CO. LTD. 7/F GUANGDONG TEX TILES MANSION, NO. 168 XIAOBEI ROAD NANJING, P. R. CHINA	**CERTIFICATE OF ORIGIN OF THE PEOPLE'S REPUBLIC OF CHINA**
(3) Consignee	
FASHION FORCE CO. LTD., DUBAI(UAE)P. O. BOX No., 6093, DUBAI(UAE), FAX NO. 263745	
(4) Means of Transport and Route	(6) For Certifying Authority Use Only
FROM NANJING PORT, P. R. CHINA TO DUBAI PORT, DUBAI(UAE)BY SEA	
(5) Country/Region of Destination	

续表

(7) Marks and Numbers	(8) Number and Kind of Packages; Description of Goods	(9) H. S. Code	(10) Quantity	(11) Number and Date of Invoices
264553 DUBAI NO. 1~400	4,000 DOZEN EMBROIDERED TABLE CLOTH NO. B4010－A502 CIFC2 DUBEI USD25.5 PER DOZEN	22884690	ABOUT 50KG GUNNY BAGS EACH GROSS FOR NET	CD－TX－9057 JAN. 02, 2023

(12) Declaration by the Exporter	(13) Certification
The undersigned hereby declares that the above details and statements are correct, that all the goods were produced in China and that they comply with the Rules of Origin of the People's Republic of China GUANGDONG TANG TEXTILE GARMENT CO. LTD. (SIGNATURE) ZHAOMING　JAN. 02, 2023	It is hereby certified that the declaration by the exporter is correct. (OFFICIAL STAMP) (SIGNATURE) GUANGDONG JAN. 02, 2023
Place and date, signature and stamp of authorized signatory	Place and date, signature and stamp of certifying authority

Section Two　Generalized System of Preferences Certificate of Origin(Form A) 普惠制产地证(格式 A)

1. About the Certificate of Origin(Form A) 认识普惠制产地证(格式 A)

The Generalized System of Preferences(GSP)certificate of origin is a tariff preferential guidance implemented by developing countries for exporting goods to developed countries. Its purpose is to make developing country exports competitive in developed countries. A certificate of origin provided to developed countries for preferential treatment. Abbreviated as G. S. P Certificate of Origin or Form A Certificate of Origin. The principles of the Generalized System of Preferences include ordinary principles, non-reciprocity principles, and non-discrimination principles.

普惠制产地证书是发展中国家向发达国家出口货物实行的一种关税优惠指导。其目的是使发展中国家出口商品在发达国家具有竞争力，向发达国家(给优惠)提供的一种原产地证明书。其简称 G. S. P 产地证或者 Form A 产地证。普惠制的原则有普通原则、非互惠原则和非歧视原则。

截至 2019 年 5 月，世界上有 39 个国家给予我国普惠制关税减免优惠待遇，分别是欧盟 28 个成员国(奥地利、卢森堡、比利时、荷兰、丹麦、芬兰、葡萄牙、西班牙、法国、瑞典、德国、英国、希腊、爱尔兰、意大利、波兰、捷克、斯洛伐克、保加利亚、罗马尼亚、匈牙利、马耳他、斯洛文尼亚、立陶宛、拉脱维亚、爱沙尼亚、塞浦路斯、克罗地亚）、挪威、瑞士、澳大利亚、新西兰、加拿大、俄罗斯、白俄罗斯、哈萨克斯坦、乌克兰、土耳其和列支敦士登公国。美国直没有给予我国普惠制待遇，日本自 2019 年 4 月 1 日起不再给予我国输日货物普惠制关税优惠。

2. Specimen 样单

Certificate of Origin, Form A

(3) Goods consigned from (Exporter's Business Name, Address, County)	(1) Reference No. GENERALIZED SYSTEM OF PREFERENCES CERTIFICATE OF ORIGIN (Combined declaration and certificate) FORM A			
(4) Goods consigned to (Consignee's Name, Address, County)	(2) Issued in (country) See Notes. overleaf			
(5) Means of Transport and Route (as far as known)	(6) For Official Use			
(7) Item Number	(8) Marks and Numbers of Package	(9) Number and Kind of Packages; Description of Goods	(10) Origin Criterion	(11) Gross Weight/ Other Quantity	(12) Number and Date of Invoices
(13) Certification It is hereby certified, on the basis of control carried out, that the declaration by the exporter is correct. (OFFICIAL STAMP) Place and date, signature and stamp of certifying authority	(14) Declaration by the Exporter The undersigned hereby declares that the above details and statements are correct; that all the goods were produced in (Country) And that they comply with the origin requirements specified for those goods in the Generalized System of Preferences for goods exported to (importing country) Place and date, signature of authorized signature			

3. The Contents of General System of Preferential Certificate of Origin (Form A)
样单拆解：普惠制产地证 (格式 A) 的主要内容

(1) Reference No.: It is located in the above right Conner, the serial number given by the Exit and Entry Inspection and Quarantine Bureau.

编号：位于证书右上方，填出入境检验检疫局指定的编号。

(2) Issued in: "The People's Republic of China" is usually filled. In most of time it is pre-printed by the China Exit and Entry Inspection and Quarantine Bureau.

签发国别：本栏填上"The People's Republic of China"（中华人民共和国），一般出入境检验检疫局在印刷证书时多数已印妥。

(3) Goods Consigned from. (Exporter's Business Name, Address and Country): Fill in the exporter's name, address, and country. If the letter of credit does not specify a detailed address, this column can be filled with the shipper's address and country name.

发货人（出口商的业务名称、地址、国别）：按出口商的名称、地址、国别填入，一定要填入详细地址，包括街道名、门牌号。如果信用证未规定详细地址，本栏可填发货人地址和国名。

(4) Goods Consigned to(Consignee's Name, Address, Country): Fill in the name, address, and country of the final destination consignee of the actual beneficiary country, and do not fill in the name of the intermediary.

收货人（收货人名称、地址、国别）：填写实际给惠国的最终目的地收货人名称、地址和国别，不得填中间商名称。

(5) Means of Transport and Route: Fill in the loading, destination port, and means of transportation, such as: "by sea" or "by steam"; Land transportation can be filled in as "by train", "by railway" or "by truck"; airway transportation "by air", etc. For transhipment goods, a transhipment port should be added, such as "With shipment at Hong Kong" or "via Hong Kong".

运输方式及线路：填装货、到货地点及运输方式，如海运填："by sea"或"by steam"；陆运可填："by train""by railway"或"by truck"；空运填："by air"等。对转运商品应加上转运港，如："With transhipment at Hong Kong"或"via Hong Kong"。

(6) For Certificate Authority Use Only: This column should be left blank for use by the issuing authority—Entry Exit Inspection and Quarantine Bureau when necessary.

供官方使用：本栏应留空不填，供出证机构——出入检验检疫局在必要时填用。

(7) Item Number: If there are different kinds of goods, then list separately.

项目号：在本证书范围内如有不同的商品种类，则应分别按序号列出。

(8) Marks and Packing Number: This information should be consistent with the shipping mark and number on the packaging of the goods. You cannot simply fill in "as per invoice No. ×××" or "as per B/L No. ×××"; If there is no transportation mark for this batch of goods, fill in "Unmarked," "No Mark(N/M)", "No Number(N/N)" or "NIL", this column cannot be left blank.

唛头与包装编号：该信息应与货物包装上的唛头及编号一致。不可简单填写"按照发票（as per invoice No. ×××)"或者"按照提单（As per B/L NO. ×××)"；如果本批货物无运输标志，则填"Unmarked""No Mark(N/M)""No Number(N/N)"或者"NIL"，此栏不能留空。

(9) Number & Kind of Packages, Description of goods: The description of the goods clearly indicates the description of the exported product. The packaging quantity must be displayed in figures and capital words. For example, "FIVE THOUSAND(5,000) CARTONS OF MOTORCYCLE", the product name should be specific and cannot use general terms such as "GARMENT,"

"MACHINE," "FURNITURE," etc. The size and item number of the product can be left blank.

The product name and other contents should be filled in and followed by a symbol indicating the end on the next line(××××××××)to prevent the addition of forged content. In addition, if the letter of credit requires the addition of contract number, letter of credit number, it can be added below the end symbol. The description of the goods should be consistent with the description of the commercial invoice. An accurate description of the goods helps the destination country's customs to quickly clear the products. For example:

ONE HUNDRED AND FIFTY(150)CARTONS OF MEN'S

T/C PRINTED JACKET SIXTY-SEVEN(67)CARTONS OF BOY'S T/C PRINTED JACKET

OR

150 CARTONS(ONE HUNDRED AND FIFTY CATRTONS ONLY)

OF MEN'S T/C PRINTED JACKET

67 CARTONS(SIXTY-SEVEN CARTONS ONLY)OF BOY'S

T/C PRINTED JACKET

包装件数、包装种类及商品名称，货物描述明确注明出口产品的货物描述：包装数量必须用大小写同时显示，如"FIVE THOUSAND(5 000)CARTONS OF MOTORCYCLE"；商品名称要具体，不能使用如"服装(GARMENT)""机器(MACHINE)""家具(FURNITURE)"等概括性用语；商品的型号、货号等可以不填。商品名称等内容填完后紧跟着下一行要打上表示结束的符号(××××××××)，以防添加伪造内容。另外，如果信用证要求加注合同号、信用证号码等，可加注在结束符号下方。货物描述应与发票上对出口产品的描述相一致。准确的货物描述有助于目的国海关对产品的快速清关。如：

ONE HUNDRED AND FIFTY(150)CARTONS OF MEN'S

T/C PRINTED JACKET SIXTY-SEVEN(67)CARTONS OF BOY'S T/C PRINTED JACKET

OR

150 CARTONS(ONE HUNDRED AND FIFTY CATRTONS ONLY)

OF MEN'S T/C PRINTED JACKET

67 CARTONS(SIXTY-SEVEN CARTONS ONLY)OF BOY'S

T/C PRINTED JACKET

(10)Origin Criterion: This column is the core item for foreign customs review. For goods containing imported ingredients, foreign requirements are strict, and once made wrong, it can easily lead to a refund inquiry.

原产地标准：此栏是国外海关审核的核心项目。对含有进口成分的商品，国外要求严格，一旦弄错容易导致退证查询。

• If this product is entirely produced by the exporting country and does not contain any imported ingredients, and is exported to all beneficiary countries, fill in "P". 如果本商品完全是出口国自产的，不含任何进口成分，出口到所有给惠国，填写"P"。

• If the exported product contains imported ingredients and is exported to the European Union, Norway, Switzerland, and Japan, fill in "W" followed by the HS item number of the exported product, such as "W 87. 11". Conditions: ① The product is listed in the "processing list" of the beneficiary country mentioned above and meets its processing conditions; ② The product is not included in the "processing list", but the imported raw materials and components used in the production process of the product must undergo sufficient processing, and the HS item number of the product is different from the HS item number of the raw materials or components used. 如果出口产品有进口成分，出口到欧盟、挪威、瑞士和日本，填"W"，其后加上出口产品的 HS 品目号，如"W 87. 11"。条件：①产品列入了上述给惠国的"加工清单"，符合其加工条件；②产品未列入"加工清单"，但产品生产过程中使用的进口原材料和零部件要经过充分的加工，产品的 HS 品目号不同于所用的原材料或零部件的 HS 品目号。

- For products containing imported ingredients exported to Canada, fill in "F". Condition：The value of imported ingredients does not exceed 40% of the product's factory price. 含有进口成分的产品，出口到加拿大，填"F"。条件：进口成分的价值未超过产品出厂价的 40%。

- For products containing imported ingredients exported to Poland, fill in "W" followed by the HS tax number of the product. Condition：The value of the imported ingredients does not exceed 50% of the FOB price. 含有进口成分的产品，出口到波兰，填"W"，后面加上产品的 HS 税号。条件：进口成分价值未超过离岸价的 50%。

- For products containing imported ingredients exported to Russia, Ukraine, Kazakhstan, Czech Republic, Slovakia, fill in "Y", followed by the percentage of the value of imported ingredients in the offshore price of the product, such as "Y 40%". Condition：The value of imported ingredients does not exceed 50% of the product's FOB price. 含有进口成分的产品，出口到俄罗斯、乌克兰、哈萨克斯坦、捷克、斯洛伐克，填"Y"，其后加上进口成分价值占该产品离岸价格的百分比，如"Y 40%"。条件：进口成分的价值未超过产品离岸价的 50%。

- This column can be left blank for goods shipped to Australia and New Zealand. 输往澳大利亚、新西兰的产品，此栏可以留空。

(11) Gross Weight or Other Quantity：This column should indicate the quantity of the product, such as "1,000 PIECES(SETS/PARIS/DOZ)". If calculated by weight, fill in the gross weight. If there is only net weight, fill in the net weight, but indicate "N. W. (NET weight)".

毛重和其他数量：此栏应填写产品的数量，如"1,000 PIECES(SETS/ PARIS/ DOZ)"等。如以重量计算的则填毛重，只有净重的，填净重亦可，但要注明"N. W. (NET WEIGHT)"。

(12) Number and Date of Invoices：Fill in the date and number of the Commercial invoice of the goods in this column, with the number in the first line and the date in the second line. This column must not be left blank. To avoid misunderstandings about months and dates, month is expressed in English abbreviations, such as "JAN. 10, 2022".

发票日期和号码：此栏填写出口货物的商业发票日期和号码，第一行填号码，第二行填日期。此栏不得留空。为避免对月份、日期的误解，月份一律用英文缩写表述，如"JAN. 10, 2022"。

(13) Certification：The unit must fill in the location and date of the Commodity Inspection Bureau. After verification, the certification holder of the Commodity Inspection Bureau will be signed his name in this column(original) and stamped with the seal. The date in this column should not be earlier than the invoice date(column 10) and declaration date(column 12), and should be earlier than the shipment date(column 3).

签证当局的证明：签证单位要填写商检局的签证地点、日期。商检局签证人经审核后在此栏（正本）签名盖签证印章。本栏日期不得早于发票日期（第 10 栏）和申报日期（第 12 栏），而且应早于货物的出运日期（第 3 栏）。

（14）Declaration by the Exporter：The term "Exporter" refers to the shipper who can either be a trader or a manufacturer. Type the name of the producing country and the importing country and the place and date when the declaration is made. The date is not later than the date of B/L and not earlier than the date of invoice. This box must be signed by the Company's authorized signatory. Any declaration by the exporter should be stated here. Usually three items may be filled in：

●The name of producing country：usually fill "China", general Commodity Inspection Bureau seal is printed beforehand.

●The name of importing countries：Fill the favor country name usually is the same with 4th/5th blank.

●The place and date of applicant and the exporters' signature.

出口商声明："出口商"一词是指发货人，可以是贸易商，也可以是制造商。键入生产国和进口国的名称以及申报的地点和日期。日期不迟于提单日期，也不早于发票日期。此方框必须由公司授权签字人签字。出口商的任何声明都应在此说明。通常可以填写三项：

本栏需要填三个项目：
●生产国别：通常填"中国"，商检总局盖章。
●进口国别：填优惠国的国名，该国名与第 4 栏、第 5 栏的国名一致。
●出口商申请日期、地点及签章。

4. Case Study 案例实训

FORM OF DOC. CREDIT   *40A：IRREVOCABLE COX：0M 3O1OVAi D
DOC. CREDIT NUMBER   *20：33416852
DATE OF ISSUE   31C：20220112
DATE AND PLACE OF EXPIRY   31D：DATE 20220317 PLACE IN THE COUNTRY OF BENEFICIARY
APPLICANT   *50：TKAMLA CORPORATION 6-7, KAWARA MACH OSAKA, JAPAN
ISSUING BANK   52A：FUJI BANK LTD. 1013, S. AKULA OTOLKNGZA MACHI TOKYO, JAPAN
BENEFICIARY   59：JIANGSU FASHION INTERNATIONAL TRADE CORPORATION #35 ZHUSHAN ROAD, JIANGNING DISTRICT, NANJING, CHINA.

AMOUNT   *32B：AMOUNT USD 12,500.00
AVAILABLE WITH/BY   *41A：ANY BANK IN CHINA BY NEGOTIATION
DRAFTS AT...   42C：AT SIGHT
DRAWEE   42A：FUJI BANK LTD.
PARTIAL SHIPMENTS   43P：PROHIBITED
TRANSSHIPMENT   43T：PROHIBITED
LOADING ON BOARD   44A：SHANGHAI PORT
FOR TRANSPORTATION TO...   44B：OSAKA PORT

FOR LATEST DATE OF SHIPMENT　44C：20220316

DESCRIPTION OF GOODS　　　　45A：COTTON BLANKET

　　　　ART. NO. H666 500 PCS USD 5. 50/PC

　　　　ART. NO. HX88 500 PCS USD 4. 50/PC

　　　　ART. NO. HE21 500 PCS USD 4. 80/PC

　　　　ART. NO. HA56 500 PCS USD 5. 20/PC

　　　　ART. NO. HH46 500 PCS USD 5. 00/PC

CIF OSAKA

DOCUMENTS REQUIRED　　46A：+CERTIFICATE OF ORIGIN GSP FORM A, ISSUED BY THE CHINA COMERCE OR OTHER AUTHORITY DULY ENTITLED FOR THIS CERTIFI-CATE.

补充资料：

（1）INVOICE NO. ：XH056671

（2）INVOICE DATE：FEB. 01, 2022

（3）PACKING：

G. W.：20. 5KGS/CTN

N. W.：20KGS/CTN

MEAS：0. 2CBM/CTN

PACEKED IN 1 CARTONS OF 100PCS EACH

PACKDIN TW0 20' CONTINER（集装箱号：TEXU 2395999 TEXU 2264000）

（4）REFRENCE NO：20220819

（5）MARKS：

　　　　ABC

　　　　OSAKA

　　　　C/NO. 1-300

Certificate of Origin（Form A）普惠制产地证格式 A

（3）Goods consigned from（Exporter's Business Name, Address, County） JIANGSU FASHION INTERNATIONAL TRADE CORPORATION #35 ZHUSHAN ROAD, JIANGNING DISTRICT, NANJING, CHINA.	（1）Reference No. XH056671 GENERALIZED SYSTEM OF PREFERENCES CERTIFICATE OF ORIGIN （Combined declaration and certificate） FORM A
（4）Goods consigned to（Consignee's Name, Address, County） TKAMLA CORPORATION 6-7, KAWARA MACH OSAKA, JAPAN	（2）Issued in：THE PEOPLE'S REPUBLIC OF CHINA （country） See Notes. overleaf
（5）Means of Transport and Route（as far as known） FROM SHANGHAI TO OSAKA BY SEA	（6）For Official Use

续表

(7)Item Number	(8)Marks and Numbers of Package	(9)Number and Kind of Packages; Description of Goods	(10)Origin Criterion (see Notes overleaf)	(11)Gross Weight or Other Quantity	(12)Number and Date of Invoices
1 2 3 4 5	ABC FC266 OSAKA C/NO. 1–300	COTTON BLANKET ART. NO. H666 500 PCS USD 5. 50/PC ART. NO. HX88 500 PCS USD 4. 50/PC ART. NO. HE21 500 PCS USD4. 80/PC ART. NO. HA56 500 PCS USD5. 20/PC ART. NO. HH46 500 PCS USD5. 00/PC	P	G. W 512. 5 CTN 25,000 PICES	XH056671 Feb. 01, 2022

(13)Certification	(14)Declaration by the Exporter
It is hereby certified, on the basis of control carried out, that the declaration by the exporter is correct. (OFFICIAL STAMP) SHANGHAI Feb. 01, 2022 Place and date, signature and stamp of certifying authority	The undersigned hereby declares that the above details and statements are correct; that all the goods were produced in ___CHINA___ (Country) And that they comply with the requirements specified for those goods in the Generalized System of Preferences for goods exported to ------------- JAPAN ------------- (importing country) SHANGHAI　Feb. 01, 2022 Place and date, signature of authorized signature

Section Three　Certificate of Origin：Asia−Pacific Trade Agreement 《亚太贸易协定》原产地证书

1. Sample Certificate Of Origin《亚太贸易协定》原产地证书样单

Asia−Pacific Trade Agreement

（Combined declaration and certificate）

(1)Goods consigned from： (Exporter's business name, address, country)	Reference No. Issued in --------------------------------- (Country)

(2) Goods consigned to: (Consignee's name, address, country)	(3) For Official use			
(4) Means of transport and route:				
(5) Tariff item number:	(6) Marks and number of Packages:	(7) Number and kind of packages/description of goods:	(8) Origin criterion: see notes overleaf	(9) Gross weight or other quantity:	(10) Number and date of invoices:

(11) Declaration by the exporter: The undersigned hereby declares that the above details and statements are correct: that all the goods were produced in ------------------------------------ (Country) and that they comply with the origin requirements specified for these goods in the Asia−Pacific Trade Agreement for goods exported to ------------------------------------ (Importing Country) ------------------------------------ Place and date, signature of authorized Signatory	(12) Certificate It is hereby certified on the basis of control carried out, that the declaration by the exporter is correct. ------------------------------------ Place and date, signature and Stamp of Certifying Authority

《亚太贸易协定》(中文文本)

(申报和证书合一)

(1)货物运自(出口人名称、地址、国家):	编号: ------------------------------------签发 (国家)
(2)货物运至(收货人名称、地址、国家):	(3)官方使用
(4)运输工具及路线	

(5)税则号列	(6)包装唛头及编号	(7)包装件数及种类;货物名称	(8)原产地标准(见背页说明)	(9)毛重或者其他数量	(10)发票编号及日期

续表

(11)出口人声明 下列签字人证明上述资料及申明正确无讹，所有货物产自 ------------------------------------- （国家） 且符合《亚太贸易协定》原产地规则的相关规定，该货物出口至 ------------------------------------- （进口国） ------------------------------------- 申报地点、日期及授权签字人的签字	(12)证明 根据所实施的监管，兹证明上述出口商的申报正确 ------------------------------------- 地点和日期，签字和签证机构印章

2. The contents of General principles of Asia-Pacific Trade Agreement 样单拆解：《亚太贸易协定》表格主要栏目及缮制

Box 1：Goods Consigned from. Type the name, address and country of the exporter. The name must be the same as the exporter described in the invoice.

第一栏：货物发运自。注明出口人的名称、地址与国别，名称须与发票上的出口人一致。

Box 2：Goods Consigned to. Type the name, address and country of the importer. The name must be the same as the importer described in the invoice. For third party trade, the words "To Order" may be typed.

第二栏：货物发运到。填入进口商的名称、地址和国家/地区。名称必须与发票中描述的进口商相同。对于第三方贸易，可以填入"To Order"字样。

Box 3：For Official Use. Reserved for use by certifying authority.

第三栏：供官方使用。此栏仅供签证当局使用。

Box 4：Means of Transport and Route. State in detail the means of transport and route for the products exported. If the L/C terms etc. do not require such details, type "By Air" or "By Sea". If the products are transported through a third country this can be indicated as follows：e. g. "By Air" "Laos to India via Bangkok".

第四栏：运输方式与详细路线。注明出口货物的运输方式和路线，如信用证条款等无此详细要求，打填上"空运"或"海运"。如货物是途经第三国运输的，可用如下方式表示：例如"空运""老挝经曼谷至印度"。

Box 5：Tariff Item Number. Type the 4-digit HS heading of the individual items.

第五栏：税则号。注明货物 4 位数的 HS 编码。

Box 6：Marks and Numbers of Packages. Type the marks and numbers of the packages covered by the Certificate. This information should be identical to the marks and numbers on the packages.

第六栏：唛头与包装编号。注明证书所载货物的包装唛头及编号，该信息应与货物包装上的唛头及编号一致。

Box 7：Number and Kind of Packages. Type clearly the description of the products exported. This should be identical to the description of the products contained in the invoice. An accurate description will help the Customs Authority of the country of destination to clear the products quickly.

第七栏：包装数量与种类：货物描述明确注明出口产品的货物描述。货物描述应与发票上对出口产品的描述相一致。确切的描述有助于目的国海关当局对产品的快速清关。

Box 8：Origin Criterion. Preference products must be wholly produced or obtained in the exporting Participating State in accordance with Rule 2 of the Asia-Pacific Trade Agreement Rules of Origin, or where not wholly produced or obtained in the exporting Participating State must be eligible under Rule 3 or Rule 4.

a）Products wholly produced or obtained：enter the letter "A" in Box 8.

b）Products not wholly produced or obtained：the entry in Box 8 should be as follows：

（1）Enter letter "B" in Box 8, for products which meet the origin criteria according to Rule 3. Entry of letter "B" would be followed by the sum of the value of materials, parts or produce originating from non-Participating States, or undetermined origin used, expressed as a percentage of the FOB value of the products（example "B" 50 percent）；

（2）Enter letter "C" in Box 8 for products which meet the origin criteria according to Rule 4. Entry of letter "C" would be followed by the sum of the aggregate content originating in the territory of the exporting Participating State expressed as a percentage of the FOB value of the exported product（example "C" 60 percent）；

（3）Enter letter "D" in Box 8 for products which meet the special origin criteria according to Rule 10.

第八栏：原产地标准：根据《亚太贸易协定》原产地规则第二条的规定，受惠产品必须是完全原产自出口成员国；若非出口成员国完全原产的产品，必须符合第三条或第四条。

a）完全原产品：在第 8 栏填写字母"A"。

b）含有进口成分的产品：第 8 栏的填写方法如下：

（1）符合第三条规定的原产地标准的产品，第 8 栏填写字母"B"。字母"B"后应填写原产于非成员国或原产地不明的原料、部件或产品的总货值占出口产品离岸价的百分比（例如"B"50%）。

（2）符合第四条规定的原产地标准的产品，第 8 栏填写字母"C"。字母"C"后应填写原产于成员国领土内的累计含量的总值与出口产品离岸价的百分比（例如"C"60%）。

（3）符合第十条特定原产地标准的产品：第 8 栏填写字母"D"。

Box 9：Gross Weight or Other Quantity. Type the gross weight or other quantity（such as pieces, kg）of the products covered by the Certificate.

第九栏：毛重或其他数量。注明证书所载产品的毛重或其他数量（如件数、千克）。

Box 10：Number and Date of Invoices. State number and date of the invoice in question. The date of the invoice attached to the Application should not be later than the date of approval on the Certificate.

第十栏：发票号码与日期。注明发票的号码与日期。发票日期不得迟于证书的签发日期。

Box 11：Declaration by the Exporter. The term "Exporter" refers to the shipper who can either be a trader or a manufacturer. Type the name of the producing country and the importing country and the place and date when the declaration is made. This box must be signed by the Company's authorized signatory.

第十一栏：出口人的声明。"出口人"指发货人，他既可以是贸易商也可以是制造商。注明生产国和进口国的国别、申报地点和申报日期。该栏必须由公司授权签字人签署。

Box 12：Certification. The certifying authority will certify in this Box.

第十二栏：签证当局的证明。该栏由签证当局签署。

Section Four　Certificate of Origin：The China-ASEAN Free Trade Zone 中国—东盟自由贸易区原产地证

1. Understanding the Certificate of Origin of China-ASEAN Free Trade Zone 认识中国—东盟自由贸易区原产地证

The certificate of origin of China-ASEAN Free Trade Zone adopts a special certificate — E (FORM E), consisting of one original and three carbon free copies. The original is beige and the copy is light green. The original and second copy of the certificate shall be provided by the exporter to the importer for use in customs clearance in the importing country. The first pair should be retained by the visa authority of the exporting party. The third copy is retained by the exporter. After customs clearance of the product, the customs of the importing Party shall annotate on the fourth column of the second copy and return the second copy to the visa authority of the exporting Party within a reasonable period of time.

中国—东盟自由贸易区原产地证书采用专用的证书——E 表(FORM E)，由一份正本及三份无碳副本组成，正本为米黄色，副本为浅绿色。证书的正本和第二副本应由出口人提供给进口人以供其在进口国通关使用。第一副本应由出口的缔约方签证机构留底。第三副本由出口人留存。产品通关后，进口的缔约方海关在第二副本第四栏上批注并在合理的期限内将第二副本返还出口缔约方的签证机构。

Two certificates of origin most widely used in China-ASEAN Free Trade Area. 在中国—东盟自贸区应用最广泛的两种原产地证书。

(1)China-ASEAN Free Trade Agreement：Certificate format：FORM E 中国—东盟自贸协定：证书格式：FORM E

Applicable countries：Brunei, Cambodia, Indonesia, Laos, Malaysia, Myanmar, Philippines, Singapore, Thailand, Vietnam. 适用国别：文莱、柬埔寨、印度尼西亚、老挝、马来西亚、缅甸、菲律宾、新加坡、泰国、越南。

(2)Special preferential tariff treatment：Certificate format：FORM SPT 特别优惠关税待遇：证书格式：FORM SPT

Applicable countries：Myanmar, Laos, Cambodia, Bangladesh. 适用国别：缅甸、老挝、柬埔寨、孟加拉国。

2. Specimen of Certificate of Origin Form E(China-ASEAN Free Trade Zone) 中国—东盟自贸区的原产地证书样单

1. 货物运自(出口人名称、地址、国家)： 例：Zhonghua Mechanic Corps. 　　No. 115, Ronghua Road, 　　Beijing, 100011, China	编号： 中国—东盟自由贸易区 优惠关税 原产地证书 (申报与证书合一) 表格 E The People's Republic of China 签发 (国家) 见背页说明
2. 货物运至(收货人名称、地址、国家)： 例：Great-Hand Mechanic Co. Ltd., 　　509 Sinsig anmara Danang, 　　00111, Jakarta, Indonesia	
3. 运输工具及路线(已知)： 离港日期：例：2022-7-23 船舶名称/飞机等：例：CZ1109 by air 卸货口岸：例：Jakarta(×× Port), Indonesia	4. 官方使用 □ 根据中国—东盟自由贸易区优惠关税协议给予优惠待遇 □ 不给予优惠待遇(请注明原因) ———————————————— 进口国有权签字人签字

5. 项目编号	6. 包装唛头及编号	7. 包装件数及种类；货品名称(包括相应数量及进口国 HS 编码)	8. 原产地标准(见背页说明)	9. 毛重或其他数量及价格(FOB)	10. 发票编号及日期
例：1	例：UG Jakarta, Product of China	例：100 pieces of parts for generators, HS No. 8452		例：100 pieces 10, 000 USD	例：2011E19A 2022-7-23

11. 出口人声明	12. 证明
下列签字人声明上述资料及申报正确无讹，所有货物产自 　　　例：China 　　　(国家) 且符合中国—东盟自由贸易区优惠关税协议所规定的原产地要求，该货物出口至 　　　例：Indonesia 　　　(进口国) ———————————————— 地点和日期，有权签字人的签字	根据所实施的监管，兹证明出口商所做申报正确无讹。 ———————————————— 地点和日期，签字和发证机构印章

The "Standard of Origin" in the eighth column of the form should include the applicable standard of origin. The different standards of origin are as follows:

表格中的第八栏"原产地标准"中应填入产品适用的原产地标准，不同的原产地标准填入的内容如下：

原产地标准	填入第 8 栏的内容
（1）完全获得产品	"×"
（2）符合增值标准的产品	单一国家成分的百分比，例如 40%
（3）符合累计增值标准的产品	中国—东盟累计成分的百分比，例如 40%
（4）符合产品特定原产地标准的产品	"产品特定原产地标准"

3. The Main Content and Key Points of Compilation of China ASEAN Certificate of Origin 样单拆解：中国—东盟原产地证主要内容及缮制要点

（1）The goods shall be shipped from（exporter name, address, country）, and the detailed address of the exporter in China, including house number, street name, place name, country, etc. The exporter must be an enterprise that has gone through the registration procedures with the local inspection and quarantine institution, and the English name shall be consistent with the registration name.

E. g. GUANGXI HEFENG IMP. & EXP. COMPANY 13, XINGHU ROAD, NANNING, GUANGXI, CHINA

货物运自（出口人名称、地址、国家），填中国境内出口人的详细地址，包括门牌号、街道名、地名、国别等。出口人必须是已在当地检验检疫机构办理注册登记手续的企业，且英文名应与注册备案的名称一致。

例如：GUANGXI HEFENG IMP. &EXP. COMPANY 13, XINGHU ROAD, NANNING, GUANGXI, CHINA

（2）When the goods are delivered to（name, address, country of the consignee）, this column shall fill in the full name and detailed address of the consignee including the country. The consignee must be a member of the preferential treatment under the preferential tariff agreement of China–ASEAN Free Trade Area.

E. g. METCH THAI CHEMICAL COMPANY LIMITED 45-7 AITRICHITR RD., BANGKOK, THAILAND.

货物运至（收货人名称、地址、国家），本栏应填收货人的全称和详细地址包括国别。收货人必须是享受中国—东盟自由贸易区优惠关税协议下优惠待遇而接受本证书的成员国。

例如：METCH THAI CHEMICAL COMPANY LIMITED 45-7 AITRICHITR RD., BANGKOK, THAILAND.

（3）The means of transport and routes（known）, including three items：date of departure, ship name/aircraft, etc., and port of unloading.

E. g. Departure date：MARCH. 6,2022

Ship name/aircraft, etc.：DONGFENG V. 0238

Unloading port：BANGKOK, THAILAND

运输工具及路线(已知)，填写内容包括三项：离港日期、船舶名称/飞机、卸货口岸。

例如：离港日期：MARCH 6,2022

船舶名称/飞机等：DONGFENG V. 0238

卸货口岸：BANGKOK, THAILAND

(4) Official use：this column has two options：(a) preferential treatment according to the preferential tariff agreement of CHINA-ASEAN free trade area；(b)no preferential treatment(the reasons must be indicated). The applicant is left blank and filled in by the customs of the importing country.

官方使用：该栏目有两项选择：(a)根据中国—东盟自由贸易区优惠关税协议给予优惠待遇；(b)不给予优惠待遇(须注明原因)。申请人留空，由进口国海关填写。

(5)Item number：If the export goods in batches have different varieties, then, "1," "2," "3" according to different varieties, invoice number, etc. For individual goods, fill in "1" in this column.

项目编号：如同批的出口货物有不同品种，则按照不同品种、发票号等分列："1""2""3"，单项商品，此栏填"1"。

(6)Packaging shipping mark and serial number：This column should be filled in accordance with the shipping mark and invoice on the outer package of the goods. If there is no shipping mark, fill in "N/M" or "NO MARK"；if the shipping mark is too much, fill in the blank below the stop lines 7,8,9 and 10.

E. g. P. T. C.

BANGKOK

INV. NO. 01A3365-754C

NO. 1-1712

包装唛头及编号：该栏目填写要与货物外包装上的唛头和发票的一致。如果没有唛头应填写"N/M"或"NO MARK"；如果唛头过多，此栏不够填写，可填在7、8、9、10栏截止线以下的空白处。

例如：P. T. C.

BANGKOK

INV. NO. 01A3365-754C

NO. 1-1712

(7)Number and type of packages and name of goods(including the corresponding quantity and HS code of the importing country)：

E. g. 1712 (ONE THOUSAND SEVEN HUNDRED AND TWELVE) BAGS LITHOPONE 30PCT ARROW BRAND.

The following when filling in this column：

(a)The number of packaging pieces must be expressed in both English and Arabic numerals.

If it is bulk goods, the words "IN BULK" should be marked(such as: 46.8MT RED MILLET IN HUSK IN BULK);

(b)The name of the goods must be detailed so that the customs officer can identify the goods. The name of the manufacturer and any trademark shall also be listed;

(c)The coordination system code shall be the code of the import member state;

(d)After the listing of the commodity name, the end symbol(×)shall be added on the next line to prevent falsification.

包装件数及种类、货品名称(包括相应数量及进口国 HS 编码):

例如：1712(ONE THOUSAND SEVEN HUNDRED AND TWELVE)BAGS LITHOPONE 30PCT ARROW BRAND.

该栏目填写时要注意以下事项：

(a)包装件数必须用英文和阿拉伯数字同时表示。如为散货，应标明"IN BULK"字样(如：46.8MT RED MILLET IN HUSK IN BULK);

(b)货品名称必须详细，以使验货的海关官员可以识别。生产商的名称及任何商标也应列明；

(c)协调制度编码应为进口成员国的编码；

(d)商品名称等项列完后，应在下一行加打结束符号(×)，以防止加填伪造内容。

(8)Standard of origin(see the description on the back page): This is the key content of the customs of the importing country, and the applicable standard of origin of the product should be filled in the standard. Different origin standards contain different contents.

原产地标准(见背页说明)：这是进口国海关重点审核的内容，应填入产品适用的原产地标准。不同的原产地标准填入的内容不同。

(9)Gross weight or other quantity and price(FOB): This column is filled in the normal unit of measurement of goods. Such as: "DOZ," "PCS," "L," etc., to the weight of the commodity gross weight, if it is bulk, can only fill the net weight, but to indicate N. W. (NET WEIGHT).

E. g. 42.80MT FOB USD 15,430.00

毛重或其他数量及价格(FOB)：此栏以商品正常的计量单位填写。如："DOZ""PCS""L"等，以重量计量的商品填写毛重，如果是散货，只能填净重，但要标明 N. W(. NET WEIGHT)。

例如：42.80MT FOB USD 15,430.00

(10)Invoice number and date: This column should be the same number and date on the invoice submitted to the local inspection and quarantine agency when applying for FORM E.

E. g. 01A3365-754C FEB. 16,2020

发票编号及日期：此栏要与申请 FORM E 时提交给当地检验检疫机构的发票上的号码和日期相同。

例如：01A3365-754C FEB. 16,2020

(11)Exporter statement: Fill in "CHINA" on the horizontal line of the producing country and the name of the final importing country, the importing country must be the same as the country of the consignee in column 2 and the country of the unloading port in column 3. If transferred to an inland destination, it should be consistent with the country of the inland destination. The applicant shall stamp the Chinese and English reference seal of the applicant and hand sign in this column. The declaration date shall not be earlier than the invoice date, and the seal shall avoid covering the name of the importing country and the signature of the applicant.

出口人声明：在生产国横线上填"CHINA"，在进口国横线上填最终进口国的名称，进口国必须与第 2 栏的收货人的国别相同，也与第 3 栏的卸货口岸的国别一致。如转运到内陆目的地，则应与内陆目的地的国别一致。申请单位的申报员在此栏加盖申请单位的中英文对照章并手签，其中申报日期不得早于发票日，盖章应避免覆盖进口国名称和手签人签字。

（12）Certificate：The applicant should fill in the place and time of the visa. After reviewing the visa personnel of the inspection and quarantine institution, the applicant should sign in the column of the original and stamp the visa seal. The visa date in this column shall not be earlier than the invoice date and the application date.

证明：申请单位要填写签证地点和时间，检验检疫机构的签证人审核后，在正本的此栏签名并加盖签证印章。本栏目的签证日期不得早于发票日期和申请日期。

Section Five　Certificate of Origin Form RCEP RCEP 原产地证

1. RCEP 的定义、作用和成员国

RCEP stands for Regional Comprehensive Economic Partnership. The RCEP aims to remove internal trade barriers, create and improve a free investment environment and expand trade in services. It will also cover a wide range of areas, including intellectual property protection and competition policy.

RCEP 是 Regional Comprehensive Economic Partnership 的缩写，即区域全面经济伙伴关系协定。RCEP 的目标是消除内部贸易壁垒、创造和完善自由的投资环境、扩大服务贸易，还将涉及知识产权保护、竞争政策等多领域。

The effective implementation of RCEP marks the official landing of the world's most populous, largest economic and trade scale, and most promising free trade zone, fully reflecting the confidence and determination of all parties to jointly uphold multilateralism and free trade, promote regional economic integration, and make important contributions to regional and even global trade and investment growth, economic recovery, and prosperity development. Its members are: China, Korea, Japan, Thailand, Indonesia, Vietnam, Laos, Brunei, Myanmar, Singapore, Cambodia, the Philippines, New Zealand, Australia, and Malaysia.

RCEP 的生效实施，标志着全球人口最多、经贸规模最大、最具发展潜力的自由贸易区正式落地，充分体现了各方共同维护多边主义和自由贸易、促进区域经济一体化的信心和决心，将为区域乃至全球贸易投资增长、经济复苏和繁荣发展做出重要贡献。其成员国包括中国、韩国、日本、泰国、印尼、越南、老挝、文莱、缅甸、新加坡、柬埔寨、菲律宾、新西兰、澳大利亚、马来西亚。

2. Specimen: Certificate of Origin Form RCEP

RCEP 原产地证样单

1. Goods Consigned from (Exporter's name, address and country)(出口商)	Certificate No.	Form RCEP
2 Goods Consigned to (Importer's/ Consignee's name, address, country)(收货人)	REGIONAL. COMPREHENSIVE ECONOMIC PARTNERSHIP AGREEMENT CERTIFICATE OF ORIGIN	
3. Producer's name, address and country (if known)(制造商)	issued in ----------------- (Country)	
4. Means of transport and route(if known) Departure Date(开船日期): Vessel's name/Aircraft flight number, etc.: (船名航次) Port of Discharge:	5. For Official Use Preferential Treatment: ☐Given ☐Not Given(Please state reason/s) --- Signature of Authorized Signatory of the Customs Authority of importing country	

6. Item number	7. Marks and numbers packages (唛头)	8. Number and kind of packages; and description of goods. (包装数和货物描述)	9. HS Code of the goods (6 digit-level) (前六位海关编码)	10. Original offering criterion (原产地标准)	11. RCEP Country of Origin (出口国)	12. Quantity (Gross weight or other measurement), and value (FOB) where RVC is applied	13. Invoice number(s) and date of invoice(s) (发票号和发票日期)

14. Remarks(第三方离岸公司及境外公司)

15. Declaration by the exporter or producer The undersigned hereby declares that the above details and statements are correct and that the goods covered in this Certificate comply with the requirements specified for these goods in the Regional Comprehensive Economic Partnership Agreement. These goods are exported to: -- (importing country) -- Place and date, and signature of authorized signatory	16. Certification On the basis of control carried out, it is hereby certified that the information herein is correct and that the goods described comply with the origin requirements specified in the Regional Comprehensive Economic Partnership Agreement. -- Place and date, signature and seal or stamp of issuing body

17. ☐Back-to-back Certificate of Origin   ☐Third-party invoicing   ☐Issued RETROACTIVELY

3. The Contents and the Key Points of the Origin of RCEP 样单拆解：RCEP 的原产地证的主要内容及缮制要点

（1）Goods Consigned from（Exporter's name，address and country）. 出口商名称、地址和国家。

（2）Goods Consigned to（Importer's/ Consignee's name，address，country）. 进口商/收货人的名称、地址、国家。

（3）Producer's name，address and county（if known）. If there are multiple manufacturers，"SEE BOX 8" is indicated in column 3 and the manufacturer information for each item is listed in column 8；if the manufacturer requests the confidentiality of the information，it can be marked as "CONFIDENTIAL"，but the relevant department or authorized agency may request the manufacturer information；if the manufacturer details are unknown，it can be marked as "NOT AVAILABLE".

生产商的详细信息，包括名称、地址和国家。如有多个生产商，则在第 3 栏注明"详见第 8 栏"（SEE BOX 8），并在第 8 栏列明每项的生产商信息；如生产商要求信息保密，则可注明"保密"，但相关部门或授权机构可要求提供生产商信息；如生产商详细信息未知，则可注明"无法提供"。

（4）Means of transport and route（if known）. 运输工具和路线。

Departure Date 发货日期

Vessel's name/Aircraft flight number，etc. 船只名称/飞机航班号等

Port of Discharge 卸货港

（5）For official use. 用于官方用途。

Preferential Treatment 优先处理

□Given 给出理由

□Not Given（Please state reason/s）未给出（请说明理由）

Signature of Authorized Signatory of the Customs Authority of the Importing Country 海关授权签字人签署进口国

（6）Item number. 条款编号。

（7）Marks and numbers on packages. 唛头和包装数量。

（8）Number and kind of packages；and description of the goods：The name of each item must be detailed so that it can be recognized by the customs officer who inspects the goods.

编号/包装种类、货物描述：每项货物名称必须详细以使验货的海关关员可以识别。

（9）HS Code of the goods（6 digit-level）：The harmonization of trade names and codes（HS）shall be completed in accordance with the 6-digit HS code of the export goods in accordance with Annex Ⅰ of Chapter Ⅲ of the Agreement

货物 HS 编码（6 位数级）：商品名称及编码协调度（HS）应根据协定第三章附件一填写出口货物的 6 位 HS 编码。

（10）Origin Conferring Criterion：Goods that are Fully acquired or produced "Fully acquired"（WO）goods produced using only originating materials "Fully produced"（PE）comply with specific origin standards（PSRs）Goods produced using non-originating materials "Tariff Classification Change"（CTC）"Regional Value Ingredient"（RVC）"Chemical Reaction"（CR）Applicable Member State Material Accumulation "Cumulative Rules" (ACU) that do not meet the requirements of specific rules of origin tariff change but apply to tiny content "Tiny Content" (DMI) details, See Chapter Ⅲ, Rules of Origin, of the RCEP Agreement Text.

原产地授予标准：完全获得或生产的货物"完全获得"（WO）仅使用原产材料生产的货物"完全生产"（PE）符合特定原产地标准（PSRs）使用非原产材料生产的货物"税则归类改变"（CTC）"区域价值成分"（RVC）"化学反应"（CR）适用成员国材料累积的"累积规则"（ACU）不满足特定原产地规则税则改变要求但适用于微小含量的"微小含量"（DMI）详细内容，可参考《RCEP 协定文本》第三章，原产地规则。

(a) Full acquisition of the goods ("WO"):

"Fully acquired goods" means goods obtained only from a Party, including natural products obtained entirely in one Party or goods made from natural products. Article 3 of the RCEP Rules of Origin lists 10 types of goods that can be considered fully acquired. When the goods are fully obtained to apply for the RCEP Certificate of Origin, fill in "WO" in the Origin Criteria column. Export of RCEP members of the Chinese planted and harvested rich bamboo, can be regarded as a complete acquisition of goods in China, enterprises in the application for RCEP certificate of origin, the certificate of origin standard column filled in "WO". For example, picking cotton grown in Xinjiang, processing and texting in China to export the RCEP member, the goods can be regarded as fully obtained goods, and the origin standard is filled in "WO".

完全获得货物（"WO"）：

"完全获得货物"是指仅从一成员方获得的货物，包括了完全在一方获得的天然产品或由天然产品制成的货物。RCEP 原产地规则第三条列明了可视为完全获得的 10 种货物。完全获得货物申办 RCEP 原产地证书时，原产地标准栏填写"WO"。出口 RCEP 成员方的中国境内种植、收获的富贵竹，可视为中国境内完全获得货物，企业在申办 RCEP 原产地证书时，证书原产地标准栏填写"WO"。例如：采摘新疆种植的棉花，在国内加工、纺织制成坯布出口 RCEP 成员方，货物可视为完全获得货物，原产地标准填写"WO"。

(b) Fully produced goods ("PE"):

"Fully produced goods" means goods produced solely from materials originating from the RCEP Member, i. e. all raw materials used in the production of goods for which an RCEP Certificate of Origin is applied for shall be manufactured by the RCEP Member and shall be eligible for RCEP Origin in accordance with the RCEP Rules of Origin. Unlike "fully acquired goods" in Article (1), the "fully produced goods" here only needs to confirm that the raw materials used in the production of the goods are the origin of the RCEP member, and do not require that the higher production raw materials used in the production of the original materials must be RCEP origin until the original natural raw materials. For "Fully produced goods", fill in "PE" in the Origin Criteria column. For example, cotton produced in India (HS52. 03) is processed into cotton yarn (HS52. 06) at Factory A in China and sold to Factory B for export to other RCEP members through textile processing (HS52. 09) Factory A cotton yarn processing has met the RCEP rules of origin requirements for the product number change standard, cotton yarn can be regarded as Chinese origin. Factory B uses cotton yarn qualified for RCEP origin to make cotton blank cloth, and the origin standard on the certificate of origin of the export blank cloth is filled in "PE".

完全生产货物（"PE"）：

"完全生产货物"是指仅使用 RCEP 成员方原产材料生产的货物，即申请办理 RCEP 原产地证书的货物生产过程中所采用的所有原材料应当在 RCEP 成员方生产制造而成并且符合 RCEP 原产地规则，具备 RCEP 原产资格。与第（一）条的"完全获得货物"不同，这里的"完全生产货物"只需确认生产该货物所用的原材料为 RCEP 成员方原产即可，不要求生产该原产材料所使用的上一级生产原料直至最初天然原材料必须为 RCEP 原产。对于"完全生产货物"，原产地标准栏填写"PE"。例如：印度生产的棉花（HS52.03）在中国境内 A 工厂加工制成棉纱线（HS52.06）后，出售给 B 厂通过纺织加工制成全棉坯布（HS52.09）出口其他 RCEP 成员方。A 工厂棉纱线加工已满足了 RCEP 原产地规则对该项商品所要求的品目号改变标准，棉纱线可视为中国原产。B 工厂采用具备 RCEP 原产资格的棉纱线制成棉坯布，其出口坯布的原产地证书上的原产地标准填写"PE"。

（c）Use in accordance with RCEP origin standards：

Goods that comply with the RCEP standard of origin and are produced using non-originating materials are filled in the origin standard according to the following three different situations.

01 If the goods are applicable and meet the origin standard of "change in tariff classification", fill in "CTC". Example：The RCEP Rules of Origin stipulate that the origin standard for cotton cloth（HS52.09）is "change of quality", if the factory purchases cotton yarn from India and processes cotton and then exports it to the RCEP member, the cotton meets the "change of tariff classification" standard, and the origin standard is filled in "CTC".

02 If the goods are suitable and meet the origin standard of "regional value ingredient", fill in "RVC". Example：The origin standard for aluminum alloy strips, rods and profiles（HS76.04）stipulated in the RCEP Rules of Origin is "change of heading or regional value component 40", if the factory produces aluminum alloy strips made of non-originating aluminum alloy ingots and then exported to RCEP members, and the standard of "regional value component 40"（that is, regional value component 40% or more）is used to determine that the product meets the Chinese origin qualification, the origin standard should be filled in "RVC".

03 If the goods are suitable and meet the "chemical reaction" origin standard, fill in "CR". Example：The origin standard specified in the RCEP Rules of Origin for other non-metallic inorganic esters（excluding esters of hydrogen halide）（HS29.20）is "change of heading, regional value component 40, or chemical reaction", if the factory produces the finished product processed from non-originating materials and re-exported to the RCEP member, the "chemical reaction" standard is used to determine that the product meets the Chinese origin qualification, the origin standard is filled in "CR".

根据 RCEP 原产地标准使用：

符合 RCEP 原产地标准使用非原产材料生产的货物根据下列三种不同情况分别填写原产地标准。

01 货物适用且符合"税则归类改变"原产地标准的，填"CTC"。例子：RCEP 原产地规则对棉布（HS52.09）所规定的原产地标准为"品目改变"，如果工厂采购了印度产棉纱加工制成棉布再出口到 RCEP 成员方，棉布符合"税则归类改变"标准，原产地标准填写"CTC"。

02 货物适用且符合"区域价值成分"原产地标准的，填"RVC"。例子：RCEP 原产地规则中对铝合金条、杆和型材（HS76.04）所规定的原产地标准为"品目改变或区域价值成分 40"，如果工厂生产采用了非原产的铝合金锭加工制成铝合金条再出口到 RCEP 成员方，采用了"区域价值成分 40"（即区域价值成分 40%或以上）的标准来判定产品符合中国原产资格的，原产地标准应当填写"RVC"。

03 货物适用且符合"化学反应"原产地标准的，填"CR"。例子：RCEP 原产地规则中对其他非金属无机酸酯（不包括卤化氢的酯）（HS29.20）所规定的原产地标准为"品目改变，区域价值成分 40，或化学反应"，如果工厂生产采用了非原产材料加工制成该成品再出口 RCEP 成员方，采用了"化学反应"的标准判定产品符合中国原产资格的，原产地标准填写"CR"。

(d) Goods that have been qualified for origin using the rules for the accumulation of origin ("ACU"):

The RCEP Rules of Origin "Accumulation" provide that when materials originating from other members of the Agreement are used in the production of a product, that party's material may be considered to be the originating material of the member in which the product was produced. The rule makes it easier for the final product to qualify for origin. In terms of filling in the origin standard, if the enterprise's goods use the origin accumulation rules to obtain the origin qualification in the production, in addition to filling in the letter symbols applicable to the relevant origin standards, it is also necessary to fill in the "ACU". Example: A Chinese enterprise produces and exports Thai H products(origin standard: regional value ingredient 40), and the proportion of Japanese raw materials in the production of FOB values is 40%, New Zealand raw materials are 15%, Chinese value-added parts account for 30%, and other non-members account for 15%. In this example, the value-added portion of China does not exceed 40%, but the aggregate regional value component of all members involved in the production using the cumulative rule(China, Japan, New Zealand) exceeds 40%, which meets the RCEP origin standard. Origin Standard Fill in: RVC ACU.

运用了原产地累积规则取得原产资格的货物（"ACU"）：

RCEP 原产地"累积"规则规定，产品生产中使用了协定其他成员方原产材料时，该成员方材料可视为产品生产所在成员方的原产材料。该规则使最终产品更加容易取得原产资格。在原产地标准填写方面，如企业货物在生产中运用了原产地累积规则取得原产资格的，在填写了符合相关原产地标准所适用字母符号外，还需要填写"ACU"。例子：我国某企业生产出口泰国 H 产品（原产地标准：区域价值成分 40），生产所用原料中日本原料占产品 FOB 值的比例为 40%，新西兰原料 15%，中国增值部分占 30%，其他非成员方占 15%。该例子中，中国增值部分不超过 40%，但使用累积规则参与生产所有成员方（中国、日本、新西兰）合计区域价值成分超过 40%，符合 RCEP 原产标准。原产地标准填写：RVC ACU。

(e) Goods eligible for origin("DMI")using the "Micro Content" rule of Origin "Micro Content":

Where the RCEP Rules of Origin "Micro Content" provide for a change in the classification of goods applicable, for goods under Chapters 1 to 97, if the value of the non-originating materials used for production without a change in tariff classification does not exceed 10% of the FOB value of the goods, or for chapters 50 to 63 goods, the weight of the non-originating materials used for production without a change in tariff classification does not exceed 10% of the total weight of the goods, The goods can still be considered original goods. The Criteria of Origin column must indicate "DMI". Example: An enterprise produces Y products (goods not specified in Chapters 50-63, and the origin standard is "change of heading") using non-RCEP origin materials a, b, c and d, accounting for 15%, 5%, 10% and 8% of the value of the finished FOB, respectively, of which the d item number is the same as the finished product Y. Since the item number of d raw material is the same as that of finished product Y, it does not meet the requirements of the origin standard of "item change", but the d raw material accounts for no more than 10% of the FOB value of the finished product, and the product Y has RCEP origin qualification using the micro content rule. The Origin Criteria column should be filled in: CTC DMI.

运用"微小含量"规则取得原产资格的货物("DMI"):

RCEP 原产地规则"微小含量"规定了货物适用税则归类改变标准的情况下，对于第 1~97 章货物，如果用于生产的未发生税则归类改变的非原产材料的价值不超过货物 FOB 价值的 10%，或者对于第 50~63 章货物，用于生产的未发生税则归类改变的非原产材料的重量不超过货物总重量 10% 的，货物仍可视为原产货物。原产地标准栏须注明"DMI"。例子：某企业生产 Y 产品(非第 50~63 章规定的货物，原产地标准为"品目改变")使用了非 RCEP 原产材料 a、b、c、d，占成品 FOB 价值比例分别为 15%、5%、10%、8%，其中 d 品目号与成品 Y 一样。由于 d 原料的品目号与成品 Y 一样，因此不符合"品目改变"的原产地标准要求，但 d 原料占成品 FOB 价值不超过 10%，运用微小含量规则，产品 Y 具备 RCEP 原产资格。原产地标准栏应填写：CTC DMI 。

(11) RCEP Country of Origin: This item is the exclusive content of the RCEP certificate, located in column 11 of the certificate, when the enterprise applies for the certificate in the single window, the "country of origin of the agreement" defaults to "CHINA", and the "maximum tax rate type defaults" to empty, when the product determines the origin qualification, the country of origin under the agreement of the goods can be determined in order.

原产国：该项为 RCEP 证书独有内容，位置在证书第 11 栏，企业在单一窗口申请证书时，"协定原产国"默认为"CHINA"，"最高税率类型默认"为空，当产品确定原产资格后，可以按顺序判定货物的协定项下原产国。

(12) Quantity (Gross weight or other measurement), and value (FOB) where RVC is applied. Only if the applicable origin criterion for the goods is a regional value component, the FOB price needs to be indicated in column.

数量：毛重或体积以及适用 RVC 时的 FOB 值。只有当货物的适用原产地标准是区域价值组成部分时，才需要在栏中注明 FOB 价格。

(13) Invoice number(s) and date of invoice(s): The invoice number and date corresponding to each item should be indicated. If there are multiple invoices, the invoice number and date for each item should be indicated separately. This invoice is an invoice issued for the importing party to import the goods. If the import invoice is not issued by the exporter or manufacturer, the "third party invoice" in column 17 shall be ticked(√) in accordance with Article 20 of Chapter III of the Agreement and the name of the company issuing the invoice and the country shall be indicated in

column 14.

发票编号和发票日期：应注明每项商品对应的发票编号和日期。如果有多个发票，应分别注明每项商品对应的发票编号和日期。此发票是指为进口成员方进口货物而签发的发票。如进口发票不是由出口商或生产商签发的，根据协定第三章第二十条规定，第 17 栏"第三方发票"应打钩(√)，且签发发票的公司名称及国家应在第 14 栏注明。

(14) Remarks：In the case of a back-to-back certificate of origin issued in accordance with Article 19 of Chapter Ⅲ of the Agreement, the "back-to-back certificate" in column 17 shall be ticked(√) and the number, date of issue, country of origin, country of origin(region) issued by the first exporting party shall be indicated in column 14. If an approved exporter number is available, it should also be indicated in column 14. This should only be filled in as necessary and includes the information specified in items 10, 11 and 13 of this back page.

附注：如为根据协定第三章第十九条签发的背对背原产地证书，第 17 栏的"背对背证书"应打钩(√)，且第一个出口成员方开具的原始原产地证明的编号、签发日期、签发国家、《协定》项下原产国(地区)应在第 14 栏注明。如有经核准出口商编号，也应在第 14 栏注明。此处仅应在必要时填写，并包括本背页说明第 10、11、13 项所规定的信息。

(15) Declaration by the exporter or producer：The undersigned hereby declares that the above details and statements are correct and that the goods covered in this Certificate comply with the requirements specified for these goods in the Regional Comprehensive Economic Partnership Agreement.

出口商或生产商的声明：以下签字人特此声明上述细节和声明是正确的，并且本证书中涵盖的货物符合《区域全面经济伙伴关系协定》中对这些货物规定的要求。

These goods are exported to：货物出口到进口国(importing country)

(16) Certification：On the basis of control carried out, it is hereby certified that the information herein is correct and that the goods described comply with the origin requirements specified in the Regional Comprehensive Economic Partnership Agreement.

认证：在进行控制的基础上，特此证明此处的信息是正确的，并且所描述的货物符合《区域全面经济伙伴关系协定》中规定的原产地要求。

(17)

☐Back-to-back Certificate of Origin 背对背原产地证书

☐Third-party invoicing 第三方开具发票

☐Issued Retroactively 补发

Exercises 练习

一、Useful Words and Expressions 常用词语和表达

1. Certificate of origin 原产地证书。

2. Certificate of origin form A 原产地证书格式 A。

3. Generalized system of preference certificate of origin form A 普惠制产地证格式 A。

4. In addition to the ordinary shipping document, please also submit certificate of origin of each shipment. 除一般装运文件外，还应提交每批货物的原产地证明书。

5. Certificate of origin in two fold indicating that goods of Chinese origin issued by of Commerce. 该条款要求由商会签发的产地证一式两份，证明货物的原产地在中国。

6. Who issues the inspection certificate in case the quality do not confirm to the contract? 如果货物的质量与合同不符，由谁出具检验证明书呢？

7. Certificate of origin(Form A), one original and one copy, certifying that the origin of the goods is China 原产地证书(格式 A)一正一副，证明货物的原产地为中国。

8. China certificate of origin, issued by the relevant authorities. 中国原产地证书，由相关的当局出具。

9. The certificate of origin must state that the goods do not contain any Israeli raw materials or processing ingredients, and that the exporter or supplier has no direct or indirect contact with Israel. 产地证明书，须声明货物中不含任何以色列的原料和加工成分，出口商或供应商不曾与以色列有任何直接或间接联系。

10. Two certificates of origin issued by the Chamber of Commerce, certifying that the origin of the goods is China. 有商会出具的产地证书两份，证明货物原产地为中国。

二、Making out a Certificate of Origin According to the Following Information 根据以下信息缮制一份原产地证书

APPLICANT: INDIA NEW DELHI JINXIN DEVELOPMENT CO., LTD. 5303 SHASHA STREET DELHI

BENEFICIAL: XING LONG IMPORT AND EXPORT COOPERATION 676 LIAOHE EAST ROAD. DALIAN, CHINA

L/C NO. 121201N10028

S/C NO. WQ(DTR)0311

DESCRIPTION OF GOODS /SERVICES:

CHINESE LIGHT SPECKLED KIDNEY BEANS 2022 CROP. (INNER MONGOLIA ORIGIN)

ADMIXTURE: 1PCT. MAX

MOISTURE: 16PCT. MAX

IMPERFECT GRAINS, OTHER COLOUR BEANS AND WATER STAIN BEANS: 5PCT. MAX

FOB DALIAN

PACKING: ABOUT 50KG GUNNY BAGS EACH GROSS FOR NET

THE LATEST SHIPMENT: OCTOBER 30TH, 2022,

EXPIRY DATE: NOVEMBER 15TH, 2022

DOCUMENTS REQUIRED

+CIQ CERTIFICATE OF WEIGHT ALLOWED BEFORE SHIPMENT IN ONE ORIGINAL PLUS TWO COPIES.

SHIPPING DATE NOVEMBER 10TH, 2022

SHIPMENT: S. S. VICTORY　　VOYAGE. 146E

THE CONTAINER NUMBER: HDMU2132707/2147245/2166420.

MARKS: N/M

Certificate of Origin

(2) Exporter	(1) Certificate No.
	CERTIFICATE OF ORIGIN OF THE PEOPLE'S REPUBLIC OF CHINA
(3) Consignee	
(4) Means of Transport and Route	(6) For Certifying Authority Use Only
(5) Country /Region of Destination	

(7) Marks and Numbers	(8) Number and Kind of Packages; Description of Goods	(9) H. S. Code	(10) Quantity	(11) Number and Date of Invoices

(12) Declaration by the Exporter The undersigned hereby declares that the above details and statements are correct, that all the goods were produced in China and that they comply with the Rules of Origin of the People's Republic of China	(13) Certification It is hereby certified that the declaration by the exporter is correct. (OFFICIAL STAMP) (SIGNATURE)
Place and date, signature and stamp of authorized signatory	Place and date, signature and stamp of certifying authority

三、**Making out a Certificate of Origin (Form A) According to the Following Information** 根据下面信息缮制一份普惠制原产地证书(格式 A)

APPLICANT: CROFT TEXTILE IMPORT AND EXPORT CO., LTD., 88 CHAMPS ELYSEES, ERFURT BUILDING, PARIS, FRANCE

BENEFICIAL: ZHEJIANG YUXI TRADING CO., LTD., 100 ZHONGSHAN ROAD, HANGZHOU, CHINA

L/C NO. 3344B99SS12

S/C NO. CC5768R

DESCRIPTION OF GOODS: MEN'S AND WOMEN'S DENIM CLOTHING,

　　　　MEN'S JEAN 500 PCS USD 55. 00/PC

　　　　WOMEN'S SHIRT 500 PCS USD 45. 00/PC

PORT OF DEPARTURE: SHANGHAI, CHINA

PORT OF DESTINATION: MARSEILLES, FRANCE

THE LATEST SHIPMENT: OCTOBER 30TH, 2022

EXPIRY DATE: NOVEMBER 15TH, 2022

SHIPPING DATE: NOVEMBER 10TH, 2022

DOCUMENTS REQUIRED

　　+CERTIFICATE OF PREFERENCES CERTIFICATE OF ORIGIN ISSUED BY

　　COMPLEMENT AUTHORITY IN ONE ORIGINAL PLUS TWO COPIES.

相关资料

(1) INVOICE NO. : XH056671

(2) INVOICE DATE: FEB. 01, 2022

（3）PACKING：

G. W.：20KGS/CTN

N. W.：19KGS/CTN

MEAS：0. 2CBM/CTN

PACEED IN 1 CARTONS OF 100PCS EACH

PACKED IN TWO 20'CONTAINER（集装箱号：FSCU3524968/FSCU3524973/FSCU352506）

（4）REFRENCE NO：20220819

（5）MARKS：

　　　ABF

　　　MARSEILLES

　　　NO. 1-300

（6）SHIP NAME：VICTORIA；VOYAGE：V. 008A

Certificate of Origin（Form A）

（3）Goods consigned from（Exporter's Business Name, Address, County）				（1） GENERALIZED SYSTEM OF PREFERENCES CERTIFICATE OF ORIGIN （Combined declaration and certificate） FORM A		
（4）Goods consigned to（Consignee's Name, Address, County）				Issued in（2） 　　　（country） See Notes. overleaf		
（5）Means of Transport and Route（as far as known）				（6）For Official Use		
（7）Item Number	（8）Marks and Numbers of Package	（9）Number and Kind of Packages; Description of Goods	（10）Origin Criterion （see Notes overleaf）	（11）Gross Weight or Other Quantity		（12）Number and Date of Invoices
（13）Certification It is hereby certified, on the basis of control carried out, that the declaration by the exporter is correct. 　　　（OFFICIAL STAMP） 　　　_____ Place and date, signature and stamp of certifying authority				（14）Declaration by the Exporter The undersigned hereby declares that the above details and statements are correct; that all the goods were produced in _____ （Country） And that they comply with the requirements specified for those goods in the Generalized System of Preferences for goods exported to _____ （importing country） _____ Place and date, signature of authorized signatory		

Chapter 7 Official Inspection Documents
官方检验单据

Key Points and Difficulties

- To Know the Functions of Inspection Certificates
- To Understand the Classifications of Inspection Certificates
- To Make out Inspection Certificates

Learning Objectives

- To Know the Functions of all kinds of Inspection Certificates
- Make out Inspection Certificates

Section One   Official Inspection Documents 官方检验单据

A variety of official inspection documents may be required to meet the requirements of the exporting and importing countries' customs or foreign exchange regulations. Documents relating to origin, quality, fumigation, health, weight, inspection and export licenses are some examples of official documents. The documentation required to ensure prompt clearance through customs will vary with countries, buyers and goods traded. Traders should, therefore, familiarize themselves with the respective import/export regulations in their countries.

要求各种官方检查文件以满足进出口国海关或外汇法规的要求。与原产地、质量、熏蒸、卫生、重量、检验和出口许可证有关的检验证都是官方文件。确保及时通关所需的文件因国家、买家和交易货物而异。因此，贸易商应熟悉各自国家的进出口法规。

1. Inspection Certificates 检验证书

The Inspection Certificate, also known as the Commodity Inspection Certificate, is a written document issued and signed by a government or notary institution after inspecting, quarantining, or identifying imported and exported goods based on different inspection results or identification items, proving that the goods meet specific standards in terms of quality, quantity, weight, or hygiene.

商品检验检疫证书，简称商检证书，是由政府或公证机构对进出口商品进行检验检疫或鉴定后，根据不同的检验结果或鉴定项目出具并签署的，证明货物在品质、数量、重量或卫生等方面符合特定标准的书面凭证。

Internationally, import and export commodity inspections are executed by a third party generally known as surveyor. Some of the surveyors are governmental organization, others are run by individuals or trade associations.

在国际上，进出口商品的检验检疫由第三方负责，第三方为检验方，例如政府组织、个人或行业贸易协会。

In our country, the China Exit and Entry Inspection and Quarantine Bureau (CIQ) are the main institution authorized to examine the quality, quantity, packing etc. The purpose of the inspection is to ensure that the goods are in accordance with the relative laws and decrees of the country. The most commonly used inspection certificates in international trade are as follows:

在我国，中国进出口检验检疫局是进行商品质量、数量和包装等检验的主要机构。其检验是为了证明货物符合本国相关的法律法规。在我国，最常用的检验证书如下：

- Inspection Certificate of Quality(质量检验证)
- Inspection Certificate of Weight(重量检验证)
- Inspection Certificate of Quantity(数量检验证)
- Inspection Certificate of Sanitary/Health(卫生/健康检验证书)
- Inspection Certificate of Veterinary(兽医检验证)
- Inspection Certificate of Phytosanitary(植物检疫证)
- Inspection Certificate of Disinfection(消毒检验证书)

It is those inspection certificates issued by the authorities show that the seller has met the requirements specified in the trade contract, as well help buyer or his issuing bank decide to effect payment or not. Accordingly, under a letter of credit, it is vital to specify types and issuing authorities of certain inspection certificates, so as to reduce the risks relating to each party and cut down the transaction cost as well.

权威机构出具检验证书，表明卖方已符合贸易合同中的要求，同时帮助买方或开证银行决定支付与否。因此，在信用证下，注明检验证书的类型和权威发布部门对降低相关方责任风险和节约交易成本等都是很重要的。

2. Key Elements of Inspection Certificate 检验证书的关键要素

In documentary credit transactions an inspection certificate should include the following elements: 在跟单信用证交易中，检验证书应包括以下要素：

- Key details(typically consignor, consignee and description of goods) regarding the shipment. Also, such details to be in conformity with other documents (e. g. documentary credit, commercial invoice)关于装运的关键细节(通常是发货人、收货人和货物描述)。此外，此类细节内容必须与其他单据(如跟单信用证、商业发票)保持一致
- Date and place of the inspection 检查日期和地点

- Statement of sampling methodology 抽样方法说明
- Statement of the results of the inspection 检查结果说明
- The name, signature and/or stamp or seal of the inspecting entity 检查机构的名称、签名和/或印章

Notes 注意

In the case of certain countries and certain commodities the inspection certificate must be issued by an appropriate government entity. Buyers should avoid the use of such terms as "first class," "well-know," "qualified," "independent," "official," "competent" or "local" when referring to an acceptable inspection authority. It is preferable to agree beforehand as to a specific inspection organization or entity and for the buyer to name the required certifying organization or entity in the documentary credit.

在某些国家和针对某些商品，检验证必须由适当的政府机构颁发。当提交到可接受检验的机构时，买方应避免使用"一流""熟知""合格""独立""官方""主管"或"当地"等术语。最好事先就具体的检验机构或实体机构达成一致，并由买方在跟单信用证中指定所需的检验证明机构或实体机构。

【知识链接】检验检疫常用术语

(1)进出口商品检验(IMPORT AND EXPORT COMMODITY INSPECTION)

(2)进口商品认证管理(IMPORT COMMODITY CERTIFICATION MANAGEMENT)

(3)进口废物原料装运前检验(IMPORT WASTE RAW MATERIALS PRE-SHIPMENT INSPECTION)

(4)出口商品质量许可(EXPORT COMMODITY QUALITY PERMIT)

(5)食品卫生监督检验(FOOD HYGIENE SUPERVISION AND INSPECTION)

(6)动植物检疫(ANIMAL AND PLANT QUARANTINE)

(7)出口商品运输包装检验(INSPECTION OF TRANSPORT PACKAGING OF EXPORT COMMODITIES)

(8)外商投资财产鉴定(PROPERTY APPRAISAL WITH FOREIGN INVESTMENT)

(9)货物装载和残损鉴定(CARGO LOADING AND DAMAGE IDENTIFICATION)

(10)卫生检疫与处理(HEALTH QUARANTINE EPIDEMIC AND TREATMENT)

(11)涉外检验检疫、鉴定、认证机构审核认可和监督(EXAMINATION, APPROVAL AND SUPERVISION BY FOREIGN-RELATED INSPECTION AND QUARANTINE, APPRAISAL AND CERTIFICATION BODIES)

(12)与国外和国际组织开展合作(COOPERATION WITH FOREIGN AND INTERNATIONAL ORGANIZATIONS)

Section Two　Inspection Certificate of Quality 品质检验证书

Inspection Certificate of Quality is the basic for seller to deliver the goods and the buyer to receive the goods, which is issued by the General Administration of Quality Supervision, Inspection and Quarantine of the People's Republic of China or its local office all over the country, proved that the quality and inspection of exported goods has meet the requirement of the contract stipulation.

品质证明书是买方收发货物的基础。此证由国家市场监督管理总局、中华人民共和国检验检疫局，或它们的地方办事处出具。其可以用来证明出口货物的质量和检验已符合合同规定的要求。

1. Specimen 品质检验证的样单

中华人民共和国出入境检验检疫
ENTRY-EXIT INSPECTION AND QUARANTINE
OF THE PEOPLE'S REPUBLIC OF CHINA 共 1 页 第 1 页 page1 of 1

编号 NO. (1)

CERTIFICATE OF QUALITY (2)

Consignor(3)

Consignee(4)

Description of Goods(5)

Quantity/Weight Declared(7)

Number and Type of Packages(8)

Means of conveyance(9)

Mark & No. (6)

This is to certify that we, did, at the request of consignor, attend at the warehouse of commodity on _____ the representative sample was drawn at random for inspection according to the stipulations of the L/C, the results were as follows: (10)

Moisture:

Max, damaged:

Max, stained:

Conclusion: the quality of the above commodity conforms with the stipulations of the stipulations of the

****

Place of Issue(11)　　　　　　　　　　　　　　　　Date of Issue(12)

Official Stamp(13)

Authorized Officer(14)　　　　　　　　　　　　　　Signature(15)

All inspections are carried out conscientiously to the best of our knowledge and ability. This certificate does not in any respect absolve the seller and other related parties from his contractual and legal obligations especially when product quality is concerned.

---

2. Contents of Certificate of Quality 样单拆解：品质检验证的主要内容及缮制方法

(1)No.: The number is issued by Inspection and Quarantine Bureau.
由检验检疫局编定的号码。

(2)Name of the Certificate.
证书名称：检验检疫局所签发的商检证书的名称。

(3)Consignor: The Consignor's name and address. Usually it is the seller's name and address.
发货人的名称和地址：通常也是信用证的受益人的名称和地址。

(4) Consignee：The Consignee's name and address. Usually it is the buyer's name and address.

收货人的名称和地址：合同的买方或信用证的开证申请人的名称和地址。

(5) Description of Goods：The goods must coincide with that in the Letter of Credit.

品名：填写所列的品名，必须与信用证及其单据的一致。

(6) Mark & No.：The mark & No. must be in conformity with the bill of lading and the Letter of Credit.

标记及号码：填写实际货物外包装上的运输标记，必须与提单和信用证规定的一致。

(7) Quantity/Weight Declared：The quantity/Weight must coincide with that in L/C and the other documents.

报验数量/重量：填写发票所列的数量/重量必须与信用证及其单据一致。

(8) Number and Type of Packages.

包装种类及数量。

(9) Means of Conveyance：The name and the number of conveyance.

运输工具：填写运输货物的运输工具的名称及其航次。

(10) Result of Inspection：Here mainly prove the results of the examinations of the goods, usually the test results consistent with the provision of L/C.

检验结果：本栏目主要证明本批货物经检验后的实际品质的结果，一般情况下检验结果与信用证规定保持一致。

(11) Place of Issue：General it is the place of the Exit and Entry Inspection and Quarantine Bureau where issues the certificate.

签证地点：一般填写签发检验证书的检验检疫机构所在地。

(12) Date of Issue：General the date of issue is later than the date of inspection, so the date of issue is no later than the date of shipment.

签证日期：一般情况下签证日期比检验日期晚，所以本栏日期不得晚于运输单上的装运日期。

(13) Official Stamp.

检验检疫局的盖章。

(14) Authorized Officer.

授权签字人。

(15) Signature.

签名。

3. Case Study 案例实训

APPLICANT：YANMAR AGRICULTURAL CO. LTD. 1-33, CHAYAMCHI, KITA-KU, OSAKA 530, JAPAN.

BENEFICIAL：XINHUA TRADING COMPANY LIMITED

L/C NO. 1202N22078

S/C NO. ST0322

：45/DESCRIPTION OF GOODS/SERVICES：

CHINESE RED KIDNEY BEANS 2022 CROP.

ADMIXTURE：1PCT. MAX

MOISTURE：16PCT. MAX

INPERFECT GRAINS, OTHER COLOUR BEANS AND WATER STAIN BEANS：5PCT. MAX

FOB DALIAN

THE LATEST SHIPMENT DATE：NOVEMBER 10, 2022,

EXPIRY DATE：NOVEMBER 25, 2022.

PACKING：ABOUT 50KG GUNNY BAGS EACH GROSS FOR NET

：46/DOCUMENTS REQUIRED

+ CIQ CERTIFICATE OF QUALITY ALLOWED BEFORE SHIPMENT IN ONE ORIGINAL PLUS TWO COPIES.

卖方于 11 月 10 日装船完毕，取得提单。货物明细如下：

重量：180.600MT, 2 700 GUNNY BAGS, 以毛作净。货装 S. S SUNNY V. 146 E 轮，集装箱号码为：HDMU2345209/2346589/2355621/2488613/2628006。

唛头：无

中华人民共和国出入境检验检疫

ENTRY-EXIT INSPECTION AND QUARANTINE OF THE PEOPLE'S REPUBLIC OF CHINA

共 1 页 第 1 页 Page of 1

编号 No.：××××××

CERTIFICATE OF QUALITY

发货人

Consignor　XINHUA TRADING COMPANY LIMITED

收货人

Consignee：YANMAR AGRICULTURAL CO. LTD. 1-33,

Chayamchi, Kita-ku, OSAKA 530, JAPAN

标记及号码 Mark & No. N/M

品名

Description of Goods　CHINESE RED KIDNEY BEANS 2022 CROP

报检数量/重量

Quantity/Weight declared　180.600MT

包装种类及数量

Number and Type of Packages　2, 700 GUNNY BAGS

运输工具

Means of conveyance　SUNNY V. 146 E

This is to certify that we, did, at the request of consignor, attend at the warehouse of commodity on 7 Nov, 2022. The representative sample was drawn at random for inspection according to the stipulation of the L/C, the result were as follows：

Moisture 16. PCT. MAX

Admixture 1PCT. MAX

INPERFECT GRAINS, OTHER COLOUR BEANS AND WATER STAIN BEANS：5PCT. MAX

Conclusion：The quality of the above commodity conforms with the stipulations of the L/C No. 1202N22078

****

续表

印章	签证地点 Place of Issue __DALIAN CHINA__

签证日期 Date of Issue __8 Nov., 2022__

Official Stamp

授权签字人 Authorized Officer ___Zhang hong___　　　签字 Signature ___Li ming___

我们已尽所知和最大能力实施上述检验，不能因为我们签发本证而免除卖方或其他方根据合同和法律所承担的产品质量和其他责任。All inspection is carried out conscientiously to the best of our knowledge and ability. This certificate does not in any respect absolve the seller and other related parties from his contractual and legal obligations when product quality is concerned.

Section Three　Inspection Certificate of Weight 重量检验证书

Certificate of Weight/Weight Certificate：This certificate proves the weight of delivery of goods should be compliance with the weight in invoice/ bill of lading/indicated on the certificate of insurance. Delivery of cargoes in bulk is usually accompanying with this certificate.

重量证明书：此证明书证明付运的货品与提单/发票/保险证明书上注明的重量一致。付运散装货物时通常要随附此证明书。

Specimen 样单

中华人民共和国出入境检验检疫
ENTRY–EXIT INSPECTION AND QUARANTINE OF THE PEOPLE'S REPUBLIC OF CHINA

共 1 页 第 1 页 Page of 1

编号 No.：

WEIGHT CERTIFICATE

发货人
Consignor

收货人
Consignee

品名
Description of Goods

报检数量/重量　　　　　　　　　　　　　　　　　　　　　　　　　标记及号码
Quantity/Weight Declared　　　　　　　　　　　　　　　　　　　　Mark & No.

包装种类及数量
Number and Type of Packages

运输工具
Means of Conveyance

Results of Weight：

****

印章　　　　签证地点 Place of Issue　　　　　签证日期 Date of Issue

续表

Official Stamp

授权签字人 Authorized Officer　　　　　　　　签字 Signature

我们已尽所知和最大能力实施上述检验，不能因为我们签发本证而免除卖方或其他方根据合同和法律所承担的产品质量和其他责任。All inspection is carried out conscientiously to the best of our knowledge and ability . This certificate does not in any respect absolve the seller and other related parties from his contractual and legal obligations when product quality is concerned.

Section Four　Phytosanitary Certificate 植物检疫证书

Phytosantiary Certificate：Plants and plant products that should be quarantined include：Forest seeds, seedlings, and other reproductive materials；Trees, shrubs, bamboo, flowers, and other forest plants；Wood, bamboo, medicinal herbs, fruits, bonsai, and other forest products. This certificate proves that the consignment of food such as fruit, vegetables and horticultural products has been examined, confirm that no part of pest or plant disease. This certificate issued by the Agriculture and Fisheries Department.

植物检疫证书：应施检疫的植物、植物产品包括林木种子、苗木和其他繁殖材料；乔木、灌木、竹类、花卉和其他森林植物；木材、竹材、药材、果品、盆景和其他林产品。此证明书证明托运的水果、蔬菜和园艺产品等食品已经检验，确实证明没有沾染害虫或植物疾病。此证书由渔农处签发。

Specimen 植物检疫证书样单

中华人民共和国出入境检验检疫

ENTRY-EXIT INSPECTION AND QUARANTINE

OF THE PEOPLE'S REPUBLIC OF CHINA

植物检疫证书　　　　　　　　编号_____

PHYTOSANITARY CERTIFICATE

发货人名称及地址

Name and address of consignor _____

收货人名称及地址

Name and address of consignor _____

品名　　　　　　　　　　　植物学名

Name of Produce _____　Botanical Name of Plants _____

报检数量

Quantity Declared _____

包装的种类

Number and Type of Packages _____

产地

Place of Origin _____

到达口岸

Port of Destination _____

标记及号码

Mark & No.

运输工具	检验日期
Means of Conveyance ＿＿＿＿＿＿＿＿	Date of Inspection ＿＿＿＿＿＿＿＿

兹证明＿＿＿＿或其他检疫已经按照规定程序进行检查和/或检验，被认为不带有输入国或地区的检疫性有害生物，并且基本不带有其他的有害生物，因而符合输入国或地区现行的植物检疫要求。

This is to certify that the plants, plant products or other regulated article described above have been inspected and/or tested according to appropriate procedures and are considered to be free from quarantine pests specified by the importing country /region, and practically free from other injurious pests; and that they are considered to conform with the current phytosanitary requirements of the importing country/region.

杀虫和/或灭菌处理 DISINFESTATION AND/OR DISINFECTION TREATMENT

日期	药剂及浓度
Date ×××××××	Chemical and Concentration ××××××××
处理方法	持续时间及温度
Treatment ×××××××	Duration and Temperature ×××××××××

印章	签证地点 Place of Issue ＿＿＿＿＿＿	签证日期 Date of Issue ＿＿＿＿＿＿
Official Stamp	授权签字人 Authorized Officer ＿＿＿＿	签名 Signature ＿＿＿＿

中华人民共和国出入境检验检疫机关及其官员或代表不承担签发本证的任何财经责任。No financial liability with respect to this certificate shall attach to the entry-exit inspection and quarantine authorities of the P. R. China or to any of its officers or representatives.

Section Five　Fumigation/ Disinfection Certificate 熏蒸/消毒证书

Fumigation/Disinfection Certification：It is a certificate which proves that the export products (such as products of animals and plants, the timber for package and the plant filler, etc.) have been sterilized or disinfected by fumigation. It specifies the medicine used and the time of fumigating and sterilizing, etc. so that the products are qualified for exports.

熏蒸/消毒证书是证明出口动植物产品（如动植物产品、包装用木材、植物填料等）经过熏蒸灭菌或消毒的证明，经过消毒处理或经过熏蒸灭虫、保证卫生安全的证件。主要用于说明使用的药物、熏蒸消毒的时间等，以使产品品质达到出口条件，方便出口。

1. Specimen 熏蒸/消毒证书样单

中华人民共和国出入境检验检疫

ENTRY-EXIT INSPECTION AND QUARANTINE

OF THE PEOPLE'S REPUBLIC OF CHINA

熏蒸/消毒证书　　　　编号 No.

FUMIGATION/DISINFECTION CERTIFICATE

发货人名称和地址

Name and Address of Consignor ＿＿＿＿＿＿＿＿＿＿＿＿＿＿＿＿＿＿＿＿＿＿

收货人名称及地址
Name and Address of Consignee _____

品名   产地
Description of Good _____   Place of Origin _____

报检数量
Quantity Declared _____   标记及号码
起运地   Mark & No.
Quantity Despatch _____   N/M
到达口岸
Port of Destination _____
运输工具
Means of Conveyance _____

熏蒸/消毒处理
FUMIGATION/DISINFECTION TREATMENT

日期   处理时间及温度
Date   Duration &Temperature
处理方法   药剂及浓度
Treatment   Chemical & Concentration

附加声明
ADDITIONAL DECLARATION

印章   签证地点 Place of Issue _____   签证日期 Date of Issue _____
Official Stamp 授权签字人 Authorized Officer _____   签名_____

中华人民共和国出入境检验检疫机关及其官员或代表不承担签发本证书的任何财经责任。No financial liability with respect to this certificate shall attach to the entry-exit inspection and quarantine authorities of the P. R. China or to any of its officers or representatives.

2. The Contents of Fumigation/Disinfection Certificate 样单拆解：熏蒸/消毒证书的主要内容及缮制要点

（1）No.：The number is issued by Inspection and Quarantine Bureau.
编号：由检验检疫局编定的号码。
（2）Name and Address of Consignor.
实际发货人的名称及地址。
（3）Name and address of Consignee：Usually it is the buyer's name and address.
实际收货人的名称和地址：合同买方的名称和地址。
（4）Name of Produce：The name of goods must coincide with that in the Letter of Credit.
产品名称：货物名称必须与信用证上的名称一致。填写发票所列的品名，必须与信用证及其单据一致。

（5）Place of Origin.

产地。

（6）Quantity Declared：The quantity must coincide with that in L/C and the other documents.

货物的原产地：填写发票所列的数量，必须与信用证及其单据一致。

（7）Place of Despatch：The port of despatch, and also the port of shipment stipulated in the shipping documents.

货物起运地：也是运输单据上的起运地。

（8）Port of Destination：The port of destination should be the port of destination which consistent with that stipulated in Letter of Credit.

货物到达口岸：也就是运输单据上的目的地，必须与信用证规定一致。

（9）Means of Conveyance.：The name and the number of conveyance.

运输工具：填写运输货物的运输工具的名称及其航次。

（10）Mark & No.：The mark & No. must be in conformity with the bill of lading and the Letter of Credit.

标记及记号：填写实际货物外包装上的运输标记，必须与提单和信用证规定的一致。

（11）Duration & Temperature：It is the main content of the certificate, fill in the duration, temperature of fumigation and disinfection time.

持续时间和温度：这是证书的主要内容，填写熏蒸的持续时间、温度和消毒时间等。

（12）Treatment.

处理方法。

（13）Chemical & Concentration.

药剂及浓度。

（14）Official Stamp.

印章。

（15）Place of Issue.

签证地点。

（16）Date of Issue.

签证日期。

（17）Authorized Officer.

授权签字人。

3. Case Study 案例实训

APPLICANT：OVERSEAS. CO., LTD. 1-33 BUILDING SWEET ROAD, VANCOUVER, CANADA.

BENEFICIAL：XINHUA TRADING COMPANY LIMITED 676 LIAOHE EAST ROAD, DALIAN, CHINA

L/C NO. 334499SE12

S/C NO. ST5768

DESCRIPTION OF GOODS/SERVICES：CHINESE RED KIDNEY BEANS 2022 CROP SOUND AND MERCHANTABLE QUALITY

MOISTURE：16PCT. MAX, FOREIGN MATTER：1PCT, MAX, DAMAGED：3PCT.

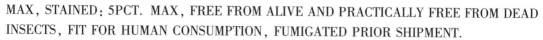

MAX, STAINED: 5PCT. MAX, FREE FROM ALIVE AND PRACTICALLY FREE FROM DEAD INSECTS, FIT FOR HUMAN CONSUMPTION, FUMIGATED PRIOR SHIPMENT.

FOB DALIAN

PACKING: ABOUT 50KG GUNNY BAGS EACH GROSS FOR NET

THE LATEST SHIPMENT: OCTOBER 30TH, 2022,

EXPIRY DATE: NOVEMBER 15TH, 2022

DOCUMENTS REQUIRED

+ CIQ CERTIFICATE OF QUALITY ALLOWED BEFORE SHIPMENT IN ONE ORIGINAL PLUS

+ CIQ CERTIFICATE OF WEIGHT ALLOWED BEFORE SHIPMENT IN ONE ORIGINAL PLUS TWO COPIES.

+ PHYTOSANITARY CERTIFICATE ISSUED BY COMPETENT AUTHORITY IN ONE ORIGINAL PLUS TWO COPIES.

+ FUMIGATION CERTIFICATE ISSUED BY ANY COMPETENT AUTHORITY IN ONE ORIGINAL PLUS TWO COPIES.

买方于10月30日装船完毕，取得提单。货物明细如下：

重量：134. 220MT, 2 700 GUNNY BAGS，以毛作净。

船名：VICTORIA 航次：V. 008A 装运港：大连

集装箱号为：

FSCU3524968/FSCU3524973/FSCU3525060/FSCU3525080/FSCU3525157/FSCU3525183。

唛头：无。

中华人民共和国出入境检验检疫

ENTRY-EXIT INSPECTION AND QUARANTINE

OF THE PEOPLE'S REPUBLIC OF CHINA

熏蒸/消毒证书　　　　　　编号 No.

FUMIGATION/DISINFECTION CERTIFICATE

发货人名称和地址

Name and Address of Consignor: XINHUA TRADING CO., LTD. 676 LIAOHE EAST ROAD, DALIAN, CHINA

收货人名称及地址

Name and Address of Consignee: OVERSEAS. CO., LTD. 1-33 BUILDING SWEET ROAD, VANCOUVER, CANADA

品名　　　　　　　　　　　　　　　　　　　　　　产地
Description of good: CHINESE RED KIDNEY BEANS 2022 CROP　　Place of Origin CHINA

报检数量　　　　2,700-GUNNY, BAGS

Quantity Declared　　134. 220 M/T　　　　　　　　　标记及号码
　　　　　　　　　　　　　　　　　　　　　　　　　Mark & No.

起运地　　　　　　　　　　　　　　　　　　　　　N/M

Quantity Despatch　　DALIAN CHINA

到达口岸

Port of Destination　　VANCOUVER, CANADA

运输工具

Means of Conveyance　　VICTORIA V. 008A

熏蒸/消毒处理

FUMIGATION/DISINFECTION TREATMENT

日期　　　　　　　　　　　　　　　　　处理时间及温度

Date 25 Oct. 2022　　　　　　　　　　Duration &Temperature 168hrs　　　10℃

处理方法　　　　　　　　　　　　　　　药剂及浓度

Treatment FUMIGATION Chemical & Concentration PHOSPHINE 1. 5g/CUBIC METER

附加声明　　　　　　　　　　　　********************

ADDITIONAL DECLARATION

* CHINESE RED KIDNEY BEANS 2022 CROP

FSCU3524968/3524973/3525060/3525080/3525157/3525183

印章签证地点 Place of Issue <u>DALIAN CHINA</u>　　　　签证日期 Date of Issue <u>26 Oct., 2022</u>

Official Stamp 授权签字人 Authorized Officer <u>Dong Chunhua</u> 签名 Signature

中华人民共和国出入境检验检疫机关及其官员或代表不承担签发本证书的任何财经责任。

No financial liability with respect to this certificate shall attach to the entry—exit inspection and quarantine authorities of the P. R. China or to any of its officers or representatives.

Exercises 练习

一、Useful Words and Expressions 常用词语和表达

1. certificate of weight 重量证明书

2. certificate of inspection certifying quality & quantity in triplicate issued by C. I. B. C. 由中国商品检验局出具的品质和数量检验证明书一式三份

3. phytosanitary certificate 植物检疫证明书

4. plant quarantine certificate 植物检疫证明书

5. fumigation certificate 熏蒸证明书

6. certificate stating that the goods are free from live weevil 无活虫证明书(熏蒸除虫证明书)

7. sanitary certificate 卫生证书

8. health certificate 卫生(健康)证书

9. analysis certificate 分析(化验)证书

10. tank inspection certificate 油仓检验证明书

11. record of ullage and oil temperature 空距及油温记录单

12. certificate of aflatoxin negative 黄曲霉素检验证书

13. non-aflatoxin certificate 无黄曲霉素证明书

14. inspection and testing certificate issued by C. I. B. C. 中国商品检验局签发的检验证

明书

15. The exporters have the right to inspect the export goods before delivery to the shipping line. 出口商在向船运公司托运前有权检验商品。

16. Who issues the inspection certificate in case the quality do not confirm to the contract? 如果货物的质量与合同不符，由谁出具检验证明书呢？

17. The certificate will be issued by china import and export commodity inspection bureau or by any of its branches. 检验证明书将由中国进出口商品检验局或其分机构出具。

18. Our inspection bureau will issue a veterinary inspection certificate to show that the shipment is in conformity with export standards. 商检局将出具动物检疫证明书以证明货物符合出口标准。

19. We have the best surveyor, china import and export commodity inspection bureau. 我们有最好的检验检疫师，即中国进出口商品检验局。

20. Our goods must be up to export standards before the inspection bureau releases them. 货物只有达到符合出口标准后，商检局才予以放行。

二、Make out a Certificate Of Quality /Phytosanitary/Fumigation/Disinfection according to the following L/C

根据以下信用证内容缮制质量/植物检疫/熏蒸/消毒证书

APPLICANT：INDIA NEW DELHI JINXIN DEVELOPMENT CO., LTD. 5303 SHASHA STREET DELHI

BENEFICIAL：XING LONG IMPORT AND EXPORT COOPERATION 676 LIAOHE EAST ROAD. DALIAN, CHINA

L/C NO. 121201N10028

S/C NO. WQ(DTR)0311

DESCRIPTION OF GOODS /SERVICES：

CHINESE RED KIDNEY BEANS 2022 CROP. (INNER MONGOLIA ORIGIN)

ADMIXTURE：1PCT. MAX

MOISTURE：16PCT. MAX

IMPERFECT GRAINS, OTHER COLOUR BEANS AND WATER STAIN BEANS：5PCT. MAX

FOB DALIAN

PACKING：ABOUT 50KG GUNNY BAGS EACH GROSS FOR NET

THE LATEST SHIPMENT：OCTOBER 30TH, 2022,

EXPIRY DATE：NOVEMBER 15TH, 2022

DOCUMENTS REQUIRED

+CIQ CERTIFICATE OF WEIGHT ALLOWED BEFORE SHIPMENT IN ONE ORIGINAL PLUS TWO COPIES.

卖方于 11 月 10 日装船完毕，取得提单。货物明细如下：

重量：108. 575MT, 2 150 GUNNY BAGS, 以毛作净。货装 S. S. VICTORY V. 146E 轮，集装箱号为：

HDMU2132707/2147245/2166420/2288198/2320978。唛头：无。

Xinhua Trading Co. Ltd., （676 Liaohe East Road, Dalian, China）与加拿大 Overseas Co. Ltd. 签订一份出口 CHINESE RED BEANS 的合同，合同号：ST5768。开证行开来信用证，号码是：334499SE12。信用证的最晚装运日期是 2021 年 10 月 30 日，有效期至 2021 年 11 月 15 日。有关的信用证条款如下：

: 45/DESCRIPTION OF GOODS: CHINESE RED KINDY BEANS 2021CROP SOUND AND MERCHANTABLE QUANLITY, MOISTURE: 16PCT. MAX, MATTER: 1PCT. MAX. DAMAGED: 3PCT. MAX. STAINED: 5PCT. MAX. FREE FROM ALIVE AND PRACTICALY FREE DEAD INSECTS, FIT FOR HUMAN CONSUMPTION, FUMIGATED PRIOR TO SHIPMENT. FOB DALIAN

PACKING: ABOUT 50KG GUNNY BAGS EACH GROSS FOR NET

: 46/DOCUMENTS REQUIRED

+CERTIFICATE OF ORIGIN ISSUED BY COMPETENT AUTHORITY IN ONE ORIGINAL PLUS TWO COPIES.

卖方于 10 月 30 日装船完毕，取得提单。货物明细如下：

重量：134. 220 MT, 2 700 GUNNY BAGS, 以毛做净。

船名：VICTORIA 航次：V. 008A 目的港：温哥华

集装箱号为：FSCU3524968/FSCU3524973/FSCU3525062/FSCU3525080/FSCU3525157/FSCU3525183。

唛头：无

+CERTIFICATE OF ORIGIN ISSUED BY COMPETENT AUTHORITY IN ONE ORIGINAL PLUS TWO COPIES.

中华人民共和国出入境检验检疫
ENTRY-EXIT INSPECTION AND QUARANTINE OF THE PEOPLE'S REPUBLIC OF CHINA

共 1 页 第 1 页 Page of 1

编号 No.: ×××××××

CERTIFICATE OF QUALITY

发货人
Consignor _____

收货人
Consignee _____

品名
Description of Goods _____

报检数量/重量
Quantity/Weight Declared _____

包装种类及数量
Number and Type of Packages _____

运输工具
Means of conveyance _____

标记及号码
Mark & No.
N/M

This is to certify that we, did, at the request of consignor, attend at the warehouse of commodity on _____
_____. The representative sample was drawn at random for inspection according to the stipulation of the
L/C, the result were as follows:

Moisture _____

Max, foreign matter _____

Max, damaged _____

Max, stained _____

Conclusion: The quality of the above commodity conforms with the stipulations of the L/C No. _____

＊＊＊＊＊＊＊＊＊＊＊＊＊＊＊＊＊＊

印章　　　　　　　　　　　　　　　　　　签证地点 Place of Issue _____

签证日期 Date of Issue _____

Official Stamp

授权签字人 Authorized Officer _____　　　签字 Signature _____

我们已尽所知和最大能力实施上述检验，不能因为我们签发本证而免除卖方或其他方根据合同和法律
所承担的产品质量和其他责任。All inspection is carried out conscientiously to the best of our knowledge and
ability. This certificate does not in any respect absolve the seller and other related parties from his contractual
and legal obligations when product quality is concerned.

中华人民共和国出入境检验检疫

ENTRY-EXIT INSPECTION AND QUARANTINE
OF THE PEOPLE'S REPUBLIC OF CHINA

植物检疫证书　　　　　　编号 ×××××××××

PHYTOSANITARY CERTIFICATE

发货人名称及地址

Name and address of consignor

收货人名称及地址

Name and address of consignee

品名　　　　　　　　　　　　　　植物学名

Name of product　　　　　　　　Botanical Name of Plants ××××××

报检数量

Quantity Declared

包装的种类　　　　　　　　　　　　　　　　　　标记及号码

Number and Type of Packages　　　　　　　　　Mark & No.

产地

Place of Origin

到达口岸

Port of Destination

运输工具

Means of Conveyance　　　　检验日期　　　　　　Date of Inspection

　　兹证明上述植物、植物产品或其他检疫已经按照规定程序进行检查和/或检验，被认为不带有输入国或地区的检疫性有害生物，并且基本不带有其他的有害生物，因而符合输入国或地区现行的植物检疫要求。

　　This is to certify that the plants, plant products or other regulated article described above have been inspected and/or tested according to appropriate procedures and are considered to be free from quarantine pests specified by the importing country /region, and practically free from other injurious pests; and that they are considered to conform with the current phytosanitary requirements of the importing country/region.

杀虫和/或灭菌处理 DISINFESTATION AND/OR DISINFECTION TREATMENT

日期 Date ×××××××	药剂及浓度 Chemical and Concentration ×××××××××
处理方法 Treatment ××××××××	持续时间及温度 Duration and Temperature ×××××××××

印章　　　　签证地点 Place of Issue ＿＿＿＿＿＿　　　签证日期 Date of Issue ＿＿＿＿＿＿＿＿

Official Stamp

　　　　授权签字人 Authorized Officer ××× 签名 Signature ×××

中华人民共和国出入境检验检疫机关及其官员或代表不承担签发本证的任何财经责任。

No financial liability with respect to this certificate shall attach to the entry-exit inspection and quarantine authorities of the P. R. China or to any of its officers or representatives.

中华人民共和国出入境检验检疫

ENTRY-EXIT INSPECTION AND QUARANTINE
OF THE PEOPLE'S REPUBLIC OF CHINA

熏蒸/消毒证书　　　　　　编号 No.

FUMIGATION/DISINFECTION CERTIFICATE

发货人名称和地址
Name and Address of Consignor

收货人名称及地址
Name and Address of Consignee

品名　　　　　　　　　　　　　　　　　　　产地
Description of good　　　　　　　　　　　　Place of Origin：＿＿＿＿＿＿
报检数量
Quantity Declared ＿＿＿＿＿＿＿＿＿＿＿＿＿＿＿
起运地　　　　　　　　　　　　　　　　　　标记及号码
Quantity Despatch ＿＿＿＿＿＿＿＿＿＿＿＿＿＿＿　Mark & No.
到达口岸

续表

Port of Destination _____

运输工具

Means of Conveyance _____

熏蒸/消毒处理

FUMIGATION/DISINFECTION TREATMENT

日期   处理时间及温度

                                                                                  Duration &Temperature 168hrs

处理方法   药剂及浓度

Treatment _____ Chemical & Concentration _____.

附加声明   *******************

ADDITIONAL DECLARATION

   *

印章   签证地点 Place of Issue _____   签证日期 Date of Issue _____

Official Stamp

                授权签字人 Authorized Officer _____   签名 _____

中华人民共和国出入境检验检疫机关及其官员或代表不承担签发本证书的任何财经责任。

No financial liability with respect to this certificate shall attach to the entry-exit inspection and quarantine authorities of the P. R. China or to any of its officers or representatives.

Chapter 8 | Bill of Exchange 汇票

 Key Points and Difficulties

- To Know Functions of Financial Documents
- To Understand the Contents of Bill of Exchange, Promissory Note
- To Make out Bill of Exchange, Promissory Note

Learning Objectives

- The Contents of Bill of Exchange, Promissory Note
- Making out Bill of Exchange, Promissory Note

Section One   Understanding Bill of Exchange 认识汇票

A bill of exchange is an unconditional order of writing prepared by one party(drawer) and addressed to another(drawee), signed by the person giving it, requiring the person to whom it is addressed to pay on demand or at a fixed or determinable future time a sum certain in money to the order or specified person or to bearer.

汇票是一种由债权人开给债务人的要求即期或者定期或可以确定的将来时间，不以任何条件为前提，对某人或某指定人或持有人支付一定金额的书面支付命令。

1. The Parties to a Bill of Exchange 汇票的相关当事人

It will be seen that there are three basic parties to a bill of exchange：汇票通常有三个基本当事方：

The drawer. The person who draws the bill and he is usually the exporter or his banker in international trade.

出票人。通常是国际贸易中的出口方或出口方的银行。

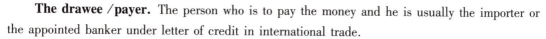
The drawee /payer. The person who is to pay the money and he is usually the importer or the appointed banker under letter of credit in international trade.

付款人。通常是国际贸易中信用证项下的进口方或指定的银行方。

The payee. The person who is to receive the money, he may be, and often is, the same person as the drawer and he is usually the exporter himself or his appointed banker in international trade or he may be the bearer of the bill.

收款人。收款人可能是，而且通常是，与出票人相同的人，通常是出口方本人或出口方指定的在国际贸易中的银行方，或者可能是汇票的持票人。

Notes：注意

The bill is drawn by A on B payable to C. Here, the Drawer is A, the Drawee is B, and the Payee is C. 该汇票由 A 对 B 开出，付款给 C. 在这种情况下，出票人是 A，付款人是 B，收款人是 C.

If A and C are the same person, it may be read：the bill is drawn by us on you payable to ourselves. 如果 A 和 C 是同一个人，可以认为：汇票由自己开出，支付给自己。

If A and B are the same person, it may be read：the bill is drawn by us on ourselves payable to you. 如果 A 和 B 是同一个人，可以认为：汇票由我们自己开出，支付给你。

Moreover, there are five derivative parties to a bill of exchange.

此外，汇票还有五个衍生交易方。

The endorser(背书人). A payee or a holder who signs his name on the back of a bill of the purpose of negotiation.

背书人。在有谈判目的的汇票背面签名的收款人或持票人。

The endorsee(被背书人). The party to whom the instrument is transferred.

被背书人。该汇票被转让给的一方。

The guarantor(保证人). The person who guarantees the payment or acceptance of an instrument.

保证人。保证支付或接受票据的一方。

The acceptor(承兑人). The drawee that has accepted a usance bill.

承兑人。已接受远期汇票承兑的付款人。

The holder(持有人). The person who possesses an instrument.

持有人。持有票据的一方。

2. Key Elements of a Bill of Exchange 汇票中的关键因素

To be a valid negotiable instrument, a bill of exchange or draft has to be drawn properly. According to the Bill of Exchange Act 1882, a bill of exchange or draft must conform to the following requirements：要成为一份有效的可转让的票据，汇票必须正确开具。根据 1882 年的《汇票法》，汇票必须符合以下要求：

● It must contain the wording like Draft or even Bill of Exchange.

必须标明"Draft"或"Bill of Exchange"字样。

● It must write unambiguously the name and address of the drawee.

必须清晰明确填写付款人的名称和地址。

- It must contain an unconditional order to pay a definite sum of money.

必须包含一个无条件命令，以支付一定的金额。

- It must be in writing and signed by the drawer.

必须为书面形式，并由出票人签名。

- It must be payable on demand or at a fixed or determinable future time.

必须按要求支付，或在固定或可确定的未来时间内支付。

- It must be payable to or to the order of a specific person or to bearer.

必须支付给特定的人或持票人，或按照特定的人的指示支付。

- It must indicate the amount to be paid in words and in figures.

必须用文字和数字标明支付金额。

In addition, there are also some other elements to be written in the draft:

此外，汇票中还应有一些其他内容：

- Number of bill of exchange: those bills have the same contents, if one of them is paid, the others will be null and void, such wording can be seen in the first copy of exchange in duplicate: "Second of the same tenor and date unpaid", and in the second copy could be "First of the same tenor and date unpaid."

汇票份数：这些汇票的内容相同，如果其中一张已付款，其他的将无效，这样的措辞在第一份一式两份的汇票中表达为"付一不付二"，在第二份中表达为"付二不付一"。

- Reason of issuing: Drafts under L/C normally indicate the reason of issuance, i. e., according to which L/C of which bank the bills of exchange are issued.

签发原因：信用证项下的汇票通常表明签发原因，即根据哪个银行的信用证签发汇票。

3. The Classification of a Bill of Exchange 汇票的种类

- **Clear or Documentary Bills of Exchange** 光票或跟单汇票

Clean Bill refers to the bill of exchange without commercial documents, above the bill except the drawer and payee without the endorsement of a third party enterprise. Among them, the bank draft is mostly a Clean Bill. Because Clean Bill signature may not be identified, it must be send to foreign collection bank to receive ticket money.

光票(Clean Bill)是指不附带商业单据的汇票，票据上面除了出票人与收款人没有第三方企业背书的票。其中，银行汇票多是光票。由于光票签章不一定能鉴定，光票必须寄送国外代收银行才可收到票款。

Documentary bill, also known as credit bills and documentary bills, are bills of exchange that can only be paid with bills of lading, warehouse receipts, insurance policies, packing lists, commercial invoice and other documents. They belong to the category of securities. Its function: firstly, it is a credit certificate related to related parties. The second is the certificate of property rights.

跟单汇票又称信用汇票、押汇汇票，是需要附带提单、仓单、保险单、装箱单、商业发票等单据，才能进行付款的汇票，属于有价证券的范畴。其作用：一是有关关系人的信用凭证。二是物权凭证。

• **Sight/Demand draft or Time/Usance/Term draft** 即期或者远期汇票

Sight/Demand draft is also called a draft payable on sight. It refers to a bill of exchange without the maturity date or clear record on the bill. Once the payee or holder requests the bill to the payer, the draft is due and the payer shall bear the liability for payment.

即期汇票也称为见票即付的汇票，是指汇票上没有到期日的记载或者明确记载见票即付，收款人或者持票人一经向付款人提示汇票、请求付款，该汇票即为到期，付款人就应当承担付款责任的汇票。

Time/Usance/Term draft is a bill paid for a certain period or on a specific date. There are several different methods of payment according to the time：（1）payment made several days after the issuance of the bill of lading（2）at … days after sight（3）at … days after date（4）payment on the specified date.

远期汇票是指在一定期限或特定日期付款的汇票。远期汇票根据时间，有几种不同的付款方式：(1)提单签发日后若干天付款(2)见票后若干天付款(3)出票后若干天付款(4)指定日期付款。

• **Trade or Bank's draft** 商业汇票或银行汇票

Trade draft or Commercial bill of exchange refers to a type of instrument issued by the payer or depositor（or acceptance applicant）, accepted by the acceptor, and paid to the payee or endorsee on the due date. 商业汇票是指由付款人或存款人(或承兑申请人)签发，由承兑人承兑，并于到期日向收款人或被背书人支付款项的一种票据。

Bank's draft is a bill of exchange issued by a local issuing bank to which the remitter deposits the payment. It is unconditionally paid to the payee or holder based on the actual settlement amount at sight. 银行汇票是汇款人将款项交存当地出票银行，由出票银行签发的，由其在见票时，按照实际结算金额无条件支付给收款人或持票人的票据。

• **With or Without recourse** 追索或无追索权汇票

Draft with recourse, refers to the holder in the bill of exchange is not paid, due not received acceptance or other legal reasons, after the preservation rights, can request remote holder or other paper debtor repay the bill amount and the related loss of bill rights, is legal for supplementary payment claim and set the second right of claim.

追索权汇票，是指持票人在汇票到期未获付款，到期前未获承兑或其他法定原因发生时，在采取保全权利行为之后，能够请求前手或其他票据债务人偿还票据金额以及相关损失的票据权利，是法律上为补充付款请求权而设定的第二次请求权。

Draft without recourse means that the issuing bank waives the right of recourse against the drawer or the paying bank, and the issuing bank cannot perform the right of recourse against the drawer or the paying bank even if the payer on the draft does not perform the duty of payment obligations. After the bank acceptance bill is rejected by the bank, it shall have the right of recourse. The recourse of the holder of a bank acceptance bill against remote holder is 6 months from the date of denial of acceptance or denial of payment; the right of recourse is extinguished after this period.

无追索权汇票是指开证行放弃对出票人或议付行的追索权利，则即使汇票上的付款人不履行付款责任时，开证行也不能向出票人或议付行行使追索权利。银行承兑汇票被银行

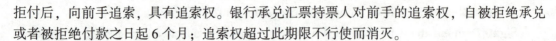

拒付后，向前手追索，具有追索权。银行承兑汇票持票人对前手的追索权，自被拒绝承兑或者被拒绝付款之日起 6 个月；追索权超过此期限不行使而消灭。

4. Legal Acts on Instruments 票据行为

Legal acts on instruments refers to the formal actions to be taken for undertaking the obligations specified in an instrument, such as issuance, endorsement, acceptance payment. Issuance is the key action among them.

票据的法律行为，是指为承担票据中规定的义务而采取的正式行为，如签发、背书、承兑付款等。出票是其中关键的票据行为。

Issue 出票

Issuing an invoice, also known as an invoice, refers to the act of creating and delivering a bill, that is, the issuer creates a bill in a legal format and delivers it to the payee. It includes two behaviors: "make" and "deliver". The so-called "making" refers to the drawer making the bill according to the legal style, recording the legal content on the bill and signing it. Due to the fact that various bills are now printed by certain authorities, the so-called "making" only involves filling in relevant content and signing. The so-called "delivery" refers to the act of handing over the bill to the payee according to the drawer's own will, and is not done out of the drawer's own will. For example, stealing a bill cannot be called "delivery", and therefore cannot be called the act of issuing the bill.

出票又称发票，是指票据创立和交付行为，即出票人依法定格式制作票据，并交付收款人的行为。它包括"做成"和"交付"两种行为。所谓"做成"就是出票人按照法定款式制作票据，在票据上记载法定内容并签名。由于现在各种票据都由一定机关印制，所以所谓"做成"只是填写有关内容和签名而已。所谓"交付"是指根据出票人本人的意愿将其交给收款人的行为，不是出于出票人本人意愿的行为如偷窃票据不能称作"交付"，因而也不能称作出票行为。

Endorsement 背书

Endorsement is also an important negotiable instrument, an act of transferring the rights of a bill for his own purpose. By endorsement, the note right passes from the endorser to the endorsee. In daily trade, an indicative draft may be endorsed and transferred multiple times. But the first endorsement assignor must be the payee, and the second hand endorsement assignor and remote holder assignee must be the same person. The completion of the endorsement includes two actions: one is to record and sign the relevant matters on the back of the bill or on the sticky bill. The second is delivery.

背书也是一项重要的票据行为，是以将汇票权利转让他人为目的的一种行为。通过背书，票据权利从背书人转让给被背书人。在日常贸易中，一张指示性抬头的汇票可以连续背书转让多次。但第一背书转让人必是收款人，而后手背书转让人和前手受让人必为同一人。背书行为的完成包括两个动作：一是在票据背面或粘单上记载有关事项并签名。二是交付。

Not all instruments can be transferred by endorsement. Instruments with restrictive title or the words "not transferable" cannot be transferred by endorsement. Instruments with title "to order of ××××" can be transferred without endorsement. The endorsement transfer can only be an indicative instrument to the order.

并不是所有票据都能背书转让，对于限制性抬头或记载有"不得转让"字样的票据是不可以背书转让的，对于"以……人为抬头"的票据，不需背书即可转让。背书转让的只能是指示性抬头的票据。

There are three types of endorsement：有三种背书：

● **Blank endorsement**：Blank endorsement only the assignor after the endorsement. The endorsee may continue to transfer. 空白背书只有转让人在背书后面签字。被背书人可继续转让。

（1）Transfer after the signature, it will be pursued. It may be registered in the column of the endorsee. 签名后转让，会被追索。可在被背书人一栏记名，也可不记名。

（2）No signature, direct delivery to the transfer, will not be pursued. It may be registered in the column of the endorsee. 不签名，直接交付转让，不会被追索。可在被背书人一栏记名，也可不记名。

● **Order endorsement**：An order endorsement is where the transferor adds a direction to pay a particular person. The bill becomes payable to, or to the order of the persons specified, e. g. say, "X signed Y". 指示背书是指背书人在提单上写明交付给某人的字样。经过指示背书的指示提单变得具有支付性，如"凭 X 指示 Y"。

● **Restrictive endorsement**：It is where the endorsement prohibits further transfer of the bill, i. e. the transferee cannot transfer his right to payment. An example of a restrictive endorsement would be "Pay X only, signed Y". 限制背书是指定某个特定的人为被背书人或记载有"不得转让"字样的背书。能否继续转让，不同票据法规定不同。

Presentation 提示（汇票）

Act of submitting bill to the payer for acceptance or payment is called presentation. As bill is a choice in action, the bill holder has to show the bill to the payer, so as to prove his right to payment. There are two types of presentation：presentation for acceptance and presentation for payment. A time bill needs to be presented for acceptance, while a sight bill or an accepted time bill needs to be presented for payment. In other words, a sight bill needs presentation once；a time bill needs presentation twice：first one for acceptance, second one for payment, presentation has to be done within the agreed period.

There are three channels to make presentation：the first one is to do over the counter of the paying bank；the second one is to exchange the bill through a clearing house；and the third one is to dispatch the bill to the paying bank for acceptance or payment.

将汇票交给付款人承兑或付款的行为称为提示。由于汇票是一种行为选择，持票人必须向付款人出示汇票，以证明其付款权。提示有两种类型：承兑提示和付款提示。定期汇票需要提示承兑，而即期汇票或已承兑的定期汇票则需要提示付款。换言之，即期汇票需要提示一次；远期汇票需要提示两次：第一次提示承兑，第二次提示付款，提示必须在约定的期限内完成。

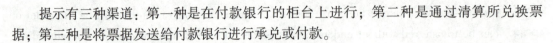

提示有三种渠道：第一种是在付款银行的柜台上进行；第二种是通过清算所兑换票据；第三种是将票据发送给付款银行进行承兑或付款。

Acceptance 承兑

Acceptance is an act by which the drawee promises to make payment at the bill maturity. Acceptance includes two acts too, that are writing and delivering. By signing his name on the bill, the payer engages that he will make payment when the bill falls due. What is more significant is that the drawee is known as the acceptor and becomes primarily liable for the payment after having signed his acceptance. Keeping mind, the bill drawer is the party primarily liable before the bill is paid in case of sight bill or accepted in case of time bill.

承兑是指付款人承诺在汇票到期时付款的行为。接受也包括两种行为，即书写和传递。付款人通过在汇票上签名，保证在汇票到期时付款。更重要的是，付款人被称为承兑人，在签署承兑后对付款承担主要责任。请记住，在即期汇票的情况下，出票人是汇票付款前的主要责任人，在定期汇票的情况中，出票人则是承兑前的主要义务人。

Acceptance can be classified into general acceptance and qualified acceptance. A general acceptance is an acceptance by which the drawee confirms the order given by the drawer without any qualification, such as, "Accepted, June 18, 2020, for bank of Tokyo LTD.". A qualified acceptance is an acceptance by which the drawee accepts the bill with conditions, that is, he revises the terms on the original bill.

承兑分为两种形式，即普通承兑和限制承兑。普通承兑指承兑人对出票人的指示不加限制地同意确认。例如"承兑，2020年6月18日，东京银行有限公司"。限制承兑是指付款人接受有条件的汇票的承兑，即修改原汇票上的条款。

Payment 付款

Act taken by the payer to pay the bill to the holder at agreed time and place is the act of payment. The so-called payment in due course signifies the payment made by the drawee in good faith on or after the maturity date to the holder thereof without perceiving his title defect. If the drawee or the acceptor does pay some person other than the holder, it does not mean the payment in due course. And thus he will be compelled to pay again to the true owner. But if he does pay the holder, whether the latter is the true owner or not, he will no longer be liable to any other party, for he has obtained the paid draft as a receipt.

付款人在约定的时间和地点向持票人支付汇票的行为称为付款行为。所谓按期付款，是指付款人在到期日当天或之后，在审核其票据没有产权纠纷的情况下，向持票人付款。如果付款人或承兑人确实向持票人以外的人付款，这并不意味着按期付款。因此，他将不得不再次向真正的主人付款。但是，如果他确实向持票人付款，无论持票人是否是真正的所有人，他将不再对任何其他方承担责任，因为他已经获得了已付款的汇票作为收据。

Dishonor 拒付

Dishonor refers to the drawee's refusal to accept and refuse to pay. The manifestation of refusal to pay includes not only the drawee's explicit refusal, but also, according to the Geneva Conventions, changes in the wording of the bill of exchange due to acceptance(excluding only the accepted part of the amount）; Regardless of whether the bill of exchange has been accepted or not, the payer has been declared bankrupt or although the ruling has not been determined, the payer has stopped payment or has no result in enforcing its property; The drawer of an unaccepted bill has gone bankrupt.

拒付是指付款人拒绝承兑和拒绝付款，拒付的表现形式除包括付款人明确的拒绝外，根据日内瓦公约的规定，还包括因承兑而变更汇票的文字（只承兑部分金额除外）；无论汇票是否已承兑，付款人已被宣告破产或裁决虽未确定，付款人已停止付款或对其财产执行尚无结果；不获承兑的票据其出票人已破产。

Notice of Dishonor 拒兑通知

Notice of dishonor refers to the act of the drawee of a bill of exchange refusing to accept it when the holder presents the bill of exchange on time. That is, the act of the payer indicating that they do not pay the amount of the bill of exchange on the due date. Although there is a financial relationship or an agreement between the invoicer and the payer to bear payment, in the law of negotiable instruments, the payer is not liable for payment due to this.

拒绝承兑，是指汇票付款人在持票人如期向其出示汇票请求表示承兑而予以拒绝的行为。亦即付款人表示于到期日不支付汇票金额的一种票据行为。发票人与付款人间虽有资金关系或虽有承担付款的约定，但在票据法上，付款人并不因此而负有付款责任。

Protest 拒绝证书

According to British Bills of Exchange Act, if a foreign bill is dishonored by the payer, the holder has to make protest within one working day. If a non-acceptance bill is protested, no presentation for payment is needed and needless to protest non-payment. Protest should be made by a notary public in the dishonor place; the holder carries out his right of recourse by means of such protest.

Charges for protest paid to the notary public should be for the account of issuer. In order to save this expenditure, issuer may add wording "Protest waived", so that the holder can carry out his recourse right without protest. Charges should be for the account of holder when he has made protest on the bill with indication of protest waived.

根据英国《汇票法》，如果外国汇票被付款人拒付，持票人必须在一个工作日内提出抗议。如果不承兑汇票被拒付，则无需提示付款，也无需抗议不付款。抗诉应当由拒付地的公证人提出；持票人通过这种抗议行使其追索权。

支付给公证人的抗议费用应由发行人承担。为了节省这笔支出，发行人可以添加"放弃抗议"的措辞，这样持有人就可以在没有抗议的情况下行使其追索权。当持票人对汇票提出抗议并表示放弃抗议时，费用应由持票人承担。

Recourse 追索

The term of recourse is used to signify the right of a draft holder to compel his prior endorsers or the drawer to perform their legal obligations of payment if dishonored by the drawee. The holder can claim the payment and related fees in succession of endorsers; alternatively, he can claim payment from any endorser, or even directly to the drawer. It needs to stress that the recourse claim should be enforced within the legal limit of time, which differs from country to country. According to the British Bill of Exchange Act, the legal limit of time is 6 years; according to the Geneva Uniform Laws, it is 1 year.

追索权是指持票人在被付款人拒付的情况下，有权迫使其前背书人或出票人履行其法定付款义务。持有人可以要求背书人的继承人支付；或者，他可以要求任何背书人付款，甚至直接向出票人付款。需要强调的是，追索权索赔应在各国不同的法律时限内强制执行。根据英国《汇票法》，法定期限为6年；根据日内瓦统一法，这是一年。

Notes 注意

• The Documentary Letter of Credit will stipulate when payment is to be made and the bill of exchange must be drawn up accordingly.

跟单信用证将规定何时付款，汇票必须据此拟定。

• The bill of exchange must conform exactly to the terms of the Letter of Credit, with the sum specified not exceeding the amount of the L/C.

汇票必须完全符合信用证的条款，所规定的金额不得超过信用证的金额。

• Unless the Documentary Letter of Credit stipulates that bills of exchange are required to be in duplicate, a single bill of exchange will be acceptable.

除非跟单信用证规定汇票必须一式两份，否则允许接受单一汇票。

• Bill of exchange forms may be purchased from printers or stationers, or they may be drawn on a company's notepaper or even a blank sheet of paper. When being presented for payment, the bill of exchange must be correctly endorsed by the payee.

汇票表格可以从打印机店或文具店购买，也可以绘制在公司的记事本上，甚至是一张空白纸上。汇票在提示付款时，必须由收款人正确背书。

Section Two   Making out Bill of Exchange under L/C
信用证项下汇票的缮制

1. The Specimen of Bill of Exchange 汇票样单

Bill of Exchange 汇票

No. 汇票编号_____(1)_____   Date：出票日期_____(2)_____

Exchange for 汇票金额_____(3)_____

At 付款期限(4)_____ Sight of this FIRST of Exchange(Second of the same tenor and date unpaid)pay to the order of 收款人(5)_____. The sum of 金额(6)_____.

Drawn under 出票条件(7)_____

To 付款人(8)_____

出票人的公司及盖章(9)_____

2. The Contents of Bill of Exchange 样单拆解：汇票的主要内容及缮制要点

（1）Draft number. This is completed in accordance with the invoice number, or writing "AS PER INVOICE".

汇票编号：此项按照发票编号填写，或写作"AS PER INVOICE"。

（2）Place and date. The date of bill of exchange is also the negotiating date under letter of credit, the place is negotiation or drawer location. It is worth noting that the bill as drawn not earlier than in other documents date, and shall not be later than 21 days after the date of the validity of the letter of credit and bills of lading.

出票日期和地点：汇票日期也是信用证项下的议付日期，地点为议付或出票地。值得注意的是，汇票的出票日期不得早于其他单据的出票日期，且不得迟于信用证和提单有效期后 21 天。

（3）Amount in figures. The amount of the draft shows that amount in figures and in words respectively. The amount in figures is followed "Exchange for". The amount may retain two decimal places, and consists of abbreviations of currency and Arabic numeral. For example：USD 7, 200.00, GBP 3,600.00, EU 7,500, JPY 4,620.00.

小写金额：汇票金额分别用数字和文字表示。小写金额后接"Exchange for"。金额可保留小数点后两位，由货币缩写和阿拉伯数字组成。例如：7 200.00 美元、3 600.00 英镑、7 500.00 欧元、4 620.00 日元。

（4）Tenor. There are two kinds of tenor. One is payable at sight, the other is payable after sight.

The draft payable at sight under the letter of credit should be marked with "××××" in the blank space between the words "At … sight" printed in this column, becoming "At sight", indicating payment at sight.

There are several main methods for the payment term of a long-term bill of exchange：

① Bills payable at ＿＿ days after sight；

② Bills payable at days after date；

③ Bills payable at ＿＿ days after stated.

期限：有两种付款期限。一种是即期付款，另一种是见票后付款。

信用证项下即期付款的汇票在本栏印就的"At … sight"之间空白处填上"××××"，变成"At sight"，表示见票即付。

远期汇票的付款期限，主要有以下几种方法：

① 见票后若干天付款；

② 出票后若干天付款；

③ 预定日期后若干天付款。

（5）Payee/pay to the order of … it is the money order, also known as payable to or payee. Usually there are three kinds of writing：

收款人：汇票受款人又称抬头人或收款人，是指接受票款的当事人。汇票常见的三种抬头表示方式：

① Restrictive rise of 限制性抬头：

"Pay to ××××× only"仅付给；"Pay to ××××× not transferable/negotiable"此种汇票不可转让，指定公司才有权收取票款。

② The indicative rise of 指示性抬头：

表示为"pay to ××××× or order""pay to the order of ×××××"，

"Pay to ×××××"

③"Pay bearer"付给持票人，也称为来人抬头"pay ××××× or bearer"，这种方式无须持背书即可转让，风险大，极少使用。

(6)Amount. Fill in capital words and currency, and plus "ONLY" at the end of the sentence.

汇票大写金额：大写金额前面注明货币名称，句末加上"ONLY"。如：

SAY U. S. DOLLARS SEVEN THOUSAND TWO HUNDRED ONLY,

SAY POUND STERLING THREE THOUSAND SIX HUNDRED ONLY,

SAY EUROPEAN DOLLARS SEVEN THOUSAND FIVE HUNDRED ONLY,

(7)Drawn Clause. The clause must be is followed the words: Drawn under … , according to the stipulation in the L/C. If there isn't any clause in the L/C, then the issuing bank name, address, credit number and issuing date must be filled respectively.

出款条款：该条款后面必须有以下字样，如根据……开具……，根据信用证的规定。如果信用证中没有任何条款，则必须分别填写开证行名称、地址、信用证号码和开证日期。

(8)Drawee or Payer. It is made out as："Drawn under ××× Bank L/C NO. ××× dated ×××" if the term of payment is L/C. It is usually the issuing bank.

付款人：汇票付款人即受票人，如果付款方式为信用证，则开具为："根据×××银行×××号×××日期的信用证开具"。银行通常是开证行。

(9)Signature of the Drawer. Drawer for letter of credit beneficiary, it is the beneficiary on L/C terms called exporters. Usually in the lower right corner of the space exporters full name must be marked. The draft is null and void without signature and seal of the drawer.

出票人签名：出票人为信用证受益人时，信用证条款下的受益人是出口商。通常在空格的右下角必须标注出口商的全名。未经出票人签字和盖章，汇票无效。

3. Case Study 案例实训

COMMODITY：GLASS WARE

CONTRACT NO. ：GX061214/89

L/C NO. ：M0389701NU30058

BILL NO. GXTSW030307241

THE DRAWER：NANNING E. T. D. Z. GUANGFA TRADING CO., LTD. (RED STAR EAST ROAD, NANNING DEVELOPMENT ZONE, NANNING, CHINA)

SHIPPING DATE：15 DEC, 2022

VALIDITY DATE：1 JAN., 2023

BILL DATE：15 JAN., 2023

L/C TERMS：

: 328/AMOUNT　　　　　　　　　: USD 1,185,00
: 41D/AVAILABLE WITH /BY　　　: ANY BANK BY NEGOTIATION
: 42 C/DRAFTS AT …　　　　　　: SIGHT FOR 100 PCT INVOICE VALUE
: 42 D/ DRAWEE　　　　　　　　: INDUSTRIAL BANK OF KOREA(HEAD OF-
　　　　　　　　　　　　　　　　FICE SEOUL)SEOUL 50, ULCHIRO 2-GA,
　　　　　　　　　　　　　　　　CHUNG-GU SEOUL, KOREA.

Bill of Exchange 汇票

No. 汇票编号 GXTSW030307241(1)　　　Date：出票日期 15 JAN., 2023　(2)

Exchange for 汇票金额 USD 1, 185, 00(3)

At 付款期限 AT SIGHT(4)Sight of this FIRST of Exchange(Second of the same tenor and date unpaid)pay to the order of BANK OF CHINA, NANNING BRANCH(5)the sum of US DOLLARS ONE THOUSAND ONE HUNDRED EIGHTY FIVE ONLY(6)

Drawn under 出票条件(7)INDUSTRIAL BANK OF KOREA(HEAD OFFICE SEOUL)SEOUL 50, ULCHIRO 2-GA, CHUNG-GU SEOUL, KOREA.
L/C NO.：M0389701NU30058 DATE 15 Nov, 2022

To 付款人　(8)INDUSTRIAL BANK OF KOREA(HEAD OFFICE SEOUL)SEOUL 50, ULCHIRO 2-GA, CHUNG-GU SEOUL, KOREA.

出票人公司及盖章(9)
NANNING E. T. D. Z. GUANGFA TRADING CO., LTD.
RED STAR EAST ROAD, NANNING DEVELOPMENT
ZONE, NANNING, CHINA
David Huang

Section Three　Promissory Notes 本票

A promissory note is an unconditional promise in writing made by one person(the maker)to another(the payee or the holder)signed by the maker engaging to pay on demand or at a fixed or determinable future time a sum certain in money to or to the order of a specified person or bearer. From definition of promissory note, it is easy to find that there is no acceptor, only the maker and the other parties are the payee, endorser, bearer and holder. The maker has prime liability while the other parties have second liability. Should the promissory note be made by two persons, then they are jointly and severally liable on the note according to its tenor.

本票是一个人向另一个人(收款人或持有人)做出的无条件书面承诺，出票人签署该承诺，承诺按要求或在固定或可确定的未来时间向特定的人或持票人支付一定的金额。从本票的定义不难发现，本票不存在承兑人，只有出票人和其他当事人是收款人、背书人、持票人和持票人。制造商承担首要责任，而其他各方承担次要责任。如果本票是由两个人开具的，那么他们根据本票的期限对本票承担连带责任。

Promissory notes are sometimes used in international trade settlements. It is used for forward payments and loan vouchers in commodity transactions. When the customer withdraws the deposit, it replaces cash payment.

本票有时用在国际贸易结算中。它用于商品交易中的远期付款和借贷凭证。当客户提取存款时，代替现钞支付。

1. Key Elements of a Promissory Note 本票的关键要素

The words "promissory Note" clearly indicated 清楚地表明"本票"字样

- An unconditional promise to pay 无条件的付款承诺
- Name of the payee or his order 收款人或其背书人的名称
- Maker's signature 制造商签名
- Place and date of issuing 签发地点和日期
- Tenor of payment 付款期限
- A certain amount of money. 一定金额

2. The Specimen of a Promissory Note 本票的样单

Promissory Note

Leicester

15 Dec, 2022

USD118.000

Ninety days after sight we promise to pay **William Smith** or order the sum of U. S Dollars **one hundred and eight thousand only**

James Harrison.

John Martin

Florence Brown

3. The Classifications of Promissory Note 本票的种类

Bank promissory note & Trade promissory note: According to different issuers, promissory notes can be divided into commercial promissory notes and cashier's check. Cashier's check is a bill issued by a bank that promises to unconditionally pay a certain amount to the payee or holder at sight; Commercial promissory notes are promissory notes issued by industrial and commercial enterprises or individuals, also known as ordinary promissory notes.

商业本票和银行本票：按照签发者的不同，本票可分为商业本票和银行本票。银行本票由银行签发，承诺自己在见票时无条件支付确定的金额给收款人或者持票人的票据；商业本票是由工商企业或个人签发的本票，也称为普通本票。

Sight promissory note and Time promissory note：According to the tenor, promissory notes can be classified as sight promissory note and time promissory note. The former is payable at sight or on demand, the latter is payable at a fixed future date or a determinable future date.

即期和远期本票：按照本票上记载的到期日的不同，本票可分为即期和远期本票。前者是见票即付，后者是在规定时间或者未来的确定时间支付。

Notes：The Difference Between a Bill and a Note 注意：汇票与本票的区别

A Bill	A Note
An order to pay	A promise to pay
Three parties	Two parties
Time bill needs acceptance	Time note needs not acceptance
Drawn in set in case of loss	Drawn in one original only

 Exercises 练习

一、Useful Words and Expressions 常用词语和表达

1. applicant 开证人（申请开证人）

for account of Messrs. 付（某人）账

at the request of Messrs. 以应（某人）请求

on behalf of Messrs. 代表某人

by order of Messrs. 奉（某人）之命

at the request of Messrs. 应（某人）要求

2. beneficiary 受益人

in favor of … 以某人为受益人

in one's favor 以……为受益人

3. drawee 付款人

to draw on(or upon) 以（某人）为付款人

to value on 以（某人）为付款人

to issue on 以（某人）为付款人

4. drawer 出票人

5. Advising bank

（1）the notifying bank

（2）advised through … bank 通过……银行通知

（3）advised by airmail/cable through … bank 通过……银行航空信/电报通知

6. opening bank 开证行

其他表示方法有：（1）issuing bank；（2）establishing bank

7. negotiation bank 议付行

8. paying bank 付款行

9. reimbursing bank 偿付行

10. confirming bank 保兑行

二、Useful Sentences 常用语句

1. Full set of clean shipped on board negotiable Bill of Landing showing freight prepaid made out/endorsed to the order of ×××××, notifying the issuing bank and the applicant with full with full address. 全套清洁已装船的可议付提单, 注明运费已预付, 做成指示性抬头, 通知开证行和申请人的详细地址。

2. An endorsement in blank specifies no endorsee, and a bill so endorsed becomes payable to bearer. 无记名背书并不书明被背书人, 以此方式背书之汇票, 应成为以持票人为收款人之汇票。

3. We'll draw on you by our documentary draft at sight on collection basis. 我们将按托收方式向你方开出即期跟单汇票。

4. A person who makes, accepts or endorses a bill for, in the name of, on behalf of or on account of a company. 任何人士, 如代表公司、以公司名义或为该公司而开立、承兑或背书汇票。

5. If the drawer, on request as aforesaid, refuses to give such duplicate bill, he may be compelled to do so. 出票人如上述要求而拒绝交出该汇票复本, 可被强迫交出。

6. A negotiable bill may be payable either to order or to bearer. 凡可流通转让之汇票均得按记名人之指示付款或付款与持票人。

7. A bill which has been protested for non-acceptance may be subsequently protested for non-payment. 汇票如因不承兑而被拒付证明, 则其后可因不付款而被拒付。

8. The Bank will be glad to remit your repayments to the hire-purchase company by monthly Banker's Order. 银行很乐意通过每月银行汇票将您的还款汇给分期付款公司。

9. Payment will be made by paying your sight draft under our irrevocable letter of credit. 我们的付款方式, 是以不可撤销信用证见票即付汇票支付。

10. The undermentioned draft we issue on you has been declared lost, and we request you to stop encashment of it. 我们向你方开出的下述汇票已被宣布遗失, 我们要求你方停止兑现。

11. Full set shipping(company's) clean on board bill(s) of lading marked "Freight Prepaid" to order of shipper endorsed to ... Bank, notifying buyers 全套装船(公司的)洁净已装船提单应注明"运费付讫", 作为以装船人指示为抬头、背书给……银行, 通知买方。

12. Bills of exchange must be negotiated within 15 days from the date of bills of lading but not later than August 8, 2021. 汇票须在提单日起 15 天内议付, 但不得迟于 2021 年 8 月 8 日。

13. Draft(s) drawn under this credit must be presented for negotiation in China on or before 30 August, 2021. 根据本证项下开具的汇票须在 2021 年 8 月 30 日或该日前在中国交单议付。

14. This credit shall cease to be available for negotiation of beneficiary's drafts after 15th August, 2021. 本证将在 2021 年 8 月 15 日以后停止议付受益人之汇票。

15. Clean shipped on board ocean bills of lading to order and endorsed in blank marked

"Freight Prepaid" notify：importer(openers/ issuer). 洁净已装船的提单空白抬头并空白背书，注明"运费付讫"，通知进口人(开证人)。

16. Full set of clean "on board" bills of lading/cargo receipt made out to our order/to order and endorsed in blank notify buyers M/S … Co. calling for shipment from China to Hamburg marked "Freight prepaid"/"Freight Payable at Destination". 全套洁净"已装船"提单/货运收据作成以我(行)为抬头/空白抬头，空白背书，通知买方……公司，要求货物自中国运往汉堡，注明"运费付讫"/"运费在目的港付"。

17. Bills of lading must be dated not before the date of this credit and not later than Aug. 15, 2021. 提单日期不得早于本证的日期，也不得迟于 2021 年 8 月 15 日。

18. bill of lading marked notify：buyer，"Freight Prepaid"，"Liner terms" "received for shipment" B/L not acceptable. 提单注明通知买方，"运费预付""按班轮条件"，"备运提单"不接受。

三、Making out a Bill of Exchange under L/C According to the Following Information 根据以下信息缮制汇票

Issuing Bank：Society General Paris，France.

L/C No：8081 Dated April 5th，2022

L/C Amount：USD 9,998.00

Applicant：A Navy &Co. Hamburg

Advising Bank：Bank of China

Beneficiary：China National Textiles Imp & Exp. Corp.

Expiry Date：May 31，2022

B/L Dated May 5th 2022

Beneficiary's draft at sight drawn on the issuing bank and pay to the order of Bank of China for 98% of invoice value marked under this credit.

Quantity of goods：15,000 kilos net，unit price USD 680.00 per 1,000 Kilo.

Invoice No：06098

ORIGINAL

No.：_____

Exchange for _____

　　At _____sight of this FIRST of Exchange(Second of the same tenor and date unpaid)pay to the order of _____the sum of _____

Drawn under _____

To. _____

_____

Chapter 9 The Customs Declaration Invoice
报关

 Key Points and Difficulties

- To Know What is Export License
- To Understand a Customs Declaration
- To Know the Contents of Customs Declaration

Learning Objectives

- Making out an Export License
- Making out a Customs Declaration

Section One   Export License 出口许可证

Import and export license belongs to the non-tariff barrier in international trade. The government stipulates that the importer or exporter have to get the license before the special goods is imported or exported in order to maintain his own country's benefit. Licenses are no longer required for most export products now, but some import products need it. Exporters apply for an export license through the Ministry of Commerce of the People's Republic of China. The customs officer will not let the goods pass if there is no license. It is a system to control the foreign trade and a warrant for customs to release the goods.

进出口许可证属于国际贸易中的非关税壁垒。政府规定为了保障进出口方所属国的利益，进出口方必须在进出口特殊商品之前获得此许可证。现在大多数出口产品不再需要许可证，但一些进口产品需要许可证。出口方向中华人民共和国申请出口许可证。若无许可证，货物将无法通关。此许可证是监管对外贸易和海关放行货物的重要凭证。

1. Key Elements of Export License 出口许可证的关键要素

The export license of each country may have its own forms and countries. However, certain elements are likely to be included in all export licenses as follows：每个国家的出口许可证可能有自己的形式和国家。但是，某些要素可能包含在所有出口许可证中，如下所示：

Name and address of seller

Name and address of buyer

Date issuance

Validity date

Description of goods covered by license

Name of country of origin

Name of country of ultimate destination

卖方名称和地址

买方名称和地址

发布日期

有效期

许可证涵盖的货物说明

原产国名称

最终目的地国家的名称

Notes 注意

Some countries require export licenses for virtually all commodities and products. The license is a means of control and taxation. In some cases the lack of an export license can be cited as a reason why the goods cannot be shipped, even though payment has not been made. Buyers should be especially careful about buying sensitive goods from countries with a demonstrated lack of rule by law.

The export license is typically the responsibility of the seller. However, if the buyer is dealing in sensitive goods, he should research the need for an export license beforehand. Failure to secure such a license can delay or prevent shipment and jeopardize the validity of a documentary credit.

一些国家要求几乎所有商品和产品都要有出口许可证。许可证是一种控制和征税的手段。在某些情况下，即使没有付款，也可以将缺乏出口许可证作为货物无法运输的原因。买家应该特别小心从明显缺乏法治的国家购买敏感商品。

出口许可证通常由卖方负责。然而，如果买方经营的是敏感货物，他应该事先研究是否需要出口许可证。未能获得此类许可证可能会延误或阻止装运，并危及跟单信用证的有效性。

2. Specimenof Export License 出口许可证样单

中华人民共和国出口许可证
EXPORT LICENCE THE PEOPLE'S REPUBLIC OF CHINA

(1)申领许可证单位：　　　　代码： Exporter：	(3)出口许可证编号： License No.
(2)发货单位：　　　　代码： Consignor	(4)出口许可证有效截止日期： Export license expiry date
(5)贸易方式： Terms of trade	(8)进口国(地区)： Country of destination
(6)合同号： Contract No.	(9)支付方式： Terms of payment
(7)报关口岸： Port of shipment	(10)运输方式： Means of transport

(11)唛头——包装件数 Marks and numbers—No. of packages				

(12)商品名称： Description of commodity				商品编码： Commodity No.

(13)规格、等级 Specification	(14)单位 Unit	(15)数量 Quantity	(16)单价(币别)Unit price	(17)总值(币别)Amount	(18)总值折美元 Amount in USD
(19)总计 Total					

(20)备注 Supplementary details	(21)发证机关签章 Issuing authority stamp & signature
(22)申请单位盖章 The stamp of the applicant	(23)发证日期 License date

3. The Contents of Export License 许可证的主要内容及缮制要点

（1）The Exporter license and code. The full names of various import and export enterprises with export license should be filled in. Form of export license must be original instead of copy. It is required correctly and fully, and the contents cannot be revised. The code is given by the Ministry of Commerce of the P. R. C. or its branch.

出口许可证单位及代码：应该填有出口经营权的各类进出口企业的全称。此许可证必须是原件，内容准确完整，并且不得修改。代码经由中华人民共和国商务部或其分部许可。

(2) Consignor and code. The shipper and exporter of quota bidding products (including paid and unpaid bidding) must be consistent.

发货单位及代码：配额招标商品(包括有偿和无偿招标)的发货人与出口商必须一致。

(3) License No. The export license number is arranged by the issuing institution.

出口许可证编号：出口许可证编号由签发机构编订。

(4) Export license expiry date. There are two kinds of expiry date: three months and six months.

出口许可证有效截止日：有两种有效截止日，即 3 个月和 6 个月。

(5) Terms of Trade. 贸易方式。

- The contents of this column include: general trade, barter trade, compensation trade, processing with imported materials, processing with supplied materials, export of foreign-invested enterprises, border trade, processing with exported materials, re-exportation, futures trade, contracting projects, loan repayment export, international exhibition, agreement trade, and other trade.

- Fill in "Incoming Processing" in this column for the re-export of incoming processing.

- When foreign-invested enterprises import materials for processing and re-export, the trade method should be filled in as "foreign-invested enterprise export".

- 此栏内容有：一般贸易、易货贸易、补偿贸易、进料加工、来料加工、外商投资企业出口、边境贸易、出料加工、转口贸易、期货贸易、承包工程、归还贷款出口、国际展销、协定贸易、其他贸易。

- 进料加工复出口，此栏填写"进料加工"。

- 外商投资企业进料加工复出口时，贸易方式填写"外商投资企业出口"。

(6) Contract No.：Only one contract number can be filled in this column.

合同号：此处只能填写一个合同号。

(7) Port of Shipment. This column allows for filling in three ports, but customs declaration can only be made at one port.

报关口岸：此栏允许填写 3 个口岸，但仅能在 1 个口岸报关。

(8) Country of Destination. It is the country or region to which the goods are exported. This refers to the final destination, i. e. the contract destination, which is not allowed to use the domain name of the destination (such as Europe).

最终目的国/进口国(地区)：这指最终目的地，即合同目的地，不允许使用地域名(如欧洲等)。

(9) Terms of Payment. The content of this column includes letter of credit, collection, remittance, promissory note, cash, bookkeeping, and free of charge.

支付方式：此栏内容有信用证、托收、汇付、本票、现金、记账和免费等。

(10) Means of Transport. This column can be filled in for sea transportation, railway transportation, road transportation, air transportation, postal transportation, and fixed transportation.

运输方式：此栏可填写海上运输、铁路运输、公路运输、航空运输、邮政运输、固定运输。

(11) Marks and Numbers No. of Packages. 唛头——包装件数。

(12) Description of Commodity and Commodity No. The code of goods refers to the H. S.

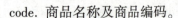

code. 商品名称及商品编码。

（13）Specification. The quality, quantity, specification, unit price must comply with the sales of contract. This item cannot be kept in blank, the contents should comply with the commodity, and "refer to contract" can also be filled in.

规格：质量、数量、规格和单价必须与销售合同一致。此项不得留空，内容应和商品一致，并且参照合同应写入。

（14）Unit. It is made out strictly according to the stipulation of the Ministry of Commerce of P. R. China. For example, the unit of weight is kilogram, the unit of volume is cubic meter, and the unit of length is meter.

单位：必须严格按照中华人民共和国商务部的规定来表示。例如，重量单位为公斤，体积单位为立方公尺，长度的单位是米。

（15）Quantity. Only one decimal is kept, other decimal is rounded down.

数量：只保留到小数点后一位，其他的小数全部省略。

（16）Unit price. As per the contract and invoice, and the unit price cannot exceed the stipulations of the Ministry of Commerce of the P. R. C.

单价：必须按照合同和发票来填写，不能超出中华人民共和国商务部所规定的价格。

（17）Amount. It should be the price multiplied by the quantity and unit price.

总值（币别）应是数量与单价相乘的价格。

（18）Amount in USD. 总价值折美元。

（19）Total. Data on the quantity, total value, and total value of goods of different specifications and grades in USD.

总计：不同规格、等级的商品数量、总值、总值折美元各自加总的数据。

（20）Supplementary details. 备注。

（21）Issuing authority stamp & signature. 发证机关签章。

（22）The stamp of the applicant. 申请单位盖章。

（23）License date 发证日期。

4. Case Study 案例实训

广州银沙贸易公司 SILVER SAND TRADING CORP. （456987）向丹麦的 F. L. SMIDTH & CO. 出口一批自行车，相关信息如下：

信用证号：FLS-JHLC06

最后装运日期：May 31, 2021

启运港：GUANGZHOU, P. R. CHINA

目的港：COPENHAGEN, DENMARK

币种：USD

贸易术语：CIF C5 COPENHAGEN

合同号：JH-FLSSC06

付款方式：L/C AT 30 DAYS AFTER SIGHT

SHIPPING MARK：N/M

HS code：87120081

数量、包装：EACH 600 SETS, ALTOGETHER 1,200 SETS IN 1,200 CARTONS

品名规格、单价：

FOREVER BRAND BICYCLE YE80326' 600 SETS USD66.00/SET

FOREVER BRAND BICYCLE YE80324' 600 SETS USD71.00/SET

中华人民共和国出口许可证

EXPORT LICENCE THE PEOPLE's REPUBLIC OF CHINA

(1) Exporter：申领许可证单位：SILVER SAND TRADING CORP. 代码：456987	(3) 出口许可证编号： License No. 2569863
(2) Consignor 发货单位：SILVER SAND TRADING CORP. 代码：456987	(4) 出口许可证有效截止日期： Export license expiry date：May 31, 2021
(5) 贸易方式：一般贸易 Terms of Trade	(8) 进口国(地区)： Country of destination：丹麦
(6) 合同号： Contract No. JH-FLSSC06	(9) 支付方式：信用证 Terms of payment
(7) 报关口岸：广州 Port of shipment	(10) 运输方式：海上运输 Means of transport：by sea

(11) 唛头——包装件数 Marks and numbers-No. of packages
N/M　EACH 600 SETS, ALTOGETHER 1,200 SETS IN 1,200 CARTONS

(12) 商品名称 Description of commodity：BICYCLE
Commodity No. 商品编码：87120081

(13) 规格、等级 Specification	(14) 单位 Unit	(15) 数量 Quantity	(16) 单价(币别) Unit price	(17) 总值(币别) Amount	(18) 总值折美元 Amount in USD
			CIFC5COPENHAGEN		
FOREVER BRAND BICYCLE YE803 26'	SET	600	USD66.00		USD39,600.00
FOREVER BRAND BICYCLE YE803 24'	SET	600	USD71.00		USD42,600.00
(19) 总计 Total		1,200			USD82,200.00

(20) 备注 Supplementary details 　　　　申请单位盖章 (22) 申领日期：2021.5.14	(21) 发证机关签章 Issuing authority stamp & signature 　　　　发证日期 (23) License date

Section Two Customs Declaration 报关单

1. Understanding the Customs Declaration 认识报关单

The Customs declaration for import and export goods refers to the legal document that the consignee or consignor of import and export goods or their agents make a written declaration on the actual situation of import and export goods in the form specified by the customs, so as to require the customs to handle customs clearance procedures for their goods in accordance with the applicable customs system. It has a very important legal status in foreign economic and trade activities. It is not only an important basis for customs supervision, taxation, statistics, and inspection and investigation, but also an important voucher for the verification of import and export goods in processing trade, as well as export tax refunds and foreign exchange management. It is also an important certificate for customs to handle smuggling and violation cases, as well as for tax and foreign exchange management departments to investigate and deal with tax fraud and arbitrage criminal activities.

进出口货物报关单是指进出口货物收发货人或其代理人，按照海关规定的格式对进出口货物的实际情况做出书面申明，以此要求海关对其货物按适用的海关制度办理通关手续的法律文书。它在对外经济贸易活动中具有十分重要的法律地位。它既是海关监管、征税、统计以及开展稽查和调查的重要依据，又是加工贸易进出口货物核销，以及出口退税和外汇管理的重要凭证，也是海关处理走私、违规案件，及税务、外汇管理部门查处骗税和套汇犯罪活动的重要证书。

The customs declaration is in different colors: the white one is made out for general trade; pink one is used for processing trade; light green paper is used for adopted in assembling and compensation trade; light blue paper is made out for enterprise invested by foreign capital. The contents of these documents are similar. The exporter has to apply to the customs for declaration of the commodity before the shipment. The customs officer will release the customs declaration if the goods are up to the requirement.

按照颜色不同，报关单分为以下几种：

(1)一般贸易及其他贸易进出口货物报关单(白色)。

(2)进料加工进出口货物报关单(粉红色)。

(3)来料加工及补偿贸易进出口货物报关单(浅绿色)。

(4)外商投资企业进出口货物报关单(浅蓝色)。

Usually there are four steps in clear Customs Declaration, they are—declaration, examination of goods, tariff and release of goods. Customs declaration can be divided into two kinds: Customs Declaration for export and Customs Declaration for import.

报关通常有四个步骤，即报关、货物检验、关税和货物放行。报关单可分为两种：出口报关单和进口报关单。

2. Specimen 样单：海关进口货物报关单

中华人民共和国海关进口货物报关单

预录入编号：   海关编号：

进口口岸 广州海关	备案号(1) C51066000019	进口日期 2021 年 8 月 15 日	申报日期 2021 年 8 月 15 日	
经营单位(440193×××) 广州昌盛电梯有限公司	运输方式(2) 江海运输	运输工具名称(3) SUI DONG FANG/ 510100607150	提运单号(4) 11XF02014	
收货单位(440193×××) 广州昌盛电梯有限公司	贸易方式(5) 一般贸易	征免性质(6) 一般征税	征税比例 T/T	
许可证号	起运国(地区)(7) 香港	装货港 香港	境内目的地 广州	
批准文号	成交方式(8) EXW	运费	保费	杂费
合同协议号 BTNU0945-46	件数(9) 13	包装种类(10) CASE	毛重(千克) (11) 7,640	净重(千克) (12) 7,073
集装箱号	随附单据(13) 商业发票、装箱单		用途(14) 销售	

标记唛码及备注

All business, whether involving transport or not, is handled subject to our general conditions.

项号(15) 商品编号 商品名称、规格型号(16) 数量及单位(17) 原产国(18) 单价 总价(19)
币制(20) 征免

1. -------6005343   ESCALATOR MACHINE   13 CASES 中国 3,706.22 51,887.08 EUR 照章征税
2. -------6005344   14.000 UNITS OF ECH3
3. -------6004843   11.0 kW-380/415V-50Hz
4. -------6005273

税费征收情况

录入员 录入单位	兹声明以上申报无讹并承担法律责任	海关审单批注及放行日期(盖章)	
报关员		审单	审价
单位地址	申报单位(盖章)	征税	统计
邮编 电话	填制日期	查验	放行

3. Specimen 样单：海关出口货物报关单

中华人民共和国海关出口货物报关单

预录入编号：   海关编号：

出口口岸 大连海关	备案号	出口日期 2021 年 6 月 11 日	申报日期(1) 2021 年 5 月 31 日	
经营单位(2)(210291×××) 大连鸿发化工贸易公司	运输方式 江海运输	运输工具名称 CSCL YANTIAN 0042S	提运单号(3)	
收货单位(4)(210291×××) 大连鸿发化工贸易公司	贸易方式 一般贸易	征免性质(5) 一般征税	结汇方式(6) T/T	
许可证号(7)	运抵国(地区)(8) 新加坡	指运港(9) 新加坡	境内货源地	
批准文号	成交方式(10) FOB	运费(11)	保费(12)	杂费(13)
合同协议号 XM2011NA266	件数 680	包装种类 DRUM	毛重（千克） (14) 294.00	净重（千克） 270.00
集装箱号	随附单据(15) 商业发票、装箱单		生产厂家	

标记唛码及备注
SINGAPORE 183.6MT CHLOROPICRIN 99.5% MIN.

项号	商品编号	商品名称、规格型号	数量及单位(16)	最终目的国(17)	单价(18)	总价(19)	币制	征免(20)
1	02/3314	CHITTANGONG BANGLADESH ACIDITY：TOPPM MAX WATER：150PPM MAX DENSITY：1.654-1.663 TOXICITY：HIGH POISONOUS	680 DRUMS	新加坡	459.00	265,302.00	USD	照章征税

税费征收情况

录入员 录入单位 报关员 单位地址 邮编 电话	兹声明以上申报无讹并承担法律责任 申报单位(盖章) 大连鸿发化工贸易公司 填制日期 2021 年 5 月 31 日	海关审单批注及放行日期(盖章) 审单 审价 征税 统计 查验 放行

4. The Components of Import/ Export Customs Declaration 样单拆解：进出口货物报关单主要内容及缮制要点

（1）预录入编号：指申报单位或预录入单位对该单位填制录入的报关单的编号，用于该单位与海关之间引用其申报后尚未批准放行的报关单。报关单录入凭单的编号规则由申报单位自行决定。预录入报关单及 EDI 报关单的预录入编号由接受申报的海关决定编号规则，计算机自动打印。

（2）海关编号：指海关接受申报时给予报关单的编号。海关编号由各海关在接受申报环节确定，应标识在报关单的每一联上。报关单海关编号为 9 位数码，其中前两位为分关（办事处）编号，第三位由各关自定义，后六位为顺序编号。各直属海关对进口报关单和出口报关单应分别编号，并确保在同一公历年度内，能按进口和出口唯一地标识本关区的每一份报关单。

（3）进口口岸/出口口岸：指货物实际进(出)我国关境口岸海关的名称。本栏目应根据货物实际进(出)口的口岸海关选择填报《关区代码表》中相应的口岸海关名称及代码。

（4）进口日期/出口日期：进口日期指运载所申报货物的运输工具申报进境的日期。本栏目填报的日期必须与相应的运输工具进境日期一致。出口日期指运载所申报货物的运输工具办结出境手续的日期。本栏目供海关打印报关单证明联用。预录入报关单及 EDI 报关单均免于填报。

无实际进出境的报关单填报办理申报手续的日期。本栏目为 6 位数，顺序为年、月、日各 2 位。

（5）申报日期：进口日期指运载所申报货物的运输工具申报进境的日期。本栏目填报的日期必须与相应的运输工具进境日期一致。出口日期指运载所申报货物的运输工具办结出境手续的日期。本栏目供海关打印报关单证明联用。预录入报关单及 EDI 报关单均免于填报。

（6）经营单位：指对外签订并执行进出口贸易合同的中国境内企业或单位。本栏目应填报经营单位名称及经营单位编码。经营单位编码为十位数字，指进出口企业在所在地主管海关办理注册登记手续时，海关给企业设置的注册登记编码。

（7）运输方式：指载运货物进出关境所使用的运输工具的分类。本栏目应根据实际运输方式按海关规定的《运输方式代码表》选择填报相应的运输方式。

（8）运输工具名称：指载运货物进出境的运输工具的名称或运输工具编号。本栏目填制内容应与运输部门向海关申报的载货清单所列相应内容一致。一份报关单只允许填报一个运输工具名称。

（9）提运单号：指进出口货物提单或运单的编号。本栏目填报的内容应与运输部门向海关申报的载货清单所列相应内容一致。一份报关单只允许填报一个提运单号，一票货物对应多个提运单时，应分单填报。具体填报要求如下：

＊江海运输填报进口提单号或出口运单号。

＊汽车运输免于填报。

＊铁路运输填报运单号。

＊航空运输填报分运单号，无分运单的填报总运单号。

＊邮政运输免于填报。

＊无实际进出境的，本栏目为空。进出口转关运输免于填报。

（10）收货单位/发货单位：收货单位指已知的进口货物在境内的最终消费、使用单位，包括：

A. 自行从境外进口货物的单位。

B. 委托有外贸进出口经营权的企业进口货物的单位。

发货单位指出口货物在境内的生产或销售单位，包括：

A 自行出口货物的单位。委托有外贸进出口经营权的企业出口货物的单位。

B 本栏目应填报收、发货单位的中文名称或其海关注册编码。加工贸易报关单的收、发货单位应与《登记手册》中的"货主单位"一致。

（11）贸易方式（监管方式）：指以国际贸易中进出口货物的交易方式为基础，结合海关对进出口货物征税、统计及监管条件综合设定的对进出口货物的管理方式。如一般贸易、易货贸易、来料加工贸易、其他贸易。

（12）征免性质：海关根据有关法则和条例对出口货物实施征、减、免管理的性质类别。

（13）征免比例/结汇方式。

征免比例用于非对口合同进料加工贸易方式下进口料、件的进口报关单，填报海关规定的实际应征税比例，例如5%填报5，15%填报15。出口报关单应该填报结汇方式，即出口货物的发货人或其代理人收结外汇的方式。本栏目应按海关的《结汇方式代码表》选择填报相应的结汇方式名称或代码。比如：电汇（代码"2"）、付款交单（代码"4"）、信用证（代码"6"）等。

（14）许可证号：应申领进出口许可证的货物，必须在此栏目填报外经贸部及其授权发证机关签发的进出口货物许可证的编号，不得为空。

（15）起运国（地区）/运抵国（地区）：

起运国（地区）指进口货物起始发出的国家（地区）。

运抵国（地区）指出口货物直接运抵的国家（地区）。

（16）装货港/指运港：

装货港指进口货物在运抵我国关境前的最后一个境外装运港。

指运港指出口货物运往境外的最终目的港；最终目的港不可预知的，可按尽可能预知的目的港填报。对应发生运输中转的货物，中转港就是装货港，指运港不受中转的影响。

（17）境内目的地/境内货源地：

境内目的地指已知的进口货物在国内的消费、使用地或最终运抵地。

境内货源地指出口货物在境内的产地或原始发货地。

（18）批准文号：

进口报关单中本栏目用于填报《进口付汇核销单》编号。

出口报关单中本栏目用于填报《出口收汇核销单》编号。

（19）成交方式：本栏目应根据实际成交价格条款按海关规定的《成交方式代码表》选择填报相应的成交方式代码。无实际进出境的，进口填报 CIF 价，出口填报 FOB 价。

(20)运费：本栏目用于成交价格中不包含运费的进口货物或成交价格中含有运费的出口货物，应填报该份报关单所含全部货物的国际运输费用。可按运费单价、总价或运费率三种方式之一填报，同时注明运费标记，并按海关规定的《货币代码表》选择填报相应的币种代码。

(21)保费：本栏目用于成交价格中不包含保险费的进口货物或成交价格中含有保险费的出口货物，应填报该份报关单所含全部货物国际运输的保险费用。可按保险费总价或保险费率两种方式之一填报，同时注明保险费标记，并按海关规定的《货币代码表》选择填报相应的币种代码。

运保费合并计算的，运保费填报在运费栏中。

(22)杂费：指成交价格以外的、应计入完税价格或应从完税价格中扣除的费用，如手续费、佣金、回扣等，可按杂费总价或杂费率两种方式之一填报，同时注明杂费标记，并按海关规定的《货币代码表》选择填报相应的币种代码。应计入完税价格的杂费填报为正值或正率，应从完税价格中扣除的杂费填报为负值或负率。杂费标记"1"表示杂费率，"3"表示杂费总价。例如：

应计入完税价格的 1.5% 的杂费率填报为 1.5；

应从完税价格中扣除的 1% 的回扣率填报为 -1；

应计入完税价格的 500 英镑杂费总价填报为 303/500/3。

(23)合同协议号：本栏目应填报进出口货物合同的全部字头和号码。

(24)件数：本栏目应填报单件运输包装的进出口货物的实际件数，即货物可以单独计数的一个外包装为单件，件是可数货物的一个计量单位。

(25)包装种类：本栏目应根据进出口货物的实际外包装种类，按海关规定的《包装种类代码表》选择填报相应的包装种类代码，如木箱、托盘、散装等包装单位。

(26)毛重：指货物及其包装材料的重量之和，即商品本身的重量加皮重。本栏目与净重、数量有连带关系。本栏目填报进(出)货物实际毛重，计量单位为公斤，不足一公斤的填报为 1。

(27)净重：指货物的毛重减去外包装材料后的重量，即商品本身的实际重量。栏目填报进(出)口货物的实际净重，计量单位为公斤，不足一公斤的填报为 1。

(28)集装箱号：集装箱号是在每个集装箱两侧标示的全球唯一的编号。

例如：　　TBXU3605231 * 1(1) 表示 1 个标准集装箱；TBXU3605231 * 2(3) 表示 2 个集装箱，折合为 3 个标准集装箱，其中一个箱号为 TBXU3605231。

(29)随附单据：指随进(出)口货物报关单一并向海关递交的单证或文件，合同、发票、装箱单、许可证等的必备的随附单证不在本栏目填报。本栏目应按海关规定的《监管证件名称代码表》选择填报相应证件的代码。

(30)生产厂家：进口货物填报用途，应根据进口货物的实际用途按海关规定的《用途代码表》选择填报相应的用途代码，如"以产顶进"填报"13"。生产厂家指出口货物的境内生产企业，本栏目供必要时手工填写。

(31)标记唛码及备注：本栏目上部用于打印以下内容：

A. 标记唛码中除图形以外的文字、数字。

B. 受外商投资企业委托代理其进口投资设备、物品的外贸企业名称。

C. 加工贸易结转货物及凭《征免税证明》转内销货物，其对应的备案号应填报在本栏目，即"转至(自)×××××××××××手册"。

D. 其他申报时必须说明的事项。

本栏目下部供填报随附单据栏中监管证件的编号，具体填报要求为：监管证件代码+"："+监管证件号码。一份报关单多个监管证件的，连续填写。

(32)项号、商品编号：本栏目分两行填报及打印。

第一行打印报关单中的商品排列序号。

第二行专用于加工贸易等已备案的货物，填报和打印该项货物在《登记手册》中的项号。

(33)商品名称、规格型号：

本栏目指按海关规定的商品分类编码规则确定的进(出)口货物的商品编号。

加工贸易《登记手册》中商品编号与实际商品编号不符的，应按实际商品编号填报。

(34)数量及单位：本栏目分两行填报及打印。

第一行打印进(出)口货物规范的中文商品名称，第二行打印规格型号，必要时可加注原文。

具体填报要求如下：

A. 商品名称及规格型号应据实填报，并与所提供的商业发票相符。

B. 商品名称应当规范，规格型号应当足够详细，以能满足海关归类、审价以及监管的要求为准。禁止、限制进出口等实施特殊管制的商品，其名称必须与交验的批准证件上的商品名称相符。

C. 加工贸易等已备案的货物，本栏目填报录入的内容必须与备案登记中同项号下货物的名称与规格型号一致。

(35)最终目的国(地区)：

原产国(地区)指进出口货物的生产、开采或加工制造国家(地区)。

最终目的国(地区)指已知的出口货物的最终实际消费、使用或进一步加工制造国家(地区)。

本栏目应按海关规定的《国别(地区)代码表》选择填报相应的国家(地区)名称或代码。

(36)单价：本栏目应填报同一项号下进(出)口货物实际成交的商品单位价格。无实际成交价格的，本栏目填报货值。

(37)总价：本栏目应填报同一项号下进(出)口货物实际成交的商品总价。无实际成交价格的，本栏目填报货值。

(38)征免：指海关对进(出)口货物进行征税、减税、免税或特案处理的实际操作方式。本栏目应按照海关核发的《征免税证明》或有关政策规定，对报关单所列每项商品选择填报海关规定的《征减免税方式代码表》中相应的征减免税方式。加工贸易报关单应根据《登记手册》中备案的征免规定填报。

(39)税费征收情况：本栏目供海关批注进(出)口货物税费征收及减免情况。

(40)申报单位(签章)：本栏目指报关单左下方用于填报申报单位有关情况的总栏目。申报单位指对申报内容的真实性直接向海关负责的企业或单位。自理报关的，应填报进

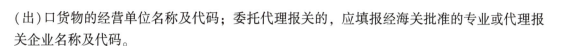

(出)口货物的经营单位名称及代码；委托代理报关的，应填报经海关批准的专业或代理报关企业名称及代码。

【知识链接1】：13个贸易术语应填写的成交方式的对应关系

发票中的贸易术语	报关单中填写的成交方式	成交方式代码
CIF、CIP以及D组的5个贸易术语填	CIF	1
CFR(CNF、C&F)、CPT填	CFR(CNF、C&F)	2
FCA、FAS、EXW、FOB填	FOB	3

注：D组5个术语为：DAF、DES、DEQ、DDU、DDP

【知识链接2】：备案号、贸易方式、征免性质、用途、征免之间的逻辑关系

贸易方式	有无备案号（标记码）	免征性质	用途	征免	说明
一般贸易 0110	无	一般征税101	外贸自营内销	照章征税	外商投资企业为生产内销产品而进口料件
			其他内销		
	有	科教用品	企业自用	全免	
		鼓励项目789			内资企业用
		自有资金799			外商投资企业在投资总额外使用自用资金进口的享受特定减免税货物

【知识链接3】：成交方式、运费、保费各栏目间的填报关系

	成交方式	运费	保费
进口	CIF	不填	不填
	CFR	不填	填
	FOB	填	填
出口	FOB	不填	不填
	CFR	填	不填
	CIF	填	填

【知识链接 4】：实际成交计量单位与法定计量单位的逻辑关系

计量单位状态	填表要求		
	第一行	第二行	第三行
成交和法定一致	法定计量单位及数量	空	空
成交和法定一致，并有第二计量单位	法定第一计量单位及数量	法定第二计量单位及数量	空
成交和法定不一致	法定计量单位及数量	空	成交计量单位及数量
成交和法定不一致且有第二计量单位	法定第一计量单位及数量	法定第二计量单位及数量	成交计量单位及数量

5. Case Study 案例实训

信用证号：FLS-JHLC06

海运提单号码：JH-FLSBL06

最后装运期限：MAY 31, 2021

收益人：SILVER SAND TRADING CORP. 6TH FLOOR, JINDU BUILDING, 135 WUXING ROAD, GUANGZHOU, P. R. CHINA

开证人：F. L. SMIDTH & CO. A/S 77, VIGERSLEV ALLE, DK-2600 VALBY, COPENHAGEN, DENMARK

启运港：GUANGZHOU, P. R. CHINA

目的港：COPENHAGEN, DENMARK

币种：USD

贸易术语：CIF C5 COPENHAGEN

合同号：JH-FLSSC06

发票号码：JH-FLSINV06

是否允许分批装运：ALLOWED；是否允许转船装运：ALLOWED

集装箱号：32345100-32345109

开证行：WEST LB(EUROPE) A. G.

议付行：BANK OF CHINA, GUANGZHOU BRANCH

付款方式：L/C AT 30 DAYS AFTER SIGHT

S CODE：87120081

唛头：FLS/9711/COPENHAGEN/CARTON1-1200

船名、航次：YIXIANG, V703

数量、包装：EACH 600 SETS, ALTOGETHER 1,200 SETS IN 1,200 CARTONS

品名规格、单价：

FOREVER BRAND BICYCLE YE803 26'　600 SETS USD66. 00/SET

FOREVER BRAND BICYCLE YE600 24'　600 SETS USD71. 00/SET

GW：39,600KGS, NW：33,600KGS

中华人民共和国海关出口货物报关单

预录入编号：　　　　　　　　　　　　　　　　　　　　　　海关编号：

出口口岸 GUANGZHOU, P. R. CHINA	备案号	出口日期 2021-5-20	申报日期 2021-5-12	
经营单位 SILVER SAND TRADING CORP.	运输方式 BY SEA	运输工具名称 YIXIANG, V703	提运单号 JH-FLSBL06	
发货单位	贸易方式 一般贸易	征免性质 一般征税	结汇方式 L/C	
许可证号	运抵(国地区) DENMARK	指运港 COPENHAGEN	境内货源地	
批准文号 654789	成交方式 CIF	运费 324,637.5	保费 6,713.69	杂费 1,800
合同协议号 JH-FLSSC06	件数 1,200 CARTONS	包装种类 CARTON	毛重(千克) 39,600	净重(千克) 33,600
集装箱号 32345100-32345109	随附单据 Export License	生产厂家		

标记唛码及备注　FLS/9711/COPENHAGEN/CARTON1-1200

项号　商品编号　商品名称　规格型号　数量及单位　最终目的国(地区)　单价　总价　币制　征免
DENMARK **COPENHAGEN** 1. 87120081.10 FOREVER BRAND BICYCLE YE803 26' 600 SETS USD66.00/SET USD39,600.00 2. 87120081.10 FOREVER BRAND BICYCLE YE600 24' 600 SETS USD71.00/SET USD42,600.00
USD82,200.00 LESS　　　　　　COMMISSION　　　　5%　　　　　　USD4,110.00
TOTAL：USD78090.00

税费征收情况

录入员　录入单位　兹声明以上申报无讹并承担法律责任 报关员　张三 　　　　　　　　　申报单位(签章) 单位地址：广东武新路京都大厦6楼 邮编：51005　　电话：020-86689898　　填制日期：2021-5-14	海关单批注及放行日期 (签章) 　　　　　审单审价 征税　　　　统计 查验　　　　放行

 **Exercises 练习**

一、Some Useful Words of Customs Declaration

海关申报的常用词语

1. A brokerage firm 报关行

2. A consumption entry 消费商品进口报关

3. Automated clearing-house 自动化结算系统

4. Anti-dump 反倾销

5. Establish the entered value 确立报关单价格

6. EDI(Electronic Data Interchange) 电子数据交换

7. Final clearance 结关放行

8. Fixed duty 固定关税

9. General Customs Administration 海关部署

10. General system of preferences 普遍优惠制

11. General tariff rate 普通税率

12. Half-duty 半税

13. High duty 高关税

14. Import taxes or duties 进口税务局或关税

15. Post entry review 出口后复审

16. Paperless summary program 海关无纸化报关程序

17. Regulatory audit 常规稽查

18. Sanction 处罚

19. Statute 法规

20. Withhold 扣留

21. Withdraw 取回

22. Declaration form 报关单

23. Three steps—declaration, examination of goods and release of goods, are taken by the Customs to exercise control over general import and export goods.

海关对进出境货物的监管一般经过申报、查验和放行三个环节。

24. Contract 合同(commodity, quantity, unit price, total amount, country of origin and manufacturer, packing, shipping mark, date of shipment, port of shipment, port of destination, insurance, payment, shipment, shipping advice, guarantee of quality, claims, force majeure, late delivery and penalty, arbitration)

25. Certificate(commodity inspection certificate) 商检证

26. Animal or plant quarantine certificate 动植物检疫证

27. Certificate of origin 原产地证

28. Import & export license 进出口许可证

29. Export drawback 出口退税

30. Processing with imported(supplied)materials 进(来)料加工

31. Goods(import& export goods, All import and export goods shall be subject to Customs examination). 商品

32. Cargo(bulk cargo, cargo in bulk, air cargo, sea cargo, bonded cargo, cargo-owner)货物

33. Commodity(commodity inspection)货品

34. Merchandise 泛指商品，不特指某一商品

35. Packing(bag 袋, bale 包, bottle 瓶, coil 圈, case 盒, crate 板条箱, dozen 打, package 件, total packages 合计件数, piece 张, roll 卷, set 套, unit 辆、台、单位, drum 桶, carton 纸箱, wooden cases 木箱, pallet 托盘, container 集装箱, in bulk 散装)

36. Weight 重量(gross weight 毛重, net weight 净重, tare 皮重)

37. Quantity 数量 The minimum quantity of an order for the goods is 500 cases.

38. Price 价格(unit price 单价, total price 总价, total amount 总价)

39. Shipper 托运人(carrier 承运人)

40. Agent 代理人(shipping agent 装运代理人, insurance agent 保险代理人, China Ocean Shipping Agency 中国外轮代理公司)

41. Shipment 装船(shipment documents 运输单据, date of shipment 装船日期, 装运期 combined transport shipment 多式联运, port to port shipment 港对港运输, freight charges 运费, air freight charge 航空运费, freight rates 运费率, extras 杂费)

42. Terms of payment 付款方式(immediate payment 即期付款)

43. Port 港口(port of dispatch 发货港, port of departure 始发港, port of loading 装货港, port of shipment 装货港, 起运地, port of delivery 交货港, port of destination 目的港, port of discharge 卸货港, port of entry 进口港, port of transhipment 转运港)

二、Some sentences of Customs Declaration 报关方面常见句子

1. Declaration for exported goods in five copies is filed by the trade enterprises with right to import &export.

一式五份的出口方报关单由有进出口经营权的企业存档。

2. Invoice, packing lists are needed for import and export customs declaration.

进出口货物报关时需随附发票、装箱单。

3. The Ethiopian Customs Declaration(ECUD)is the only declaration form.

埃塞俄比亚海关报关单(ECUD)是唯一的报关单形式。

4. When the export cargo is ready for shipment, agent should apply for quarantine, and get the Export Cargo Declaration Sheet.

当出口货物备妥待运时，代理人应申请检疫，并取得出口货物报关单。

5. Agents apply for Customs Clearance to Qingdao Customs to get release sheet.

代理人向青岛海关申请报关并取得放行单。

三、Make out an Export License/ Export Customs Declaration According to the Following Conditions. 根据下面信息缮制一份出口许可证或报关单

THE SELLER：NANJING JINSHAN GAO TRADING GORP., LTD. （南京金山高贸易有

限公司 , 3201158972）5TH FLOOR，YUDU BUILDING, 132 ZHONGSHAN ROAD NANJING, CHINA

THE BUYER：JOHNSMITH COMPANY, VIGERALEV ALLE, DK－2900 VALBY, COPENHAGEN, DENMARK

PORT OF LOADING：NANJING, CHINA；PORT OF DISCHARGE：COPENHAGEN, DENMARK；CARRIER：DONGFANG, V703

TERMS OF PAYMENT：D/P 30 DAYS AFTER SIGHT

出口发票中所列商品的情况：

NO. S OF PACKAGES	DESCRIPTION	QTY/UNIT	UNIT PRICE	AMOUNT

CIF COPENHAGEN

XINGFU BRAND BICYCLE（HS CODE：87120081）

| 600CTNS | YE803 26' | 600 SETS | USD66/SET | USD39600. 00 |
| 600CTNS | TE600 24' | 600 SETS | USD72/SET | USD43200. 00 |

TOTAL：USD82,800. 00

B/L No.：HDJH-FLSB4052, INVOICE NO.：JH-FLSINV05

NW：21,600KGS, GW：24,000KGS, 1×40'CONTAINER NO：TEXU9608490

该公司外汇核销单编号：215157263，计量单位：辆/千克

南京苏通报关有限公司于 2021 年 5 月 20 日向南京海关申报出口，提单日期为 2021 年 5 月 21 日。

该批商品的出口许可证号码为：54780, S/C NO.：JH-FLSSCO5

船公司核定的运费率为 5%，保险公司收取保费 400 美元

LATEST DATE OF SHIPMENT：MAY28, 2021

MARKS：FLS/9711/COPENHAGEN/CARTON 1-1, 200

集装箱自重：4 吨

中华人民共和国出口许可证
EXPORT LICENCE THE PEOPLE'S REPUBLIC OF CHINA

（1）Exporter：申领许可证单位： 代码：	（3）出口许可证编号： Licence No.
（2）Consignor 发货单位： 代码：	（4）出口许可证有效截止日期： Export licence expiry date
（5）贸易方式： Terms of trade	（8）进口国（地区）： Country of destination
（6）合同号： Contract No.	（9）支付方式： Terms of payment
（7）报关口岸： Port of shipment	（10）运输方式： Means of transport

(11)唛头——包装件数 Marks and numbers-No. of packages					
(12)商品名称： Description of commodity			商品编码： Commodity No.		
（13）规格/等级 Specification	（14）单位 Unit	(15)数量 Quantity	（16）单价（币别）Unit price	（17）总值（币别）Amount	(18)总值折美元 Amount in USD
(19)总计 Total					
(20)备注 Supplementary details			(21)发证机关签章 Issuing authority stamp & signature		
			发证日期		
(22)申请单位盖章			(23)License date		

中华人民共和国海关出口货物报关单

预录入编号：   海关编号：

出口口岸	备案号	出口日期	申报日期	
经营单位	运输方式	运输工具名称	提运单号	
发货单位	贸易方式	征免性质	结汇方式	
许可证号	运抵(国地区)	指运港	境内货源地	
批准文号	成交方式	运费	保费	杂费
合同协议号	件数	包装种类	毛重(千克)	净重(千克)
集装箱号	随附单据		生产厂家	
标记唛码及备注				

项号	商品编号	商品名称	规格型号	数量及单位	最终目的国（地区）	单价	总价	币制	征免

税费征收情况		
录入员　录入单位　兹声明以上申报无讹并承担法律责任 报关员 　　　　　　　　　　申报单位(签章) 单位地址 邮编　　　　　　电话　　　　　　填制日期	海关单批注及放行日期 (签章) 　　　　　审单审价	
	征税　　　　　统计	
	查验　　　　　放行	

Chapter 10　Skills of Auditing Documents
审核单证的技巧

🎯 **Key Points and Difficulties**

- To Know What is the Skills of Auditing Documents
- To Understand the Process of Auditing Documents
- Focal Points of Auditing on Some Documents

Section One　Understanding Auditing Documents 认识审核单证

一、Document Checklists 单证核对表

The following is a series of checklists for document preparation and examination by the buyer, seller, advising bank, negotiating bank and issuing bank. They are not fully comprehensive as there are an almost infinite number of transaction variations possible, some of which require specialized procedures and documentation. Therefore, they should be viewed only as a general guide. 以下是买方、卖方、通知行、押汇行和开证行准备和检查单据的一系列清单。这些清单并不全面, 因为存在着无数次交易变化的可能性, 其中一些清单需要专门的程序和文件。因此, 这些清单被视为一般指南。

Seller/Exporter/Beneficiary 卖方/出口方/受益人

The seller/exporter/beneficiary has the responsibility of preparing and presenting documents in accordance with the terms and conditions of the documentary credit or collection. If the documents are incorrect or inconsistent, there is a risk of having them refused or dishonored, wasting time and money, and possibly imperiling the transaction itself. 卖方/出口方/受益人根据信用证和托收的条款和条件, 负责单据的准备和呈交工作。如果单据信息错误或不一致, 那么卖方会承受被拒付的风险, 同时也会浪费时间和精力, 可能还会危及交易过程。

Issuing Bank 开证行

The issuing bank has the responsibility of examining the documents presented by the seller/beneficiary to make sure that they are in conformity with the terms and conditions of the documentary credit or collection. 开证行负责审核卖方和受益人呈递的单据，其目的是确保单据符合信用证和托收的条件和条款。

Advising/Negotiating Bank 通知行/议付行

The advising or negotiating bank has the responsibility of examining the documents presented by the issuing bank to determine their authentication and if they are consistent with the requirements of the documentary credit or collection. 通知行/议付行负责审核开证行呈交的单据的真实性并且审核单据是否符合信用证或托收的要求。

Buyer/Importer/Applicant 买方/进口方/申请者

The buyer/importer/applicant first has the responsibility of listing documents that are required for the seller in the documentary credit. Upon presentation by the bank the buyer examines documents for consistency and accuracy. Problems with documents often lead to problems of goods from the shipping company or customs or receiving unwanted or incorrect goods. 买方/进口方/申请者首先负责列明信用证中所要求出具的单据。一旦银行呈交，买方就应审核单据的一致性和准确性。若单据出现任何问题，将会导致装运公司的发货问题、关税问题，以及接错货物等问题。

二、Documents Examination 审单

Whether a nominated bank or confirming bank conducts its obligation to pay the beneficiary depends on the documents presented by the beneficiary being in conformity with the requirement specified in the L/C. Whether the issuing bank performs imbursement to the nominated bank which has made payment to the beneficiary depends also on documents received being in compliance with the requirements in L/C. The buyer must check the documents released by the issuing bank to him so as to decide to pay to the issuing bank. Even the seller should also carefully examine the documents after having made out them, all the documents to be submitted to the bank. In a word, one issue in common to all parties involved in a documentary L/C is to examine documents required in the L/C. Once again, to be handled, to be presented, to be transacted, and to be examined in the L/C is documents rather than goods. Examining documents must be considered as a vital step in the whole transaction.

指定银行或者保兑行是否履行对受益人付款的义务主要依赖于受益人呈交的单据是否符合信用证的要求。开证银行是否对指定银行(指定一行以支付于受益人)进行偿付取决于所收到的单据是否符合信用证要求。买方必须检查由开证行出具的单据以便决定支付开证行。卖方也应在制单之后仔细审核单据，所有的单据应呈交给银行。总之，在信用证中的各方所面临的共同问题是审核信用证下要求的单据。同时，还要处理、呈递、交易，以及审核单据。审核单据是整个交易过程中最重要的部分。

1. Principle of Examining Documents 审单的原则

* Parties by examining documents should be strictly but with reasonable care.

- All parties except the beneficiary have to complete examination within a reasonable period, normally up to seven banking days after receiving documents.

- The documents must comply with each other.

- The parties involved only check documents clearly identified in the L/C, non-document conditions would be ignored.

2. Procedure of Examining Documents 审单的程序

Procedure of examining documents differs from country to country and even from bank to bank. Procedure listed below can be considered as a reference or a remediation：审核单据的过程在每个国家和每个银行都不同。以下的程序视为参考或补充：

- To sort and count types and numbers documents received. 对收到的文件进行分类和编号。

- To write a receipt of document package in duplicate, indicating the date of receipt, one of them should be returned to party from which the documents are received. 要写一个一式两份的文件包收据，注明收到日期，其中一份应退还给收到文件的一方。

- To check the L/C and documents to make certain that 检查信用证和单据以确保：

(1)The documentary credit is advised by an advising bank. If the L/C is sent directly to the beneficiary, its authenticity should be verified by any means. 跟单信用证由通知银行通知。如果信用证是直接寄给受益人的，则应通过任何方式核实其真实性。

(2)The draft bears the correct documentary credit reference number. 汇票上有正确的跟单信用证参考号。

(3)The invoice is issued by the beneficiary of credit. 发票由信用证受益人开具。

(4)Transport document indicates the number of full set of originals. 运输单据注明全套正本的份数。

(5)Insurance document is issued in the form required in the credit, insurance policy, or insurance certificate, or cover notes plus declaration. 保险凭证按信用证、保险单或保险凭证要求的形式出具，或按保险单加声明的形式出具。

To compare documents with the credit, the sequence of comparison is firstly in vertical direction and then in horizontal direction. So-called "vertical" means that all documents are to be compared with credit, in detail, items in various documents should be consistent with to be stated in the credit. "Horizontal" means that all documents are to be compared down in the column of "discrepancies and action taken" of the list. For some simple credits, only those items that are easy to become discrepancies would be checked, as to faster the examination.

要将单据与信用证进行比较，比较的顺序是先纵向，然后横向。所谓"纵向"是指所有单据都要与信用证进行比较，详细地说，各种单据中的项目都要与在信用证中说明的项目一致。"横向"是指在列表的"不符点和采取的措施"栏中对所有文件进行向下比较。对于一些简单的信用证，只会检查那些容易出现差异的项目以加快审核。

3. Methods of Auditing Documents 审单的方法

- Vertical review method

—The document is consistent with the letter of credit

Review all required documents based on the letter of credit and UCP, and ensure that the content of each document complies with the provisions of the letter of credit and UCP

纵向审核法

—"单证一致"

—以信用证和 UCP 为基础对规定的各项单据进行审核，各单据的内容要符合信用证和 UCP 的规定

- Horizontal review method

The document matches the document

After the vertical review, other specified documents should be reviewed with the document as the center, and the relevant content should be consistent with each other

- 横向审核法

—"单单相符"

—纵向审核之后，分别以单据为中心审核其他规定的单据，有关内容要相互一致。

Section Two   Focal Points of Auditing 审核单证的要点

一、Focal points of Auditing—Invoice 审核的要点——发票

1. Invoice must be made out in favor of applicant（what stipulated in UCP600 is excluded）

2. The signer must be the beneficiary（L/C's stipulation "The third party's documents are acceptable" is excluded）

3. The description of goods must be in conformity that stipulated in L/C

4. Price Clauses must be identical with that stipulated in L/C

5. The quantity of goods must be in conformity with that stipulated in L/C

6. Unit price and price conditions must be in conformity with that stipulated in L/C

7. Unless additional clauses are stated in L/C, invoice is not signed and the date is omitted.

- 抬头人必须是申请人（UCP600 规定的除外）
- 签发人必须是受益人（信用证规定"第三方单据可接受"的除外）
- 商品的描述必须与信用证规定一致
- 价格条款必须与信用证规定一致
- 商品的数量必须符合信用证规定
- 单价和价格条件必须符合信用证规定
- 除非信用证要求，发票无需签字和日期

二、Focal Points of Auditing—Insurance Policy 审核的要点——保险单

1. Insurance policy must be issued and signed by insurance company or its agents, unless it is additionally stipulated, insurance policy issued by insurance company is not acceptable

2. Currency must be the same as that stipulated in L/C

3. The rate of insurance：the lowest amount insured must be 110% of CIF/CFR value if there is no relative stipulation in L/C

4. Insurance risks must be in conformity with that in L/C. When "all risks" are needed, the statements or clauses including all risks must be acceptable

5. Insurance obligations must cover shipment of goods, delivery and place of receiving stated in L/C

6. The distance between port of unloading and destination

- 必须由保险公司或其代理出具并签署，除非另有规定，保险经纪人出具的暂保单不予接受

- 币种必须和信用证一致

- 投保比例

—L/C 无规定：最低投保额必须是 CIF/CFR 金额的 110%

—L/C 规定投保比例：如 110%，视为最低要求

- 保险险别必须符合信用证的规定，要求"一切险"时，含有任何"一切险"批注或条款都将接受

- 保险责任至少覆盖信用证规定的货物装运、发运或接管地到卸货港或最终目的地之间的路程

7. The number of originals need not to be marked out, if marked, unless otherwise are stated, all originals must be handed out

8. Pieces and shipping marks must be the same as that stipulated in invoice and other documents

9. Transportation tool, place of departure and destination must be in conformity with L/C

10. The issuing date cannot be later than shipment date, unless "insurance obligations are effective until the end of shipment date" is stated thereon.

11. Unless otherwise is stated in L/C, franchise policy is acceptable.

- 不必注明正本份数，如果注明，除非另有规定，所有正本都必须提交

- 包装件数、唛头等必须与发票和其他单据一致

- 运输工具、起运地及目的地，必须与信用证及其他单据一致

- 出单日期不得晚于装运日期，除非表明保险责任最晚于装运之日起生效

- 除非信用证另有规定，接受含有收免赔率/额的保单

三、Focal Points of Auditing—Transportation Documents 审核的要点——运输单证

(一)Focal Points of Auditing—Ocean Bill of Lading 审核的要点——海运提单

1. The original B/L must be signed according to the stipulations of Clause B of UCP, Item 20, and the shipper's name must be on B/L, and the shipper's identity must be stated

2. If "shipped on board" is printed on B/L and the individual shipment is not stated, the issuing date of B/L is seen as the shipment date

3. If there is the individual shipment with the date stated thereon, the date is seen as the shipment date no matter whether the issuing date is earlier than that date or not

4. The date of shipment is in conformity with that in L/C

5. The port of loading and unloading must be inconformity with that in L/C

• 正本提单必须以 UCP 第 20 条 B 款规定的方式进行签字，且承运人的名称必须出现在提单的表面，以表明承运人身份

• 如果是预先印就"已装运于船"的提单，并且没有单独装船批注，提单的出具日即视为装船日

• 如带有加注日期的单独装船批注，该日期视为装船日，而不论在提单签发日之前还是之后

• 装船日是否符合信用证规定

• 装货港和卸货港必须与信用证规定一致。

（二）Focal Points of Auditing—Charter Contract B/L 审核的要点——租船合约提单

1. The bank does not audit relative charter contracts

2. Original charter contract B/L must be signed according to Clause B of UCP, Item 20 without stating the name of shipper

3. If "shipped on board" is printed on charter contract B/L and the individual shipment is not stated, the issuing date of B/L is taken as the shipment date

4. If there is the individual shipment with the date stated thereon, the date is taken as the shipment date no matter the issuing date is earlier than that date or not

5. The date of shipment is in conformity with that in L/C

6. The port of loading and unloading must be inconformity with that in L/C

• 银行不审核相关的租船合约

• 正本租船合约提单必须以 UCP 第 20 条 B 款规定的方式签署，无需显示承运人名称

• 如果是预先印就"已装运于船"的租船合约提单，没有单独装船批注，出具日即视为装运日

• 如带有加注日期的单独装船批注，该日期视为装船日，而不论在签发日之前还是之后

• 装船日是否符合信用证规定

• 装货港和卸货港必须与信用证规定一致

（三）Focal Points of Auditing—Combined Transport Document 审核的要点——多式联运单据

1. Original combined transport document must be signed according to Clause B of UCP, Item 20. The name and identity of shipper or combined transport operator must be stated thereon

2. If "shipped on board" is printed on B/L and the individual shipment is not stated, the issuing date of B/L is taken as the shipment date

3. If there is the individual shipment with the date stated thereon, the date is seen as the shipment date no matter whether the issuing date is earlier than that date or not

4. The date of shipment is in conformity with that in L/C

5. Place of receiving, place of delivering, place of loading and destination must conform to that in L/C

● 正本多式联运单据必须以 UCP 第 20 条 B 款规定的方式进行签字，且承运人或多式联运经营人的名称必须出现在提单的表面，并表明其身份

● 如果是预先印就"已装运于船"的提单，并且没有单独装船批注，提单的出具日即视为装船日

● 如带有加注日期的单独装船批注，该日期视为装船日，而不论在提单签发日之前还是之后

　● 装船日是否符合信用证规定

　● 接管地、发运地、装货地和目的地必须与信用证规定一致

6. The number of originals must be stated thereon

7. The name of commodity can be general name of goods, which is not contradictive to that in L/C

8. Audit "freight prepaid" or "fright to collect"

9. Shipping mark, pieces, net weight are the same as that stipulated in L/C

10. "The goods and/or packing conditions are defective" shouldn't be stated thereon

11. Endorsement should made out according to L/C(if any)

12. Modification and amendment must be evidenced

● 必须注明正本的份数

● 商品名称可使用与信用证不矛盾的货物的统称

● 运费预付或运费到付(如信用证要求)是否正确表明

● 唛头、件数、毛重须与其他单据一致

● 不应有货物及/或包装状况有缺陷的批注

● 背书应按照信用证要求(如有)

● 修正和变更必须经过证实

(四)Focal Points of Auditing—Airway B/L 审核的要点——空运单据

1. Original airway B/L must be signed according to Clause B of UCP Item 20, and shipper's named and identity must be stated thereon

2. Normally, the original should be "consignor's original", if additionally required, a full set of original must be submitted

3. Airway B/L must state clearly that "the goods are ready for being shipped"

4. If L/C requires that the actual date of delivery must be stated separately, the date is taken as the shipping date. If not, the issuing date is delivering date

● 正本空运单据必须以 UCP 第 20 条 B 款规定的方式签署，且承运人的名称必须出现在提单的表面，以表明承运人身份

● 在表面看来系"发货人/托运人的正本"，如果要求提交全套正本，只要提交一份表明是发货人/托运人的正本即可

● 空运单据必须表明货物已收妥待运

● 如果 L/C 要求表面必须标明发运的实际日期，并做出单独批注，该发运日期将被视为装运日期；如果没有要求，则出具日期将被视为发运日期

5. The departing airport and arriving airport must be stated according to L/C

6. IATA Code is allowed to replace words

7. B/L should not be made out to demonstrative order, the notified party must be in conformity with that in L/C

8. The name of commodity can be general name of goods, which is not contradictive to that in L/C

9. Audit "freight prepaid" or "fright to collect"

10. Shipping mark, pieces, net weight are the same as that stipulated in L/C

11. "The goods and/or packing conditions are defective" shouldn't be stated thereon

12. Modification and amendment must be evidenced

- 必须注明信用证要求的出发地机场和目的地机场
- 可使用 IATA 代码代替文字
- 不应做成指示抬头，被通知人须符合信用证规定
- 商品名称可使用与信用证不矛盾的货物的统称
- 运费预付或运费到付(如信用证要求)是否正确表明
- 唛头、件数、毛重须与其他单据一致
- 不应有货物及/或包装状况有缺陷的批注
- 修正和变更必须经过证实

四、Focal Points of Auditing—Certificate of Origin 审核的要点——原产地证

1. Certificate of origin must be issued by the person stipulated in L/C. If it is stipulated that certificate of origin should be issued by beneficiary, exporter or manufacturer, documents issued by Chamber of Commerce are acceptable as long as beneficiary, exporter or manufacturer are stated accordingly

2. If L/C does not stipulate who should issue documents, documents issued by any person including beneficiary are acceptable

3. Documents must be signed and stated the date thereon

4. The information of consignee is in conformity with that in shipping documents

5. Exporter cannot be the same as beneficiary or consignor of shipping documents

- 必须由信用证规定的人出具

—如果信用证要求由受益人、出口商或厂商来出具，则由商会出具的单据是可以接受的，只要该单据相应地注明受益人、出口商或厂商

—如果信用证没有规定由谁来出具，则由任何人包括受益人出具的单据都可接受

- 必须经过出单人签署、注明日期
- 收货人的信息如果显示，则不得与运输单据中的收货人信息相矛盾
- 出口方可以不同于受益人或运输单据的发货人

五. Focal Points of Auditing—all Certificates of Inspection 其他单据——所有检验检疫证书

1. Contents are made out according to L/C

2. Whether the date is marked depends on contents and nature of certificates

- 内容按照信用证的要求缮制
- 是否加注日期取决于单据的内容和性质

六、Focal Points of Auditing——Drafts 审核的要点——汇票

1. The issuer must be the beneficiary, and the beneficiary must sign on it

2. Whether the payer is the same as that stipulated in L/C or not

3. The amount is the same as that in commercial invoice, which is in conformity with that in L/C

4. The figure of the amount is in accordance with the words

5. The date of paying is issued according to L/C

6. Currency is in accordance with L/C

7. If necessary, endorsement is required(such as, when payee and claimer are different, the payee shall endorse to the claimer)

8. When modification and amendment are required, the issuer has to evidence the necessity of modification and amendment

- 出票人必须是受益人，由其签字或盖章加签字
- 付款人是否符合信用证的规定
- 金额和发票相同，与信用证的金额一致
- 金额的大小写如都有，则必须一致
- 付款期限要符合信用证的规定
- 币种和信用证相一致
- 如必要，需要背书(例如汇票收款人和寄单索汇人不同时，需要收款人给索汇人的背书)
- 修改和变更是否有出票人的证实

主要参考文献

[1]李贺. 外贸单证实务：应用. 技能. 案例. 实训(第四版)[M]. 上海：上海财经大学出版社，2023.

[2]王小娟. 国际贸易实务双语教程[M]. 北京：对外经贸大学出版社，2023.

[3]广银芳. 外贸单证实务(第二版)[M]. 北京：中国轻工业出版社，2022.

[4]冷柏军，李洋. 国际贸易实务双语教程(经济管理类课程教材·国际贸易系列)[M]. 北京：中国人民大学出版社，2021.

[5]周树玲，郝冠军. 外贸单证实务(第五版)[M]. 北京：对外经贸大学出版社，2021.

[6]易露霞，陈新华. 国际贸易实务双语教程(第五版)[M]. 北京：清华大学出版社，2020.

[7]何源. 跟单信用证一本通(第二版)[M]. 北京：中国海关出版社，2018.

[8]李嘉倩. 外贸单证实务[M]. 北京：北京理工大学出版社，2018.

[9]卓乃坚. 国际贸易支付与结算及其单证实务(第三版)[M]. 上海：东华大学出版社，2017.

[10]孝先，石玉川. 国际贸易实务[M]. 上海：对外经贸大学出版社，2016.

[11]孙双进，孙宪. 报关报检单证实操手册 检验检疫单证篇[M]. 北京：中国海关出版社，2016.

[12]孙双进，孙宪. 报关报检单证实操手册 海关单证篇[M]. 北京：中国海关出版社，2016.

[13]孙双进，孙宪. 报关报检单证实操手册 贸易管制单证篇[M]. 北京：中国海关出版社，2016.

[14]刘金波. 国际金融实务[M]. 北京：中国人民大学出版社，2016.

[15]姚大伟. 国际商务单证理论与实务[M]. 上海：上海交通大学出版社，2014.

[16]翟步习. 信用证英语应用分析[M]. 上海：对外经贸大学出版社，2014.

[17]童宏祥. 外贸单证操作[M]. 上海：华东师范大学出版社，2014.

[18]章安平. 进出口业务操作[M]. 北京：高等教育出版社，2014.

[19]全国国际商务单证考试专业培训考试办公室. 国际商务单证理论与实务[M]. 北京：中国商务出版社，2016.

[20]中国国际贸易促进委员会商务培训认证考试办公室. 外贸跟单理论与实务[M]. 北京：中国商务出版社，2016.